READ-ALOUD BIBLE STORIES

One-Hundred-and-One
Read-Aloud
Bible Stories

From the
Old and New Testament

By Joan C. Verniero

BLACK DOG
& LEVENTHAL
PUBLISHERS
NEW YORK

Published by
Black Dog & Leventhal Publishers, Inc.
151 West 19th Street
New York, NY 10011

Distributed by
Workman Publishing Company
708 Broadway
New York, NY 10003

Editorial Consultants:
Dr. Larry Richards
Dr. Mary Manz Simon
Dr. John H. Walton

Design by Liz Trovato

Illustrations on pages 20, 51, 81, 136, 196, 201, 217, 221, 298, 327, 332, 347
from A First Bible © 1934, illustrated by Helen Sewell

Cover and additional art by Pat Pardini

Manufactured in the United States of America

ISBN: 1-57912-024-5

j i h g f e d c b a

Library of Congress Cataloging-in-Publication Data
Verniero, Joan C.
101 read-aloud Bible stories: from the Old and
New Testament / by Joan C. Verniero
p.   cm.
Summary: A collection of Bible stories each of which can be read aloud in
under ten minutes.
ISBN 1–57912–024–5
1. Bible stories, English. [1. Bible stories.] I. Title.
BS551.2.V47   1998
220.9'505– –dc21   98–5112
CIP
AC

CONTENTS

INTRODUCTION

One-Hundred-and-One Read-Aloud Bible Stories is a collection of timeless adventures that beg to be told. These are ancient stories for today's young people. The stories are intended to be read aloud by an adult or an older child so that the young listener can hear their important themes.

While the Bible is the most widely published book in the English language, it is not necessarily the most widely understood book in our language. The wording is ancient and the context is based in a historical time that is strange to most people. Many of us relate the reading of the Bible to religious study only. Children too often do not appreciate the Bible as a great story that is itself a collection of intriguing relationships, exciting expeditions, and meaningful encounters .

The purpose of this volume is to present players in the story as accessible characters to whom children can relate. The lessons the characters learn are lessons that a listener might learn in a similar situation. I've tried to make the geographical locations come alive so that a modern-day child, and the adult that reads to that child, can see and feel some of what it was like to be alive at the time of the story.

I've used quite a bit of dialogue to engage the listener. The passages are true to the text of the Bible, while some of the language has been updated to correspond with a contemporary conversational style. At the same time, the beauty of the biblical writers' speech patterns remains intact.

How are these Bible stories for children different from other collections? Because the selections are intended as read-aloud stories of similar lengths, the challenge was to recount the familiar stories of the Bible with an ear for the synergy of narrative and pace. When elements of history were needed, they have been included, as was often necessary with the Old Testament. When familiar passages were too short, as was often the case with the parables of the New Testament, they have been grouped together in a thematic telling.

In the style of contemporary literature for children, I've intentionally not expounded upon the morals, lessons and pitfalls that the characters in the stories encounter. Instead, I've chosen to place the story in a context that a child listener can understand by perhaps beginning with "This is a story about . . . ." In many instances, I've let the story unfold to tell the listener what it is about. Interested adult readers can take it upon themselves to explain any lessons or draw any theological conclusions which they may see fit to add to the telling.

The stories in this volume are derived from *New Revised Standard Version of the Bible*. This version is the authorized revision of the *Revised Standard Version of 1952*, a revision of the *American Standard Version of 1901*, which reflected earlier revisions of the *King James Version of 1611*. As my source, I used the *HarperCollins Study Bible*, published in 1993, which is a project sponsored by the Society of Biblical Literature. The Society of Biblical Literature was founded in 1880 and has 5,500 members from over 80 countries.

JOAN C. VERNIERO
1998

THE OLD TESTAMENT

The Creation

God created the world and every living thing in the world in just six days. On the seventh day, he rested from all the work he had done.

God began with a formless void. The nothingness was made of darkness without any pattern. God blew a wind into the void. The wind swept across the deep, dark waters. One by one, God was about to create wonders out of the stillness like a conductor making music with an orchestra.

"Let there be light," said God into the darkness.

Light filled the void, and God saw that the light was good for what he was about to create. On that first evening, God separated the darkness from the light. He called the darkness Night. And he called the light Day. There was an evening and a morning. This was the first day.

"Let there be a dome," said God on the second day.

Across the waters of the void, God placed the dome. He called the dome Sky. There was an evening and a morning. This was the second day. And into the void of yesterday came the Sky.

"Let the waters under the Sky gather into one place, and let the dry land appear," said God on the third day.

The waters pulled together at their edges. The land beneath bared itself to the Sky, and it became dry. God called the dry land Earth. He called the waters that had gathered the Seas. When God saw that what he had done would benefit what he was about to create, he spoke again on the third day.

"Let the Earth produce vegetation, both plants that yield seed and fruit trees of every type that bears fruit with seeds," said God on the third day.

Fruit trees and plants of all species sprouted forth from the Earth. God watched the unfolding and saw that it was good for what he was about to create. There was an evening and a morning. This was the third day. On it, God created Earth, the Seas and vegetation.

"Let there be lights in the dome of the sky to separate the day from the evening. Let the lights be for signs and seasons, for days and years. And let the lights in the dome give light to the Earth," said God on the fourth day.

God made the two great lights, and the lesser light to rule the night—the Moon , and the greater light to rule the day—the Sun. Then, he made the stars. God again saw that what he had done was good for what he was about to create. There was an evening and a morning. This was the fourth day. On it, a new moon was surrounded by the stars, and the Sun shined bright.

"Let the waters bring forth swarms of living creatures. Let birds fly above the Earth across the dome of the Sky," said God on the fifth day.

Great sea monsters, every winged bird of every kind and every living creature that moved took a breath at the sound of the words. Wild animals of every type, cattle of every kind and everything that crept upon the ground came alive. God recognized that what he made was good for what he was about to create. There was an evening and a morning. This was the fifth day. It had new creatures flying and crawling and stampeding on the Earth, and swimming through the Seas.

"Let us make humankind in our image, according to our likeness. Let them have dominion over the fish of the sea, the birds of the air, the cattle, the wild animals and the creeping things of the Earth," said God on the sixth day.

And, in his likeness, he created a male and a female, and they breathed like all the other living creatures and the green plants he had created. God put the man and the woman over the other creatures, and he gave them the plants and the trees that bore fruit with seeds. There was an evening and a morning. The sixth day marked the creation of human beings. God saw that man and woman he created were good.

On the seventh day, God was finished. He had made the heavens and the earth. He had created multitudes to inhabit the earth. He had made the food for them to eat, and he had gathered the waters for them to drink. God blessed the seventh day. On it, he rested from all the work he had done in creating the world.

ADAM AND EVE IN THE GARDEN OF EDEN

*A*fter God made the man out of the dust of the ground and breathed into his nostrils the breath of life, he planted a garden in the eastern land of Eden for the man. Underground springs gave the garden water. Every tree was pleasant to see and nourishing as food grew in this garden. In the middle of the trees was the tree of life. Also in the garden was the tree of the knowledge of good and evil.

The underground spring was fed by a river with four tributaries. The first tributary was called Pishon. It flowed around the land of Havilah, a land plentiful in gold and onyx. The second river was the Gihon, which flowed around the land of Cush. The Tigris was the third river, flowing east to Assyria. The fourth tributary was the Euphrates.

When God put the man in the garden, he gave him instructions. "You may eat freely of every tree in the garden. But of the tree of the knowledge of good and evil, you may not eat. On the day that you eat of that tree, you will be doomed to die."

And the man listened to God. Then God called to the man every animal of the land and every bird of the air. The man named the creatures, and the names he gave them were how they were called. God saw that the man needed a partner. He made a deep sleep come upon the man. From the man's chest, God took one of his ribs. Then, he closed over the hole in the man's chest cavity with the man's flesh. God took the man's rib and made it into a woman.

"This at last is bone of my bones and flesh of my flesh; this one shall be called Woman, for out of Man this one was taken," said the Man.

The man and the woman were both naked but they were not ashamed. Rather, they enjoyed each other's company in the Garden of Eden that God had made for them.

One day, the woman was startled by a serpent she had not expected to see. The serpent addressed the woman boldly.

"Did God say, 'You shall not eat from any tree in the garden?'" asked the serpent.

"God said we may eat the fruit of the trees in the garden, but not the fruit of the tree in the middle of the garden. If we touch it, we will die," answered the woman.

The serpent sneered. "You will not die. God knows instead that when you eat of that tree, your eyes will open and you will be like God. You will know good and evil," said the serpent.

The woman inspected the forbidden tree more closely. Like the other trees, this tree was pleasant to see. She wondered if, like the rest, its fruit was good to eat. She took a bite to test the fruit. Then, the woman gave the man the fruit to taste. No sooner had they both eaten than their eyes were opened in a new way. They saw how naked they were, and they rushed to make clothing for themselves by sewing fig leaves together.

With the evening breeze, they heard the sound of God walking in the garden toward them. The man and the woman hid from God among the trees. God called the man to him.

"I heard you on the breeze, but I was afraid because I was naked. So I hid myself," said the man.

"Who told you that you were naked?" God inquired. "Have you eaten fruit from the tree that I commanded you not to eat?"

The man told how the woman gave him the fruit, and God turned to the woman for an explanation.

"The serpent tricked me, and I ate the fruit you told us not to eat," she said.

Then, God cursed the serpent and ordered it to crawl upon its belly and eat dust for the rest of its days. He told the serpent he would create ill will between the woman's offspring and all serpents forever. People would strike the heads of serpents, and serpents would strike back at the heels of people. God promised to make childbearing painful for women through the rest of time. To the man, God promised a life of toil in the fields to grow what the garden had before given freely.

The man and woman were named. They were called Adam ("the man") and Eve, because she was the mother of all people. God drove Adam and Eve from the Garden of Eden for what they had done. Angels kept them from returning.

CAIN AND ABEL

ain and Abel were the children of the first humans that God created. Their mother and father were Eve and Adam. Unlike their parents, the sons had not lived in Garden of Eden. An angel with a flaming sword guarded the tree of life from them.

Cain and Abel lived with their parents after God drove them out of the garden. There was no rain. The earth was fertile and the grasslands were plenty. For generations to come, their life would be considered ordinary. Their parents farmed the land and owned pastures and livestock. They learned how to till the soil, reap the harvest and thresh the wheat. They herded the sheep, tended the goats and raised the cattle.

Cain and Abel were as different as brothers could be. They had different temperaments. Cain was proud, and Abel was easygoing. Most distinct were their destinies.

Cain was the firstborn son of Eve. He became a farmer. He was happiest when he tilled the ground. And he was proud of the crops he produced. Abel preferred being a shepherd. His favorite job was bringing the cattle to be watered at the well so the animals could drink.

One day, Cain was delighted by the choice of crop he had grown. He picked a sample and brought it to God as a gift. The same day, Abel selected a fat newborn from his flock of sheep. Abel offered the lamb to God. God praised Abel for his gift, and he ignored Cain. Feeling slighted by God, Cain said nothing. His anger showed in his actions. His shoulders drooped. His head hung low, and his face darkened into a frown. He kicked some dirt with his sandals.

"Why are you so angry? If your deeds are good, won't you be rewarded? You know that if your deeds are not good, you will find sin lurking at the door. Sin desires you to do bad, but you must rise above it," said God to Cain.

Cain was too angry by what happened and too confused by God's words to pay attention to them.

"Let's go out to the field," Cain said to Abel.

When they walked only a short distance, Cain attacked his brother. His fury was so great that he was blinded by it. Abel tried to fight back, but Cain was upon him with the strength of pure rage. Without hesitating in his passion, Cain murdered Abel. Then, he went back the way he had come.

"Where is your brother?" God asked Cain.

"I do not know. Am I my brother's keeper?" answered Cain.

"What have you done?" demanded God. "Your brother's blood is crying out to me from the ground. From now on, the ground that has opened its mouth to receive Abel's blood will curse you. It will no longer give you its strength to use. As of today, you will be a wanderer on this earth."

Cain protested. "My punishment is more than I can bear. Today you have driven me from you. I am a fugitive on the earth, and anyone who meets me can kill me."

It was God's turn to protest. "That is not so, Cain. Whoever kills you will suffer sevenfold."

God put his mark on Cain. It said to anyone who saw it that this was Cain, the same Cain of the story that people told. This was the Cain that killed his brother Abel. He was the Cain that God drove from his farm. He was the same Cain that God protected against injury with his mark. Anyone who did harm to Cain would receive seven times the injury at the hand of God.

Cain and his wife settled in the land of Nod. In Hebrew, Nod means "wandering." They had a son, whom they called Enoch. Cain loved his son dearly, so much that he built a city in his honor and called it Enoch.

The story of Cain and Abel spread widely among the new generations of people in the area. But some people had not yet learned the lesson. One of these was Lamech, who was born four generations after Cain's son Enoch. Lamech was very boastful. One day, Lamech sang a song for his wives. He bragged about killing one man who wounded him and killing another who struck him. Instead of singing of remorse, Lamech sang, "If Cain is avenged sevenfold, truly Lamech, seventy-sevenfold."

Other people heard about Cain and Abel, and they believed strongly in God. God's mark on Cain to protect him, even though he had murdered his brother, told them of God's love.

NOAH AND THE FLOOD

od was very displeased with the way people acted toward one another. They were corrupt and violent. Feeling great pain, he knew he had to send a powerful message to the world.

God said, "I will wipe humanity, whom I have created, from the face of the earth—men and animals, creatures that move along the ground and birds of the air—for I am sorry that I have made them."

Through his anger, God remembered how loving and good Noah and his family were. Noah was a farmer who had three sons, Shem, Ham and Japheth. Unlike many people on the earth at that time, Noah was a good man. He lived a proper and quiet life with his family and tried to obey God. God decided to spare them from destruction. He told Noah of his plan to send a great flood over the face of the earth to destroy all living creatures.

"Make an ark from cypress wood," he told Noah. "This is how I would like you to build it." Then, he instructed Noah to build a great ship, 450 feet long, 75 feet wide and 45 feet high. The ark was to be coated with tar so that the floodwaters could not get inside. It would have a roof and lower, middle and upper decks.

Although Noah thought that it was strange to build such a large vessel, he was a man of great faith. He knew he had to follow God's instructions, even if he did not understand why. When Noah finished building the ark, God spoke to him again.

"Everything on this earth will perish, Noah, every creature that has the breath of life in it. But this I promise you. You and your family will be spared. Take into the ark two of every kind of creature, one male and one female. Take plenty of food for your family and for the animals."

Noah did exactly as God commanded him.

When God saw that Noah had obeyed him, he told him, "Seven days from now, I will send rain on the earth for forty days and forty nights. Every person, animal and bird, except those in your ark, will die."

Noah and his wife and their three sons and their wives entered the ark. After seven days, just as God had said, the floodwaters came. Rain fell upon the earth as if the very sky had split open. Water also gushed out of the ground. Soon, the ark was lifted from the ground and began to float on the powerful waters that God had sent to destroy his own creation. The ark rose higher and higher as the rain fell for forty days and forty nights.

Noah and his family, plus the animals he had chosen, remained inside the ark. Even after the rain stopped falling, the land was covered with water for 150 days. That was a long time to be afloat in the ark. But Noah did not lose his faith in God's promise to him.

One day, Noah sent a raven to fly over the waters and look for land. The bird flew back and forth, but could only find water wherever it went, so it returned. Noah then released a small white dove from the ark. The dove flew away, but also returned without seeing dry land. Noah took the bird back inside the ark and waited.

God remembered what he had spoken to Noah. After the floodwater had covered the earth for 150 days, God sent a wind over the surface of the waves. The water began to go down, little by little. Again, Noah sent the dove out from the ark. This time, when the dove returned, it carried an olive branch in its beak. Noah knew that the water was drying up. He sent the bird out once more, but this time it did not return.

Finally, Noah's ark came to rest on the mountains of Ararat. The waters sank lower and lower until it was possible to see other mountains. Eventually, the earth was completely dry.

God spoke to Noah, "Come out of the ark with your family. Take all of the creatures you have carried with you, and set them free so they can multiply on this earth, be fruitful and increase in number upon it."

Joyfully, Noah did as God instructed. Every person and every creature left the ark. When they had disembarked, Noah built an altar to God. He selected some of the animals and birds for sacrifice and made an offering to God as thanks for remembering him and his family. When God saw what Noah had done, God was pleased that he had selected him to replenish the earth with goodness.

"Never again will I curse the ground because of humanity's sins," God said. "And never again will I destroy all the living creatures of this earth, as I have done. As long as the earth endures, seedtime and harvest, cold and heat, summer and winter, day and night, will never cease."

This was God's promise, or covenant, to Noah and the world. As a reminder of his promise, God created a rainbow to fill the sky. Noah lived a long and good life for the rest of his days. His children and their children and the offspring of the creatures who survived the great flood filled the world.

THE TOWER OF BABEL

he survivors of the great flood and their families multiplied over the years according to God's plan. Everyone on earth was descended from Noah's three sons and their wives. The sons were Shem, Ham and Japheth. The people spoke the same language and used the same words. They traveled from the east of their land to the land of Shinar, which was located on a great plain. There, they decided to settle.

The people wanted to make a new town. Because stone was very scarce in the area the people created bricks. The bricks were made of mud and baked very thoroughly. To hold the bricks in place, the people used a type of mortar made out of tar. From the tar and bricks, the people built buildings.

Not content to simply build homes, the people from the East decided to build a great city with many buildings. In the center of this city, they made plans to build a very high tower. The tower would show everyone how powerful they were.

"Come, let us build ourselves a city, with a tower that reaches to the heavens, so we will be famous. Then we won't be scattered over the face of the whole earth," they said.

Their tower, sometimes called a "ziggurat," was square at its base. The sides were sloped with many steps that led to a shrine at the top. The people believed that the steps represented a staircase leading from earth to heaven. The magnificent tower, visible throughout the city, represented God's path to the temple, and was a symbol of the people's power.

The people were not happy to just build a city and tower. They then began to worship other gods and idols. They forgot the punishment God had sent through the great flood. Even though they were the descendants of Noah, they forgot Noah's obedience to God.

God came down to the city that the people were building. He saw the buildings made of brick and tar. More importantly, he saw the great tower. God knew that the people were proud and ambitious. He knew they believed that by building the city and the great tower they would control their own lives, forgetting their obligation to God. The kingdom of people would start thinking of God as being much like themselves. He decided to stop this rebellious action.

God thought, "This is only the beginning of what they will try to do. They will believe that nothing is impossible for them to try."

To teach the people who built the great tower that they could not defy the power of heaven, God chose to scatter them all over the earth.

"I will go down and confuse them so they will not understand each other," God said. "If as one people speaking the same language they have begun to do this, then nothing they plan to do will be impossible for them."

God's action had a great impact on the people. They were forced to travel to many different lands and began to speak different languages. This made it difficult for them to understand each other. They could not talk to each other and could not work well together.

The city the people had attempted to build was abandoned. Their great tower was also abandoned. The city was then known as "Babel," which is from the Hebrew word "Babylon," and also sounds like the word in Hebrew for "confused."

By preventing the people of Babel from speaking the same language, God stopped their plan to build a mighty city on earth and a tower to symbolize their pride. They no longer spoke the same words. They were unable to communicate with each other. They could not live in one place. The people spread across the lands of the earth, leaving behind the city they had started.

The "Tower of Babel" then became a symbol of people trying to control God. The story of the tower provides a vivid explanation of why people, to this very day, speak so many different languages and have different customs.

GOD'S PROMISE TO ABRAHAM

braham was the father of the Israelite patriarchs. He was first known as "Abram." Abram and his wife Sarai were from the region today known as Iraq. They did not have any children.

Abram and Sarai lived among people who did not believe in one god. Instead the people worshipped many idols.

God spoke to Abram. "Go from your country and your family and your father's house to the land that I will show you. I will make you into a great nation, and I will bless you and make your name great."

Abram was seventy-five years old when he left Haran. He traveled with his wife Sarai and Lot, the son of his brother. They took all of their possessions with them. God led them to the land of Canaan. Canaan is now part of present-day Israel.

On a hill east of Bethel, Abram built an altar to worship God. God had told him that the land of Canaan would belong to Abram and to all of his offspring. In Hebrew, Bethel means "house of God." Abram then settled in the Negeb.

Abram left Canaan during a severe famine, but he returned once the trouble had passed. By that time Abram was a wealthy man, owning many herds and flocks. He was also rich with gold and silver. Lot, his nephew, was also wealthy, possessing flocks, herds and many tents. Abram realized that the land could not support both his herds and the herds of Lot. The shepherds who were in charge of watching the flocks began to argue.

Abram spoke to his nephew: "Let there be no fighting between you and me and between your herders and my herders. We are family. Is not the whole land before you? Separate yourself from me. If you go to the left, I will go to the right."

Lot looked around at the land before him, and he saw that it was vast and fertile. Choosing the plains of Jordan, Lot took his herds and left Abram. After Lot left, God instructed Abram to look around.

"Raise your eyes now and look from the place where you are, northward, southward, and eastward and westward. All the land you see, I will give to you and to your offspring forever. I will make your offspring like the dust of the earth. It is impossible to count the grains of dust and so it will be impossible to count all your descendants," said God.

Abram settled near the oaks of Mamre, which are at Hebron. There, he built an altar to God.

During this time, fighting broke out in the area of the Dead Sea, or Salt Sea, as it was also called. Rulers in the region tried to rebel against Chedorlaomer, who was a great warrior. Chedorlaomer and his allies were victorious in defeating the other rulers, and they took the possessions and land of those they conquered. Among the conquered was Lot, who lost his belongings and was captured.

When Abram learned of his nephew's misfortune, he set out with many men to rescue him. Abram successfully defeated Chedorlaomer, and he freed Lot. Following Lot's rescue, Abram received a vision from God. In his dream, God said to him, "Do not be afraid Abram, I am your shield. Your reward will be very great."

But Abram responded to the vision, "How can I be great when I have no children? The only child I have is with a slave woman. Sarai is unable to bear a child. Is the son of a slave to be my heir?"

God replied to Abram's question. "No, this child will not be your heir, Abram. Look at the stars in the sky tonight. They are plentiful. So shall your offspring be."

Abram heeded the words of God. He offered a sacrifice to God of a heifer, a female goat, a ram and a turtledove. As the sun set, he returned to his tent and fell into a deep sleep. While he was sleeping, a great darkness spread before him. Through it, God spoke.

"Know this for certain, Abram. Your offspring will be foreigners in a land that is not theirs. They will be slaves there for four hundred years. But then, I will bring judgment on the people who oppress them, and they will be given many possessions.

"As for you, Abram, you will join your ancestors in peace, because you have been a good man. To your descendants, I give this land, from the river of Egypt to the great river of the Euphrates, to the land of the Kenites, the Kenizzites, the Kadmonites, the Hittites, the Perizzites, the Rephaim, the Amorites, the Canaanites, the Girgashites and the Jebusites."

Abram was pleased with what God had told him. He remained faithful to God's plan.

When Abram was ninety-nine years old, God appeared to him again.

"Abram," God spoke to him, "walk with me and be blameless. I will make a covenant with you, a special agreement." Awestruck, Abram fell to his knees.

God continued, "Your name will no longer be Abram. From now on you will be known as 'Abraham.' You will be the ancestor of a multitude of nations. I will establish my covenant between you and me and your off-spring after you, throughout their generations. Forever, I will be God to you and to your offspring. I will give to your offspring the land where you are now an alien, all the land of Canaan, forever. And I will be their God."

Abram, who was now called Abraham, was very humbled. God also said to him, "Your wife Sarai will now be know as 'Sarah.' I will bless her, and I will give you a son with her. She shall give rise to nations, and kings of people will come to her."

Abraham believed God's promise, and God was pleased that Abraham trusted him to do something that seemed impossible.

ABRAHAM'S SON ISAAC

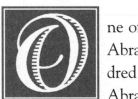

One of the many descendants of Noah was called Abraham. Abraham was a great man. When Abraham was one hundred years old, God kept a promise he had made with him. Abraham's wife, Sarah, became pregnant and gave birth to a son. The child was named Isaac. Sarah and Abraham were very happy that God had blessed them with a baby in their old age.

Sarah said, "God has brought laughter for me. Everyone who hears the sound will laugh with me. Who would ever have said that I would nurse children? And yet, I have a son for Abraham in his old age!"

There was a celebration when the child grew and was no longer nursed by Sarah. Their neighbors joined in the great feast Abraham had arranged. But Sarah noticed that Isaac was playing with Ishmael, the son of Hagar, an Egyptian woman. This disturbed Sarah, because the boy was the child of Hagar and her husband Abraham. He was a painful reminder that Abraham and Hagar had been together.

Sarah approached her husband and said, "Send away this slave woman with her son. Her son shall not inherit along with my son Isaac."

Sarah's request troubled Abraham. Hagar's child was also his son. How could he do as Sarah asked?

God said to Abraham, "Do not be distressed because of the boy and your slave woman. Whatever Sarah says to you, do as she tells you, because it is through Isaac that offspring shall be named for you. You do not have to worry about Hagar and her son. I will make this child the leader of a powerful nation, because he is also yours."

Abraham listened to God, and he sent Hagar and their child Ishmael away. He gave them food to eat and water to drink for the journey. Hagar and Ishmael traveled through the wilderness, but God protected them. When he was an adult, the son of Hagar and Abraham married an Egyptian woman. Abraham and Sarah and their son Isaac lived well for many years. But, one day, God decided to test Abraham's faith.

God said to Abraham, "Take your son Isaac, whom you love, and go to the land of Moriah. There, I wish you to offer him as a sacrifice, a burnt offering on the mountain that I will show you."

In the morning, Abraham collected wood for the offering. He mounted a donkey with his son Isaac. Two men went with them to the place where God had asked Abraham to go. On the third day of their journey, Abraham stopped and told the men to stay with the donkey.

"The boy and I will go over there to worship," he said. "Then, we will return."

He and Isaac took the wood for the offering, as well as a torch and a knife. They walked on together. Isaac looked at his father curiously.

"I see that we have everything for the offering to God. But where is the lamb that we will sacrifice?" Isaac asked him.

Abraham answered, "God will provide the lamb for the burnt offering, my son."

They continued to walk together. When they came to the place where God wished them to go, Abraham built an altar and put the wood on top of it. He turned to his son Isaac and bound him with ropes. Placing Isaac on the altar as God had asked him to do was a great test of Abraham's devotion to God. He loved his son Isaac very much. With a heavy heart, Abraham picked up the knife, and held it over Isaac.

An angel called to him from heaven, "Abraham, Abraham!"

"Here I am," Abraham answered.

"Do not lay your hand on the boy or do anything to him!" said the angel. "I now know that you fear and love God, because you were willing to sacrifice your son Isaac."

Abraham lowered his hand. He looked up past the altar and saw a ram with its horns caught in a bush. Abraham untied Isaac. Knife in hand, he approached the ram. Then, he killed the animal and made a burned offering of its flesh. Abraham called the place where he was, "God will provide."

The angel spoke to Abraham a second time. "God is pleased with what you have done, Abraham. He will reward you because you've listened to his voice. Your offspring will be as numerous as the stars of heaven and as the sand that is the seashore. All the peoples of the earth, in every nation, will gain a special blessing through your children."

Abraham and Isaac joyfully returned to the spot where the two men were waiting with the donkey. Then, they left together, grateful to God.

THE MARRIAGE OF ISAAC AND REBEKAH

hen Isaac was grown, he wished to marry. He spoke to his father Abraham about his desire. Abraham was a very old man at this time. His wife Sarah had died and was buried in the land of Canaan. Abraham knew it was important for his son to marry. So he spoke to his most trusted servant.

"Swear a solemn oath to me," he commanded the servant, "that you will help me find a suitable wife for my son. I do not wish him to marry anyone from the land of Canaan. I would prefer that you seek his bride from my relatives, in the country where I was born."

The servant was very willing to help Abraham. However, he knew that it might be difficult to convince a woman to leave Abraham's homeland and travel with him to meet Isaac.

"Sir," he asked Abraham, "What should I do if I find a woman but she does not wish to leave her family and follow me here?"

Abraham thought for a moment and then answered his servant. "In that case, you are free from any obligation to me."

The servant began his journey to find Isaac a wife. He collected ten of Abraham's camels. He packed up the many fine gifts Abraham had chosen for his new daughter-in-law and her family. Then he traveled to to the city of Nahor in Mesopotamia. When he arrived in the city, he went directly to the well to water his camels. It was evening, the time when women traditionally came to the well to get water for their households.

The servant began to pray. "O God of my master Abraham," he began, "please help me find a good wife for Isaac. I have chosen this spot in the city of Nahor. I pray that among the women who will come here tonight, I may find the right wife for Isaac. Give me a sign. When I ask for water, may she offer to water all of my camels as well. Then I will know that she is the one you have chosen."

Before he had finished praying, a beautiful young woman appeared at the well. She carried a water jug on her shoulders. She began to fill the vessel with water from the well.

Abraham's servant ran to her. "I would like to sip some water from your jar," he told her.

"Drink, my lord," she responded, not knowing who he was.

When the servant had finished drinking, the young woman spoke to him again. "Please allow me to give water to your thirsty camels, too."

The servant watched her draw water for his animals. He wondered if she was the one God had chosen for Isaac. When the camels finished drinking, the servant took a gold nose ring and two bracelets from the parcels that he carried. He offered them to the young woman.

"Tell me whose daughter you are," he said to her. "Is there room in your father's house for me to spend the night?"

The woman responded, "I am Rebekah, the daughter of Bethuel, son of Milcah and Nahor. Of course, we have plenty of straw and fodder and a place for you to spend the night."

The servant of Abraham was deeply touched by the young woman's kindness. He silently thanked God for directing him to young Rebekah. In the meantime, Rebekah ran to her house to tell her family about the man she had met at the well. Her family welcomed the servant into their house. They were curious about the jewelry that he had offered to Rebekah. They helped him unload his camels, and they offered him water to wash his tired feet. Then, they prepared delicious food for him to eat.

But the servant refused the food, saying, "I cannot accept your hospitality until I have told you why I have come here. I am the servant of Abraham, a powerful and good man, whom God has blessed with many wonderful things such as flocks and herds, silver and gold. God has also blessed Abraham and his wife Sarah with a son, Isaac. It is because of Isaac that I am here. I have promised my master to find a suitable wife for his beloved son. It is Abraham's wish that the young woman come from the land of his birth."

The servant explained to Rebekah's family how he had remained at the well in the city of Nahor to observe the women who would go there in the evening. He told them how he had prayed to God to find a suitable wife for Isaac.

"I was delighted when Rebekah came to the well," he told them. "I believe she is the one whom God has chosen for Abraham's son. However, I understand if Rebekah does not want to leave her home here and travel with me."

Rebekah's family asked her. "Do you wish to go with this man?"

"I will," she answered.

With her consent, Rebekah's family sent her with the man to Abraham and Isaac. One of her own servants traveled with her. Near their destination, Rebekah saw a young man approaching them.

"Who is that young man over there, walking in the fields to greet us?" Rebekah asked the servant.

"That is Isaac, the son of my master Abraham," the servant told her.

Rebekah covered her face with a veil. Then the servant greeted Isaac. He told him of his journey to Abraham's homeland and how he had found Rebekah. Isaac was very happy to meet this lovely young woman. He made her comfortable in his mother Sarah's tent. Soon, he fell in love with Rebekah and married her. Abraham was filled with delight that Isaac had found a bride, since his son would inherit all of his wealth and lands.

ESAU
AND JACOB

fter Sarah's death, Abraham married another woman, called Keturah. He and Keturah had many children. Isaac was still Abraham's only heir. It was Isaac and his descendants who would inherit the wealth of Abraham.

Abraham was very generous to all his sons and daughters. However, out of fairness to Isaac, Abraham gave gifts to his other children and sent them away to a land in the East.

Abraham died when he was 175 years old. He had lived a long and prosperous life. His son Isaac and his son Ishmael, whose mother was the Egyptian woman Hagar, joined together to bury their father. They took his body to the field Abraham had purchased from the Hittites near Mamre. He was laid to rest in the cave of Machpelah with his wife Sarah.

After Abraham's death, God blessed his son Isaac and sent him to live at Beer-lahai-roi. When Isaac's wife Rebekah was unable to have children,

Isaac prayed to God that he and Rebekah would be able to have children in order to continue the line of his father. Soon afterwards, Rebekah became pregnant. However, Rebekah's pregnancy was a difficult one, and she was in great pain. She asked God why she suffered so much.

"If this is how it is to be, how can I possibly endure the pain?" she implored.

God answered, "Two nations are in your womb, and the two peoples born of you shall be divided. The one shall be stronger than the other. The elder shall serve the younger."

Rebekah gave birth to twin sons. Although the delivery was difficult and long, Rebekah and Isaac were filled with joy. The first child to be born was called Esau. Because Esau's bright red hair also covered his arms and legs, it appeared that he was wearing a garment. Esau was also known as Edom, a play on the word "red." The second child was born holding onto Esau's heel. He was named Jacob. In the Hebrew language, the name Jacob has its roots in the word, "heel."

Although they were twins, Esau and Jacob were very different in nature. Esau liked to hunt and was a man of the fields. Jacob was a quiet man who liked living in tents. Isaac was very fond of his son Esau, because he, too, liked to hunt and to be in the wilderness. Jacob was Rebekah's favorite son.

One day, Jacob was sitting by his tent cooking some stew. Esau came in from the open country where he had been for many, many days. He was very tired, and he was extremely hungry. He smelled his brother's stew and approached him.

"Jacob," said Esau, "I have been in the wilderness for a long time, and I would like to share some of your meal. Quick, let me have some of that red lentil stew that smells so delicious, before I die of hunger!"

Jacob looked up at his brother. Although he was a quiet man, Jacob was also a schemer. He thought about the fact that, even though he and his brother were twins, Esau was the firstborn son. In ancient times, being the firstborn was very important. The eldest son received certain birthrights, including the right to inherit his father's wealth. This troubled Jacob. He knew that Esau was Isaac's favorite. Jacob decided to take advantage of the situation before him.

"I shall give you some of this stew, Esau," Jacob told him. "But first, you must sell me your birthright."

Esau was puzzled by Jacob's request. He could not understand why his brother would ask such a thing of him.

"Jacob," Esau spoke, "Why are you asking this of me? I am only hungry. So hungry, I feel that I might die of hunger! What good is my birthright to me now?"

Again, Jacob was aware of the advantage he had over the hungry Esau.

"Swear to me, that you will give me your birthright, Esau," he said. "If you do so, I will let you eat some of this food that I have prepared."

Esau was so overcome by hunger that still he did not see the full meaning of what Jacob was trying to do.

"If that is what you wish, then so be it, Jacob," Esau said to him. "I swear that you may have my birthright as the first son of Isaac."

Jacob was happy that his plan had worked and that Esau had sworn to give him the rights of a firstborn son. He offered his brother some of the lentil stew he had made, and also some bread. Esau hastily ate and drank. Then, he got up and left Jacob at his tent. Esau made his way back into the wilderness. Isaac was wrong to trick Esau. But Esau was wrong too. His actions showed he didn't think God's promise to Abraham was important at all.

ISAAC'S PEACE WITH THE PHILISTINE KING

great famine occurred in the land where Isaac lived. It was so severe that it was impossible to grow anything in the dry soil. Isaac's herds were hungry and thirsty. He knew that he had to leave the area. God spoke to Isaac and told him where he should go.

"Do not go down to Egypt. Settle in the land that I show you. If you stay there, even though you are a foreigner, I will be with you and I will bless you. I will give lands to you and your descendants. I will fulfill the oath I gave to your father Abraham, because he was good to me and obeyed my voice."

Isaac listened to the words of God. Gerar, where God directed him to go, was ruled by Abimelech of the Philistines. The people of the place were suspicious of Isaac, because he was a foreigner. Isaac was afraid to tell the Philistines that Rebekah was his wife, because he feared they would kill him in order to be with her. Instead, he called her his sister.

After he had planted seeds in the new land, Isaac enjoyed a bountiful harvest. God had blessed him, and he became very wealthy. He had many herds and flocks and a great household. The Philistines were not only suspicious of the foreigner and his sister, they were envious of Isaac's prosperity, as well.

Finally, Abimelech said to Isaac, "Why did you trick us and tell us that Rebekah was your sister? When I looked out of my window this morning, I saw that you were with her as her husband. Go away from us. We do not trust you, and you have become too powerful."

Isaac departed from the land of the Philistines. He camped in the valley of Gerar and settled there. He noticed that the Philistines had filled the wells that his father Abraham had dug in the valley with mud and dirt. So, he opened them up again, and he called them by the names his father had given them.

Isaac's servants also dug for water in other parts of the valley. They discovered a well of spring water under the ground, but the local herdsmen did not want them to have it, saying, "This water is ours." Isaac called the well "Esek," because the men had argued with him over it. Esek meant "dispute" in Hebrew. He instructed his servants to dig elsewhere.

When they had come upon another well, the herders also claimed it as their own. Isaac named that well "Sitnah" or "opposition," because of the bad feelings of the herders. Finally, Isaac's servants found a third well. The locals did not claim this one, and Isaac was pleased. Isaac called the well "Rehoboth," meaning a "broad place or room."

"God has made room for us and we shall be fruitful in the land," he said. Because of the difficulty with the Philistine herdsmen over the wells, Isaac decided to move to a place called Beersheba. That evening, God appeared to him.

"I am the God of your father Abraham," God told Isaac. "Don't be afraid, because I am with you. I will bless you and make your offspring numerous for my servant Abraham's sake."

Isaac was comforted by the words, and he pitched a tent in the place where he heard God's voice. Building an altar there, he told his servants to dig another well. Eventually, Abimelech came from Gerar to find Isaac. He traveled with Ahuzzath, his advisor, and Phicol, the commander of his army. The sight of Abimelech and his men troubled Isaac.

"Why have you come to me?" Isaac demanded. "You did not trust me, and sent me away from you."

Abimelech answered, "That is true. We did not trust you. But now we can see that God has been with you, Isaac. Therefore, we wish to make an oath with you. The covenant between us will be that you will not harm us, since we did not harm you, but we sent you away peacefully."

Isaac was pleased by Abimelech's offer of an oath. He had no quarrel with him. To celebrate the happy news, he ordered his servants to prepare a great feast for Abimelech and his men. That evening, everyone had much to eat and drink. Then, they went to sleep. Early the next morning, Isaac and Abimelech rose early and repeated the vow to live together peacefully. Then, Abimelech and his men departed.

Isaac's servants approached him. They had dug a well as he had instructed them. "Come and see the water we have found!" they told him.

Isaac went to the new well with them and named it "Shibah," which is similar to the Hebrew word for "oath." This well would commemorate the covenant between Isaac and the Philistines.

The city of Beersheba was named after Isaac's well. It was at Beersheba that Isaac and Rebekah finally found peace.

JACOB'S TRICK

s Isaac grew older, his eyesight began to fail. One day he called his eldest son Esau to him.

"My son," he said. "I am old and cannot see very well. I don't know how many days I have left. Please, take your bow and arrows and go into open country and hunt for me. When you return home, you can prepare the game that you've hunted. Then I will give you a special blessing. It is important to me that I bless you before I die."

Isaac's blessing was very important. It meant that he recognized Esau as the eldest son and his legal heir. When Rebekah overheard what Isaac had said, she began to worry about her favorite son, Jacob. As soon as Esau left to go hunting, Rebekah called Jacob to her.

"Jacob," she said to him. "Your father has asked your brother to go into the wilderness and hunt for him. He has instructed him to cook the game exactly as he likes it. Then he will give Esau his special blessing."

Rebekah continued, "Do as I say, Jacob. Go out into the field and bring me two young goats, so that I can prepare them as your father likes. Once I do, you will go to your father, present him with the food and receive his blessing."

Jacob was confused by his mother's request. "If I go to my father," he reasoned, "he will know it is me and not Esau, because I have very smooth skin. Esau has red, hairy skin. Our father cannot see well and will touch me to know if I am Esau. When he finds out that I am not my brother, he may curse me for trying to deceive him."

"Don't worry," Rebekah said. "I have a plan, Jacob. I will take the skin from these young goats and make a garment for you to wear on your arms, so that your skin will appear hairy. Then, if Isaac touches you, he will think that you are your brother Esau. He will bless you, which is very important. And, if he should discover who you are, it is me that he will curse."

Rebekah knew the seriousness of what she planned. If Isaac discovered her actions, she might never see Jacob again. Yet Rebekah wanted Jacob, not Esau to inherit the wealth of Isaac.

Jacob went out and did as his mother commanded. He brought two young goats to her, and she prepared them as a tasty meal that would please her husband Isaac. Rebekah collected some of Esau's clothing and told Jacob to change into the clothes.

She took the skin from the animals Jacob had killed and made a covering for Jacob's hands and arms and his neck. She handed Jacob the food, and she sent him to his father.

"Father," Jacob said, "I am Esau, your firstborn child. I have brought you the delicious food that you requested. I am ready to receive your special blessing."

Isaac was startled by Esau's appearance. "Esau, did you find the game so quickly?"

Jacob replied, "I was able to do it so quickly, father, because God helped me."

Then, Isaac asked Jacob to bend down near him. "Esau, come close to me so that I may touch you and know that you are truly my eldest son."

Isaac touched him on his hands, arms and neck. "This is strange to me," Isaac said. "Your voice is so much like Jacob's. Yet, you feel like my son Esau. Are you really Esau?"

Jacob answered nervously, "Yes, father, I am."

Isaac asked Jacob to bring him the food that he had prepared. He ate the savory meal and drank some wine.

When he was finished eating, Isaac asked Jacob to come close to him again. "Come near and kiss me, my son," Isaac instructed him.

When Jacob leaned over to kiss his father, Isaac could smell that it was Esau from the odor of the garments that he wore.

"Ah, the smell of Esau is like a field that God has blessed," he said. "May God give you the dew of heaven, the fatness of the earth and plenty of grain and wine. Let people serve you and nations bow down to you. Be lord over your offspring and may your mother's children bow down to you. Cursed be everyone who curses you, and blessed be everyone who blesses you."

When Jacob received his father's blessing, he left. No sooner had he gone than Esau returned from the fields with game that he had prepared for his father.

"Father," Esau said to Isaac, "I have returned with the game that you asked me to kill. I am ready to receive your special blessing."

"Who are you?" asked the very confused Isaac.

Esau answered, "I am your firstborn son, Esau, of course."

Isaac trembled violently. "How can this be? Who was it that hunted game just a short time ago and brought it to me and asked for my blessing?" he asked. "Who was it that I gave my blessing to?"

When Esau heard this, he was filled with a terrible anger. Esau understood how important it was that Isaac recognize him as his heir.

"Father!" he yelled, "how could you give your special blessing to anyone else but me? Surely, you can give me a blessing, too! Was it to Jacob that you gave your blessing? Has he tricked me yet another time? Was it not enough for him to fool me into giving him my birthright?" Esau began to weep.

What had occurred deeply saddened Isaac, but he knew that he could not undue the blessing and promise he had bestowed upon his son Jacob.

Isaac tried to comfort Esau. "I am sorry this happened, my son," he said. "You shall not live by the fatness of the earth or the dew from heaven. By your sword, you will live. And you will serve your brother as is now proper. But someday," he continued, "you will break free of Jacob's control over you."

Esau was filled with hatred for his brother Jacob. He waited for the time when he could get revenge against his brother.

JACOB'S DREAM

J acob's life changed quickly after he tricked his father into blessing him by pretending to be his brother Esau.

"Leave at once," Rebekah told Jacob. "Go, my son, to my brother Laban in Haran until your brother's anger passes and he forgets what you have done to him."

Esau was furious. He hated Jacob for receiving the blessing as the first-born son of his father Isaac. To make matters worse, Isaac had said that Esau would serve Jacob. Rebekah, his mother, overheard the news that Esau plotted to kill Jacob as soon as Isaac died, and after Esau finished mourning the death.

Rebekah schemed to save her one son from the wrath of the other. She told Isaac that Jacob was going to Paddan-aram to the household of Laban. There he would find a wife and settle for a time. With this plan, Jacob would be safe. Again, Isaac blessed Jacob and wished him prosperity and many children. Isaac also prayed that Jacob would return to live in the country God promised to Abraham. For, although they lived in the promised land, they were governed by another people.

"May God bless you and make you fruitful and numerous so that you become a company of peoples. May you and your offspring take possession of the land that God gave to Abraham, the land where you now live as a stranger," said Isaac to his son Jacob.

Jacob obeyed his mother, accepted his father's blessing and set off for his uncle's household.

Esau understood from Jacob's departure that his parents frowned upon taking a wife from the people of the area, the Canaanites. To please Isaac and Rebekah, Esau married Mahalath, the daughter of Abraham's son Ishmael.

As Jacob travelled, the sun had set so he decided to rest for the night. He found a shelter near some rocks. He was exhausted from the fast pace he had taken to get away from Esau's wrath. Jacob was eager to sleep. In the collection of small rocks scattered about his shelter, he selected one upon which to lay his head.

In only moments, Jacob was asleep. He dreamed a dream from God. He saw a ladder with so many steps that it reached from the floor of the earth through the clouds and into heaven. Some angels were going up the ladder, while others were going down the ladder. Jacob stood near the ladder with God.

In the dream, God told Jacob, "I am the God of Abraham and Isaac. The land on which you lie I will give to you and your offspring. Your children shall be like the dust of the earth, and you shall spread abroad to the west and the east, to the north and the south. Know that I am with you and I will bring you back to this land. I will not leave you until I have done what I promised you."

Then, Jacob awoke and spoke to himself. "This is no place other than the house of God. It is the gate of heaven."

The place had the name of Luz before Jacob arrived. But Jacob called it Bethel, because in Hebrew, Bethel means "the house of God." With great care, Jacob built a pillar of stones as high as he could reach. Then, he set the stone on top which had been his pillow. Jacob poured oil over the stone, and he prayed.

For the first time, Jacob stopped to feel how sad he was to leave his father's house. He asked God to protect him where he went until he could return. He vowed to honor God in gratitude.

Jacob said, "God, be with me, keep me where I go and give me bread to eat and clothing to wear until I come again to my father's house in peace. You are my God, and this stone which I have set up as a pillar will be God's house. Of all that you have given me, I will surely give one-tenth to you."

Jacob was a changed man. He continued on his journey. He saw from his dream that he was not only running from Esau. He was beginning a new life in the land of the East. He would have many children, and they would move away in all directions. God had blessed his family, and Jacob had promised to honor God in return.

He walked until he came to a well where three flocks of sheep were resting. Jacob talked with the shepherds. They were from the town where his uncle lived. As they talked, the shepherds said, "Look! Here comes your cousin, Rachel, with your uncle's sheep." Jacob was glad, because he knew that God had guided his journey thus far.

RACHEL AND JACOB

Jacob first caught a glimpse of Rachel at the well where she had brought her father's sheep to be watered. She was the daughter of his mother's brother Laban. Jacob told the young woman that he was her kinsman. They kissed, and Jacob wept at finding a member of his family after his long, hard journey from the house of his father Isaac.

News of Jacob's arrival reached Laban, Rachel's father. The uncle ran to meet his nephew.

"Surely you are my bone and my flesh," said Laban, in the expression of the time.

Jacob remained as a visitor in his uncle's house for about a month. Rachel was the younger of his two daughters. Her sister's name was Leah. Jacob fell in love with Rachel. Since it was the custom at the time for cousins to marry, Jacob was eager to make Rachel his wife.

At the end of the month, Jacob's uncle invited him to remain as part of the household. Jacob began to shepherd Laban's flocks like the others in the service of household. But, Laban was careful not to abuse Jacob's good nature.

"Just because you are my kinsman, should you serve me for nothing?" asked Laban.

"I will serve you seven years for the hand of your daughter Rachel," said Jacob.

"It is better that Rachel marries you than any other man," agreed Laban.

The following seven years of Jacob's life were as sweet as the spring rain. Jacob loved Laban's younger daughter Rachel so much that Jacob worked for love without any attention to how hard he worked or how many years he tended the flocks. The seven years ended at last. Jacob hurried to claim Rachel for his wife. Laban arranged a large wedding feast to celebrate the union. But Laban tricked Jacob. After the dinner was eaten, Laban brought Leah instead of Rachel to Jacob's room. When the morning arrived, Jacob saw what his dishonest father-in-law had done.

"What have you done to me? Did I not serve you for Rachel's hand as we agreed? Why did you deceive me?" protested Jacob to Laban.

"In our country, we do not give the younger sister in marriage before the firstborn. But, complete this week of wedding celebrations, and I promise you also the hand of Rachel, in return for seven years' more work," said Laban.

When the guests left Laban's house, Jacob took Rachel as his wife. He began to serve his father-in-law for an additional seven years. Now Jacob had two wives, Leah and Rachel. But, Jacob only loved Rachel. In a short time, God saw that Leah was unloved, so she conceived a child by Jacob. Rachel, on the other hand, was childless. Leah hoped that now Jacob would love her more than her sister. She gave birth and conceived again.

It happened again a third time. Now, Leah had three sons. Rachel was still childless, even though Jacob continued to love her more.

"Give me children or I shall die!" cried Rachel one day to her husband.

"Am I God?" protested Jacob.

Rachel prayed night and day for a child. After many years, she conceived and gave birth to a son. Rachel and Jacob named him Joseph.

It was time for Jacob and his wives and children to leave the home of Laban. While Jacob lived in Laban's household, his uncle prospered. Laban did not want to see his prosperity suffer upon Jacob's leaving, so once again he was dishonest with his son-in-law. When Jacob went to say goodbye to Laban, Laban asked Jacob what wages he was owed.

Instead of wages, Jacob asked his uncle for the right to remove from Laban's flock the speckled and spotted sheep and the black lambs. He would leave the white animals for Laban. Laban agreed, then ordered his sons to gather all the speckled, spotted and black animals and go ahead of Jacob with them by three days. When he looked for the animals he was promised, Jacob knew he had again been tricked, but he was able to take his share of livestock from the newborns of his uncle's flock that were born. Now he had a herd to rely upon for his new life. Jacob's herd grew into large flocks.

The angel of God appeared to Jacob in a dream. "I am the God of Bethel where you anointed a pillar and made a vow to me. Now leave this land at once and return to the land of your birth."

Jacob gathered his family and his worldly possessions and set out for the hilly country over which he had traveled many years earlier. When Laban learned that Jacob was fleeing with his daughters, he followed at a rapid pace behind them. Unknown to Jacob, Rachel had stolen her father's household gods and brought them with her on the trip. Laban overtook Jacob's party and accused Jacob of stealing from him. Of course he had not stolen anything, Jacob protested.

He was very angry at Laban's words, because it was Laban who had cheated Jacob many times. Jacob told Laban to enter his tent and see for himself that none of his belongings were there. And Laban never found them, because Rachel hid them so well.

The two men made an agreement that day to mend the anger between them. Jacob reached for a stone, much like the one he had used years earlier as a pillow. He placed it on top of a pillar that he built on the sandy ground. The others in the party also gathered stones and they created a great heap of stones together. Jacob called the heap "Galeed," which means "the heap of witness" in Hebrew. It was also called Mizpah, meaning "watch tower."

Laban said, "This heap and this pillar are witness (or watch tower) that I will not pass beyond here to harm you, and you will not pass beyond here to harm me."

Then, Laban kissed his grandchildren, blessed his daughters and made his way home in an easterly direction. Meanwhile, as Jacob neared Canaan, he sent messengers to his brother Esau announcing his arrival. The message in return said that Esau was coming to meet Jacob with an army of four hundred men. At the news, Jacob was frightened. He divided his animals into two herds, so that if Esau were to destroy one herd, Jacob's family would still have one herd left.

When Esau approached, Jacob was very distressed, expecting to be punished by his brother's wrath. But, instead, Esau ran to meet him. The brothers embraced and wept to see one another after so many years.

Jacob built a shelter for his family and his cattle in the valley of the Jordan River. The place was called Succoth.

JOSEPH AND HIS BROTHERS

The patriarch Jacob, who was also called Israel, had twelve sons. Rachel, Jacob's wife whom he loved very much, was mother to Joseph, the next to the youngest son, and Benjamin, the youngest. Since Rachel's death at Benjamin's birth, Joseph had become the light of his father's life. When Joseph was seventeen years old, and Jacob, a very old man, Jacob gave his favorite child a beautiful striped coat of many colors.

Jacob's other sons already saw how much their father loved Joseph. The gift of the wonderfully colored coat was too much for them to tolerate. They became extremely jealous and could not wish Joseph, "Shalom," the Hebrew word for "peace." To complicate matters, Joseph began to dream of greatness in his future, dreams he could not understand at his young age. When he shared his dreams with his brothers, their hatred toward the favorite son of Jacob grew.

"Listen to this dream I dreamed," Joseph said to his brothers the first time. "There we were, binding sheaves in the field. Suddenly my sheaf rose and stood upright; then your sheaves gathered around it, and bowed down to my sheaf."

A sheaf is a bunch of wheat or other cereal grass tied around the middle once it is cut. Jacob's sons lived in the grasslands of Canaan where they also tended flocks of animals. A sheaf would be taken from the fields to the barn, where it was stored until the wheat was to be eaten.

"Are you to reign over us?" asked his brothers angrily, and their hatred became even stronger. Joseph was innocent of what his brothers claimed he intended. In the same spirit, he shared his next dream with them, and also with his father Jacob.

"Look, I have had another dream: the sun, the moon, and the eleven stars were bowing down to me," said Joseph.

"What kind of dream is this that you have had? Shall we indeed come, I and your mother and your brothers, and bow to the ground before you?" asked Jacob.

But the old man saw that the dream was important. As for Joseph's brothers, they wanted nothing further to do with him. They were certain his intentions were to rule over them and even their father. In their opinion, Joseph did not even stop there in his ambition, because in his dream his dead mother bowed to him, too.

The brothers went to pasture their father's flock, leaving Joseph at home. After some time, Jacob asked his favorite son to go to the distant pasture and check on things.

"Are not your brothers pasturing the flock at Shechem?" Jacob asked. "Go now; see if it is well with your brothers and with the flock, and bring word back to me."

In Shechem, the place Jacob mentioned, Joseph met a man who helped him search for his brothers. Some say the stranger was a messenger of God sent to guide Joseph to his destiny.

"What are you seeking?" asked the stranger.

"I am seeking my brothers. Tell me, please, where they are pasturing the flock," said Joseph.

"They have gone away, for I heard them say, 'Let us go to Dothan,'" said the stranger.

Following the stranger's direction, Joseph found his brothers at Dothan. At Joseph's approach, the jealous brothers began to plot against him. They saw their opportunity to get even and decided to kill him.

"Here comes this dreamer," said one. "Let us kill him and throw him into one of the pits; then we shall say that a wild animal has devoured him, and we shall see what will become of his dreams."

Reuben, Jacob's firstborn, said, "Shed no blood; throw him into this pit here in the wilderness, but lay no hand on him." It was his intention to rescue Joseph from the deep hole and return him to his father.

So, the brothers stripped Joseph of his beautiful colored coat and threw him down into the deep hole without even water to drink. Then they sat down to eat out of sight of where Joseph was trapped. A caravan of merchants in the distance, carrying gum, balm and resin bound for Egypt, gave Judah, one of the brothers, an idea.

"How do we benefit if we kill our brother and conceal his blood? Come, let us sell him to the Ishmaelites, and not lay our hands on him, for he is our brother, our own flesh," said Judah.

The other brothers agreed that they might as well make some money out of their hatred for Joseph instead of merely killing him. They lifted poor Joseph out of his captivity and sold him to the caravan for twenty pieces of silver. Unknown to his brothers, Joseph was bound for Egypt.

Reuben, true to his plan to rescue Joseph, returned to the pit for Joseph and found it empty. "The boy is gone; what am I to do?" he cried to his brothers.

Now the brothers had to tell their father Joseph was missing. However, they decided not to admit that they knew he was in the hands of merchants. After all, they had done nothing to rescue Joseph. So, they slaughtered a goat and dipped Joseph's robe into its blood, making it look as though he had been taken by a wild animal and eaten.

"See what we found; is this your son's robe?" they said to their father when they returned home.

"It is my son's robe!" said the distraught Jacob. "A wild animal has devoured him; Joseph is without doubt torn to pieces."

Then Jacob tore his own clothing, which was the traditional way to show sorrow for the dead. All of his sons and daughters tried to comfort him, but he refused to be comforted. Alone, Jacob mourned for his favorite son for many days.

No one knew that on that day Joseph would be sold to Potiphar, one of the Egyptian Pharaoh's officials, the captain of the royal guard. No one expected that the family would reunite with Joseph in the future.

Joseph was the first of Jacob's family to experience slavery in Egypt. His story is found in the Bible at the end of the Book of Genesis. The entire story of Joseph, of which this story is a part, leads to the next book of the Bible, the Book of Exodus, which tells of the freeing of the Israelites from slavery in Egypt.

JOSEPH AS PRISONER

n Egypt, Joseph lived in the house of Potiphar and his wife. Although many slaves served in the fields or at construction work, Potiphar saw that with Joseph in his house, he was more prosperous than ever. His fields flourished and his house grew rich. Potiphar trusted Joseph completely, because he recognized that Joseph was blessed by God.

Joseph was handsome. After a time, Potiphar's wife wanted to show her affection for the slave. But Joseph was honorable. He explained himself to Potiphar's wife.

"My master has no concern about anything in the house. He has put everything that he has in my hand except yourself, because you are his wife. How then could I do this great wickedness, and sin against God?" asked Joseph.

Potiphar's wife, like Joseph's brothers before her, plotted against Joseph.

One day, she grabbed his clothing and commanded him to show her affection, which he refused. Instead, he turned abruptly to leave her, but she would not let go of his garment. He fled, and the garment ripped and remained torn in her grasp. Potiphar's wife was angry, and she cried out for her husband. She told him a lie about Joseph.

"The Hebrew servant, whom you have brought among us, came in to me to insult me," she claimed, showing Potiphar the garment as proof.

Potiphar was angry. But, because of his fondness for Joseph, he had Joseph jailed with the king's prisoners, instead of in the more desperate prison for slaves.

Again, Joseph showed by his goodness that he was blessed by God. Because of it, the chief jailer committed to Joseph's care all of the prisoners who were in the king's prison.

Shortly afterward, the Pharaoh grew angry with his cupbearer and his baker, and he imprisoned them. The chief jailer put the two officers in Joseph's charge. One night, the cupbearer and the baker had disturbing dreams.

"Why are you so sad today?" asked Joseph when he came to them the following morning.

"We have had dreams, and there is no one to interpret them," they said.

"Do not interpretations belong to God? Please tell me the dreams," answered Joseph.

The chief cupbearer told his dream first. "In my dream there was a vine before me, and on the vine there were three branches," he said. "As soon as it budded, its blossoms came out and the clusters ripened into grapes. Pharaoh's cup was in my hand, and I took the grapes and pressed them into Pharaoh's cup, and placed the cup in Pharaoh's hand."

Joseph told him the meaning of the dream. "The three branches are three days. Within three days Pharaoh will restore you to your office, and you shall place Pharaoh's cup in his hand, just as you used to do when you were his cupbearer."

Then, Joseph asked the cupbearer to speak to the Pharaoh about him, requesting his release, because he was stolen from the land of the Hebrews. The cupbearer agreed.

Next, the chief baker told his dream, because he saw that Joseph had given a favorable meaning to the cupbearer's dream. "I also had a dream," said the chief baker. "There were three cake baskets on my head, and in the uppermost basket, there were all sorts of baked foods for the Pharaoh. But the birds were eating it out of the basket on my head."

Joseph saw that, in the first dream, Pharaoh was nourished. But, in the second, he was deprived of food. He gave the baker his interpretation of the dream.

"The three baskets are three days. Within three days, Pharaoh will lift up your head from you—and hang you on a pole, and the birds will eat the flesh from you."

On the third day, Pharaoh celebrated his birthday. He made a feast for all of his servants. Pharaoh restored the chief cupbearer to his position, and he ordered that the baker be hanged. In spite of his promise, the cupbearer forgot to mention Joseph's request.

Two years passed, and Joseph was still in the king's prison. Then, Pharaoh had a dream. He dreamed he was standing by the Nile and out of the river came seven cows, some sleek and some fat, and they grazed in the reed grass. Seven other cows followed, some ugly and some thin. These seven stood by the first seven cows on the bank of the Nile.

After the dream, Pharaoh awoke. But, he fell asleep again and dreamed a second dream. Seven ears of corn, plump and good, grew on one stalk. Seven thin ears, blighted by the east wind, sprouted up behind them and swallowed the plump ears.

Pharaoh told his dreams to all of the magicians and all of the wise men of Egypt. But, no one could interpret the dreams. Then, the chief cupbearer remembered Joseph.

"I remember my faults today," he told Pharaoh. And the cupbearer explained about his dream and the dream of the baker. He told the Pharaoh about the young Hebrew and how he correctly read the meaning of both dreams. Then, Pharaoh sent for Joseph from the prison.

"I have had a dream, and there is no one who can interpret it. I have heard it said of you that when you hear a dream you can interpret it," Pharaoh told Joseph.

Joseph answered, "It is not I; God will give Pharaoh a favorable answer."

After Pharaoh repeated his dreams, Joseph spoke again.

"Pharaoh's dreams are one and the same; God has revealed what he is about to do. The seven good cows are seven years; and the seven good ears are seven years. The dreams are one. The seven lean and ugly cows that came up after them are seven years, as are the seven empty ears blighted by the east wind. They are seven years of famine."

Joseph told Pharaoh that God had spoken to the king. After seven years of great plenty in Egypt, seven years of famine would follow and be enough to make the plenty be forgotten in the land. The doubling of the dream, Joseph explained, meant that the events were fixed by God. Joseph suggested that Pharaoh select a very wise man and set him in charge of the land of Egypt. Pharaoh should then appoint overseers to take one-fifth of the produce of Egypt during the years of plenty and store it for use during the seven years of famine. In this way, Joseph said, the land of Egypt would not perish.

Because Pharaoh saw that Joseph spoke in the spirit of God, he appointed Joseph to supervise what had to be done in the land of Egypt.

"See, I have set you over all the land of Egypt," Pharaoh said to Joseph. "I am Pharaoh, and without your consent, no one shall lift up hand or foot in all the land of Egypt."

And Pharaoh removed the signet ring from his own hand and put it on Joseph's finger. He ordered Joseph dressed in garments of fine linen, and he put a gold chain around his neck. Joseph's fortune had changed indeed.

JOSEPH AS GOVERNOR

Joseph was thirty years old when Pharaoh appointed him governor of the land of Egypt. Pharaoh gave Joseph an Egyptian name and a wife named Asenath. He respected Joseph, and he made sure that Joseph's household was rich in furnishings and servants. During the seven years of plenty, the harvest of crops was very large. Joseph ordered that food be stored in every city from the surrounding fields. As much grain as there were sands by the sea was stored in the cities of Egypt. So much was stored during those seven years that Joseph stopped measuring its quantity.

Joseph's wife had two sons, and Joseph called them both by Hebrew names. He named the first Manasseh.

"God has made me forget all my hardship and all about my father's house," he said about the meaning of the name Manasseh.

The second son was called Ephraim.

"God has made me fruitful in the land of my misfortunes," said Joseph at the naming of the second son.

The years of plenty came to an end as Joseph had said they would. Seven years of famine followed. In the land of Egypt, the people cried out to Pharaoh about their hunger. He heard their cries, and he told them his solution.

"Go to Joseph. Do what he tells you," said Pharaoh to the Egyptians.

In response to the people's cries, Joseph opened all the storehouses in the land. He sold grain to all the people of Egypt. All the other peoples of the world came to Joseph, too, for grain, because the famine was severe in every land on earth.

When Jacob, in the land of Canaan, learned that there was grain in Egypt, he spoke to his sons.

"Why do you keep looking at one another? I have heard that there is grain in Egypt. Go down and buy some for us there, that we may live and not die," said Joseph's father, not knowing whom his sons would find when they arrived in Egypt for the grain.

Ten of Joseph's brothers traveled from Canaan to Egypt. Jacob kept his youngest, Benjamin, at home. He greatly feared that he would lose the only remaining son of his beloved wife Rachel. When Joseph saw his brothers, he recognized them. And he remembered the dreams he had about them when he was a boy. But he treated them like strangers and spoke harshly to them. For their part, the brothers did not know the powerful governor was their lost brother Joseph.

"Where do you come from?" he questioned them.

"From the land of Canaan, to buy food," they answered.

"I say you are spies," he accused them.

"No, my lord. We, your servants, have come to buy food. We are twelve brothers, the sons of a certain man in the land of Canaan. The youngest is still with our father. And one is no more," they answered.

Joseph did not relent. "It is just as I have said to you. You are spies!" he said. "Here is how you shall be tested. As Pharaoh lives, you shall not leave this place until your youngest brother comes here. Let one of you go and bring this brother. The rest of you will remain in prison until then."

They refused, and Joseph put them in prison. However, he did not wish to behave unjustly, nor did he wish for them to die in prison. On the third day of their imprisonment, he spoke to them again.

"If you are honest men, let one of you stay here. The rest of you shall go and carry grain to your household. Return with the youngest brother to me. Thus, your words will be tested and you shall not die."

They spoke among themselves.

"Alas, we are paying the penalty for what we did to our brother. We saw his pain when he pleaded with us for his life, but we would not listen. That is why this pain has come upon us," they said, talking about what they had done to Joseph.

Reuben spoke out: "Did I tell you not to wrong the boy? But you would not listen. So now we pay for his blood."

They were unaware that Joseph understood their conversation, since he spoke with them through an interpreter and had pretended to be Egyptian. Joseph turned away from them and wept. Then, he pointed to Simeon. He ordered that Simeon be bound before their eyes. The other brothers he sent away with bags full of grain. They were also given provisions for the journey to Canaan by Joseph's servants.

When the brothers opened their sacks outside the city, they saw that the money they had brought with them to Egypt to buy the grain lay inside the sacks, unspent. They turned trembling to one another.

"What is this that God has done to us?" they cried out.

JOSEPH'S ORDERS TO HIS BROTHERS

hen the brothers returned to Canaan with the grain, they told Jacob what had happened in Egypt.

"The man, the governor of the land, spoke harshly to us and charged us with spying on the land. Then he said to us, 'Leave one of your brothers with me, take grain for the famine of your household and go your way. Bring your youngest brother to me, and I shall know that you are honest men. Then I will release your brother to you.'"

Jacob said, "Joseph is no more, and Simeon is no more. And now you would take Benjamin."

Reuben tried to console their father. "You may kill my two sons if I do not bring Benjamin back to you. Put him in my hands, and I will bring him back to you."

But Jacob refused to send Benjamin, and the matter was closed. The famine continued to grow worse, and soon the all grain they had brought to Canaan was eaten. Jacob implored his sons to return to Egypt for more grain.

This time Judah spoke to his father. "The man solemnly warned us, saying, 'You shall not see my face unless your brother is with you.' Send Benjamin with me, and let us be on our way so that we may not die, you and me and also our little ones."

Jacob said, "If it must be so, then do this. Take some of the choicest fruits of the land in your bags and give them as a present to the man, a little balm and a little honey, gum, resin, pistachio nuts and almonds. Take double the money with you. Carry back with you the money that was returned in the top of your sacks. Perhaps it was an oversight. Take your brother also and may God Almighty grant you mercy before the man so that he may send back your other brother Simeon and Benjamin."

The brothers stood again before Joseph in Egypt. When Joseph saw Benjamin with them, he ordered the steward of his house to slaughter an animal and invite the travelers to dine with him at noon. His brothers were afraid and petitioned the steward to take back the money which they were sure would cause them further punishment. The steward told them not to worry.

He said, "Rest assured, do not be afraid. Your God and the God of your father must have put treasure in your sacks for you. I received your money the first time."

When Joseph arrived home at noon, all of his brothers including Simeon were in his house.

"Is your father well, the old man of whom you spoke? Is he still alive?" Joseph asked them.

They bowed their heads respectfully and told him yes. When Joseph saw Benjamin, his own mother's son, he was overcome with emotion. He hurried out of the room to weep. Upon returning, he ordered that the meal be served. The steward served Joseph first and gave portions from his table to the brothers. They did not dine together, because it was against the law for Egyptians to eat with Hebrews. Benjamin's portion was five times greater than his brothers' portions. When the meal was finished, the brothers left Joseph's house, including Simeon.

Joseph commanded his steward, "Fill the men's sacks with food, as much as they can carry, and put each man's money in the top of his sack. Put my silver cup in the top of the sack belonging to the youngest."

In the morning when the brothers had traveled only a short distance toward Canaan, they were overtaken by the steward, who spoke the words Joseph had commanded him to speak.

"Why have you returned evil for good? Why have you stolen my silver cup?" demanded the steward.

The brothers protested. So sure were they of their innocence that they told the steward that the one in whose bag the cup was found would die. They also offered that the rest of them would become the governor's servants. When they searched their sacks, they were horrified to see the silver cup in Benjamin's possession. As was the custom at the time, they tore at their clothes to show their anguish, because Benjamin would have to die. Afterwards they returned to the city.

They fell to the ground before Joseph, sure that God had found them guilty of their past deed. They offered themselves as his slaves.

"Only the one in whose possession the cup was found shall be my slave," said Joseph. "As for you," he said to the others, "go up in peace to your father."

Judah spoke to Joseph about his father. "When he sees that the boy is not with us, he will die." Then he referred to himself. "Now, therefore, please let your servant remain as a slave to my lord in place of the boy. And let the boy go back with his brothers. For how can I go back to my father if the boy is not with me?"

Joseph could no longer pretend before his brothers.

"Come closer to me. I am your brother, Joseph, whom you sold into Egypt. And now do not be angry with yourselves, for God sent me before you to save lives. Hurry and go up to my father and say to him, 'Thus says your son Joseph, God has made me lord of all Egypt. Come down to me. Do not delay.'"

Joseph promised to provide for his family in Egypt, as there were five more years of famine to come. He wept upon Benjamin's neck, and Benjamin wept upon Joseph's. The word reached Pharaoh that Joseph's brothers were in Egypt, and Pharaoh provided wagons to accompany them back to Canaan for the return trip with their wives, children and Jacob. Joseph gave new clothing to each of his brothers. To Benjamin, he gave five sets of clothing and three hundred pieces of silver. For his father, he sent ten male donkeys loaded with gifts from Egypt and ten female donkeys with grain, bread and other provisions.

When the brothers told Jacob what happened in Egypt on this trip, he said, "My son Joseph is still alive. I must go and see him before I die."

JACOB IN EGYPT

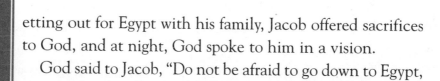

Setting out for Egypt with his family, Jacob offered sacrifices to God, and at night, God spoke to him in a vision.

God said to Jacob, "Do not be afraid to go down to Egypt, for I will make of you a great nation there. I myself will go down with you to Egypt, and I will also bring you up again. And Joseph's own hand shall close your eyes."

In all, seventy members of Jacob's family settled in the land of Egypt. Pharaoh invited them to live in Goshen, in the northern part of the Nile Delta, in an area that was green and fertile and very well-suited to the raising of sheep. Joseph prepared his chariot and met his father in Goshen. When he saw Jacob, Joseph wept on his father's neck as he had done on the day when he presented himself to his younger brother Benjamin.

"I can die now, having seen for myself that you are still alive," responded Jacob to Joseph.

Joseph presented his father to Pharaoh, and Jacob gave his blessing to the ruler of Egypt. When he settled in the new land, Jacob was 130 years old.

The famine grew more severe in all the lands. Joseph collected all the money to be found in the lands of Egypt and Canaan, and he brought it to Pharaoh's house. It was money that the residents had paid for the grain they received during the early years of the famine.

When the people came next to Joseph to ask for food, he could not request money from them. He told them instead, "Give us your livestock, and I will give you food in exchange."

And he exchanged food for livestock for one year. By the following year, Joseph had bought all the livestock. Now he bought the land from the people of Egypt in the name of Pharaoh. In exchange, he gave the people seed to plant. He made them promise that at the harvest, they would give one-fifth of the crop to Pharaoh. They were to keep the rest of the crop as food for themselves and their households. The people did as Joseph asked, and they were spared.

Jacob, now 147 years old, was close to death. He had lived in Goshen, the land where Pharaoh had sent him to raise sheep, for seventeen years. The old man called upon his son Joseph.

"If I have found favor with you, promise to deal truly with me. Do not bury me in Egypt. Carry me out of Egypt and bury me in the burial place of my ancestors."

Joseph swore to his father that he would do as he asked. Then, Joseph presented his sons to Jacob. They were called Ephraim and Manasseh. Jacob laid his right hand on the head of Ephraim and his left hand, on the head of Manasseh. Joseph protested.

"Not so, my father!" he corrected. "Since this one is the firstborn, put your right hand on his head." And Joseph attempted to place Jacob's right hand on Manasseh's head. Jacob kept the hand on the head of Ephraim.

Jacob said, "I know, my son. He also shall become a people, and he also shall be great. Nevertheless, his younger brother shall be greater than he, and his offspring shall become a multitude of nations."

Then, Jacob blessed each of his own sons, and he told them of the future. According to God's plans they were to become the twelve tribes of Israel.

After his father's death, Joseph commanded the physicians of Egypt to embalm Jacob. They spent forty days anointing the deceased body and wrapping it in cloth. The Egyptians wept for Jacob for seventy days, as was the custom. Then, Pharaoh gave Joseph permission to bury Jacob in the land of Canaan. A caravan traveled with them. It included the servants of Pharaoh and the elders of the land of Egypt, as well as Joseph's brothers and their families and many other members of his father's household.

After the burial, Joseph returned to Egypt with his brothers. They spoke to Joseph about a promise they made to their father before he died. The words were chosen by Jacob, and he had asked that they be spoken after his burial.

"Say to Joseph, 'I beg you, forgive the crime of your brothers and the wrong they did in harming you.'"

"Though you intended the worst for me," said Joseph, "God intended good to come from it."

Joseph wept, and his brothers wept. Joseph reassured them of his love and forgiveness. He promised to provide for them and their children. Joseph lived until the age of 110 years when he was embalmed and placed in a coffin in Egypt. But he made his brothers promise that when God came to them to bring them to the land promised to Abraham, Isaac and Jacob, they would carry Joseph's bones with them from Egypt.

HEBREW SLAVES IN EGYPT

acob lived in Egypt until his death. He fathered many sons who went to Egypt with him, including Reuben, Simeon, Levi, Judah, Isaachar, Zebulun, Benjamin, Dan, Naphtali, Gad and Asher. Because of his brothers' jealousy, Jacob's son Joseph already lived in Egypt when Jacob moved there from the land of Canaan. The sons of Jacob had many children. The descendants of Abraham that God promised would be as plentiful as stars in the sky were growing rapidly.

Even after Joseph and his brothers died, the Israelites continued to multiply in Egypt. They became very strong because of their numbers.

When a new king took the throne in Egypt, he became suspicious of the Israelites. He was afraid that if his country was invaded, the vast numbers of Israelites would join the conquerors and defeat the Egyptian armies.

This Pharaoh, which is the title for the king in Egypt, said to his people, "Come, let us deal wisely with the Israelites. If their numbers should grow, they would have the power to join our enemies and defeat us."

The Egyptians came to fear the growing number of foreigners among them. They made slaves of the Israelites, oppressing them with forced labor, using them to build cities such as Pithom and Rameses.

Even though they worked hard, and under terrible conditions, the Israelites continued to prosper and grow. This deeply angered the Pharaoh and the people of Egypt.

Pharaoh commanded that the Israelite slaves work even harder. They had to pump the waters of the Nile River into the fields to help the crops to grow. They worked with mortar and brick, working long hours. They were forced to work to the point of collapse, and the Egyptians showed no mercy. Under Pharaoh's command, they were ruthless in their treatment of the Israelites.

Pharaoh's decision to make slaves of the descendants of Jacob did little to lessen the ruler's fear. He needed another way to discourage them, and to prevent their population from growing.

Pharaoh had two Hebrew midwives brought before him. At the time, as is the case in some places now, midwives helped women deliver their babies.

Pharaoh said to the midwives, who were named Shiphrah and Puah, "When you act as midwives to the Hebrew women, I want you to kill the newborn child if it is a boy." The birthstool was a crude table made of two large stones, on which a woman gave birth. The Pharaoh plotted that, by ordering the execution of male children, he would wipe out the line of the Israelites, since the family's bloodline was passed from son to son to son.

Shiphrah and Puah feared God. They knew that it was wrong to kill the male children of the Hebrew women. Because God had promised Abraham that his descendants would flourish, the midwives purposely disobeyed the command of the Pharaoh. Against his orders, they let the new-born males live.

When Pharaoh discovered that the midwives had not done as he had commanded, he was extremely angry. He asked that they be brought before him for a second time. Although the midwives trembled in anticipation of Pharaoh's wrath, they knew they had done the right thing.

"Why did you disobey me?" questioned Pharaoh. "I asked you to kill all the male children born to Hebrew women. Why have you not done this?"

The midwives responded slyly, "The Hebrew women are not like the Egyptian women. They are very healthy and strong. They do not need our assistance in delivering their children. They give birth before we can even go to them."

Although the Pharaoh was not happy with the explanation given by the midwives, he did not harm them. Thus, God protected them. But Pharaoh was not finished in his dealings with the Israelites. This time, he commanded all of the people of Egypt to kill the male children born to Hebrew women.

"Every boy that is born to the Hebrews you shall throw into the Nile, but you shall let every girl live," he proclaimed to the people of Egypt.

This story begins the book of Exodus. The word "exodus" comes from the Greek language. It means "exit" or "departure." The book of Exodus continues from the stories found in the Book of Genesis. That is why it begins with the names of the sons of Jacob and the descendants of Abraham.

There are two central and important events that happen in the Book of Exodus. The first is the freeing of the Israelites from captivity in Egypt under the ruthless rule of its Pharaoh. The Israelites are finally allowed to leave, or exit, the country of their oppressors. The second event is the strengthening of the covenant between God and his people at Mount Sinai. This is the story of Moses and the ten commandments.

THE
BABY MOSES

here was danger when a baby boy was born to Jochebad, the wife of Amram, descendants of Levi living in Egypt. The woman knew that it was necessary to hide her child from the Pharaoh. He had ordered that all males born to the Hebrews be thrown into the Nile River.

Jochebad hid her baby for three months in her home. When it was no longer possible for her to hide him there, she got a basket of papyrus, a material that could float. She plastered the basket with tar and made a small boat for her baby. Then, she placed him inside. She hid the papyrus basket among the reeds that grew on the banks of the Nile river.

Jochebad also had a daughter, Miriam. She asked Miriam to stand on the river bank, a distance from where she had placed the basket, to watch over the baby.

Soon after, the daughter of the Pharaoh came to the river to bathe. She had many attendants with her. Although her father was a ruthless man, the princess was kind and compassionate. She saw the strange, floating basket among the reeds and asked one of her maids to bring it to her. When she opened the basket, she was surprised to see that it contained a baby. The baby boy was crying loudly.

Pharaoh's daughter felt sorry for the baby. "This must be one of the Hebrew children," she said.

The baby's sister watched what had happened from her place on the river bank. She hurried to the princess and asked her, "Would you like me to get a Hebrew woman to nurse this child for you?"

The princess accepted Miriam's suggestion, unaware that she was the baby's sister. The girl returned home and told her mother what had happened. Then, she told her mother to follow her to where the princess and her attendants were gathered at the river.

"Here is a nurse for you," Miriam told Pharaoh's daughter.

The princess gave the child to the woman. "Take this child and nurse it for me, and I will pay you," she said.

The baby's real mother took him and nursed the baby until he grew up. When he no longer needed to be nursed, his mother returned with the child and presented him to Pharaoh's daughter. The princess decided to adopt the child.

"I will call him Moses," she said, "because I drew him out of the water." The name Moses sounds like the Hebrew for "draw out."

Thus, the Levite woman, Jochebad, found a way to keep her son alive and well cared for.

As the child Moses grew up, he saw the oppression of the Hebrew people in Egypt. One day, he witnessed an Egyptian beating an Israelite slave. The action so angered him that, when no one was looking, he killed the Egyptian and hid his body in the sand.

The following day, Moses saw two Hebrews fighting with each other.

"Why do you strike your fellow Hebrew?" Moses asked them.

The man answered, "Who made you a ruler and judge over us? Do you mean to kill me the way you killed that Egyptian?"

The man's response frightened Moses. He wondered if everyone knew about what he had done. If that was the case, it would only be a matter of time before Pharaoh found out, too.

Moses fled to the land of Midian. The people in this land were descendants of Abraham and his second wife, Keturah.

One day, Moses went to a well in one of the Midian towns and sat down. The priest of Midian, Reuel, had seven daughters. When the young women came to the well to draw water and feed their father's flock, several shepherds tried to drive the women away.

Moses defended the daughters of Midian. He personally gave water to their animals.

When the women went home to their father, they told him what had happened.

"Where is this man who helped you?" their father asked. "Why did you just leave him there? Invite him to eat with us."

Moses agreed to stay with Reuel and his daughters. Eventually, Moses married Zipporah, Reuel's daughter. They had a child who they called Gershom. Moses liked this name because it meant, "I have been an alien in a foreign land."

Eventually, the king of Egypt died. The Israelites, however, were still slaves. When they appealed to God for deliverance from their oppression, God heard their cries. He remembered the promise he had made to Abraham, Isaac and Jacob. God decided to select Moses for a very special mission to help the Hebrews in Egypt.

THE
BURNING BUSH

oses was tending his father-in-law's sheep in the desert. He led the flock beyond the wilderness to Horeb, the mountain of God. He let the sheep graze and watched over them. Suddenly, a bush near him burst into flame. Although the bush burned, it was not consumed by the fire. An angel appeared through the burning branches.

Moses was frightened. "I must stop and look at this great sight and see why the bush is burning but does not burn up," he said aloud.

God saw that Moses was captivated by the burning bush, and he called out to him, "Moses, Moses!"

"Here I am," Moses replied.

"Come no further," God instructed him. "Remove the sandals from your feet, for the place on which you stand is holy ground."

Once Moses had done as he instructed, God continued.

"I am the God of your father, the God of Abraham, the God of Isaac and the God of Jacob," he said.

Moses was now so frightened that he hid his face.

"I have observed the misery of my people in Egypt," said God, speaking of the Israelites. "I have heard their cry on account of their taskmasters. Indeed, I know their sufferings and I have come down to deliver them up out of that land to a good and broad land, a land flowing with milk and honey. This is the country of the Canaanites. I have seen how the Egyptians treat my people. I will send you to the Pharaoh to bring my people, the Israelites, out of Egypt."

Moses questioned God, "Who am I that I should go to Pharaoh and do this task?"

"Do not fear," God consoled him. "I will be with you, and this shall be the sign for you that it is I who sent you. When you have brought the people out of Egypt, you shall worship me on this same mountain."

Moses was still uncomfortable with God's mission for him. "If I go to the Israelites and tell them what I am about to do, they will ask me, 'What is the name of the God that spoke to you, Moses?' How shall I answer them?"

"I am who I am," God said to Moses. "Thus, you shall say to the Israelites, 'I am has sent me.' You will also say, 'The God of your ancestors, the God of Abraham, the God of Isaac and the God of Jacob has sent me to you.' This is my name forever, and this is my name for all generations."

God told Moses to gather the elders of Israel and go together to the king of Egypt. He instructed him to tell the Pharaoh that the God of the Hebrews had met with his people and that they must make a three-day journey into the wilderness to sacrifice to him.

"I know that the king of Egypt will not let you go unless forced by a mighty hand," God said. "Therefore, I will strike Egypt with my wonders. After they have seen this, they will set you free."

To convince Moses of his power, God told him to touch his shepherd's staff. When Moses touched it, the staff became a snake. Then, God asked Moses to put his hand inside his cloak. Moses did this, and when he removed his hand from his cloak, it was white with disease.

He put his hand back into his cloak, and, withdrawing it a second time, he found that it was healed.

"If the Egyptians are not convinced of my powers by these actions," God said, "then you shall take some water from the Nile River and pour it on the ground. The water will become blood."

Moses was very humbled by God's special signs. But he was still afraid that he was the wrong choice to carry out God's mission.

Moses begged God, "I have never been eloquent. I am slow of speech and slow of tongue. Please, send someone else."

God responded, "Who gives speech to mortals? Who makes them mute or deaf, seeing or blind? Is it not I, your God? If you are afraid of this task, then take your brother Aaron the Levite with you. He can speak fluently. Even now, he is coming out to meet you with a glad heart.

"You shall speak to him and put the words into his mouth. I will be with both of you and teach you what to do. Aaron will speak for you to the people. He shall serve as a mouth for you and you shall serve as God for him. Take in your hand this staff, with which you shall perform the signs."

So, God spoke to Moses through the burning bush on the mountain. Moses then returned to his father-in-law. He told him of his intentions to take his wife and children back to Egypt in order to obey the commands of God.

TEN
TROUBLES

oses and Aaron went before the Pharaoh of Egypt to ask him to free the Hebrew slaves as God had asked them to do. They showed Pharaoh how God had the power to turn a staff into a snake. But Pharaoh had many magicians and sorcerers at his court who could perform the same kind of act through magic. Thus, he was not impressed with the actions of Moses and Aaron, and he would not release the Israelites.

God spoke to Moses, "Since the Pharaoh's heart is hardened and he will not let the people go, you must go back to him as he is going to the river. Say to him, 'The God of the Hebrews sent me to you to say, 'Let my people go.' But until now you have not listened. So, I will strike the Nile with my staff and it shall be turned to blood. The fish in the river shall die, the river itself shall stink, and the Egyptians shall be unable to drink water from it.'"

God continued, "Tell Aaron to take your staff and stretch it over all the waters of the land, over its rivers, canals and its ponds. The water will become blood, and there shall be blood throughout the whole land of Egypt, even in wooden buckets and stone jars."

Moses and Aaron did as God requested. Pharaoh and his officials watched as God's servants raised the staff and struck the Nile River. The river turned to blood, and the fish died. The river smelled so badly that the people could not drink from it.

But, Pharaoh's magicians were also able to perform this feat. The Egyptians began to dig for water along the river bank, and Pharaoh refused to set the Israelites free.

This was the first plague, or trouble, that God sent upon the Egyptians.

When Pharaoh still refused to set the Israelites free, God again spoke to Moses: "If the Pharaoh will not let my people go, tell him that I shall plague the entire country with frogs. The river shall swarm with frogs. They shall come up into the palace, into the bedrooms and into the houses of the officials and people. Aaron will raise the staff and stretch out his hand over the rivers and canals and pools. It will bring frogs everywhere."

The Pharaoh's magicians could also perform this feat. Pharaoh, however, was troubled by the frogs that invaded the land, so he called Moses to him.

"Tell your God that I will set his people free if he will remove the frogs," said Pharaoh.

Moses asked God to remove the frogs. God honored the request, and the frogs died in the houses, the courtyards and the fields.

Once the frogs were gone from his land, the Pharaoh still did not do as he had promised.

So, God sent a third plague to Egypt. This time, he commanded Moses and Aaron to strike the dust of the earth with the staff. Tiny gnats appeared everywhere. The bugs covered people and animals from head to toe. The

Pharaoh's magicians tried to do the same thing, but could not create the gnats, no matter how hard they tried. Nonetheless, Pharaoh's heart remained hardened, and he would not listen to Moses.

God sent other plagues to the people of Egypt. The land was covered with flies. The livestock were killed by pestilence. The skin of the Egyptians and their animals were covered with festering boils. Terrible thunderstorms with hail struck the land. And the crops were destroyed by swarms of locusts. Still, Pharaoh was deaf to the pleas of Moses.

The ninth time that Moses went before Pharaoh, God had sent a darkness over the land so thick that people could not see each other. For three days, they were unable to move from where they were.

Pharaoh was getting tired of the troubles sent by the God of the Israelites.

"Go worship your God if you must, but leave your livestock here," said Pharaoh.

Moses answered, "Our livestock must come with us. Not a hoof shall be left behind. From these animals, we will choose those for a sacrifice to God."

Pharaoh was angered by Moses's response. "Get away from me!" he said. "Be certain that you do not see my face again, because on that day, you shall die!"

But, Pharaoh did not let the Israelites go.

Finally, God said to Moses, "I will bring one more plague upon Pharaoh and Egypt. After this plague, the Pharaoh will release my people. Tell the Hebrews to ask their neighbors for objects of silver and gold before you leave the land."

By now, Moses had commanded the awe and respect of many Egyptian people and officials. He went before them and said, "At midnight, God will send the tenth plague. He will go throughout the land and every firstborn son of Egypt will die. From the firstborn child of Pharaoh to the firstborn son of the female slave who works at the handmill, all will die. You will hear a loud cry go up from everywhere in Egypt."

Again, the Pharaoh turned his back on Moses's warning.

God prepared Moses and his people for the trouble that he would send to Egypt. God commanded, "This month shall mark for you the beginning of months. It will be the first month of the year for you. Tell the people that on the tenth of this month, they are to select a lamb. On the fourteenth day of this month, they are to slaughter the lamb at twilight. They shall take some of its blood and put it on the two doorposts of their house.

"Then, they shall eat the lamb that same night, with unleavened bread and bitter herbs. Burn whatever remains in the morning. Eat the lamb quickly. For on this night, I shall pass through the land of Egypt and strike down the firstborn of humans and animals alike. The blood that marks your house will be a sign. When I see the blood, I will pass over you, and no plague will destroy you."

Just as he had said, God struck down the all the firstborn sons of Egypt. There was not a house in Egypt that was not affected by the tenth plague. Even the firstborn son of the Pharaoh died.

Pharaoh summoned Moses and Aaron before him. "Rise up and go away!" he told them. "Go worship your God as you said. Take your flocks and your herds and be gone!"

The Israelites left quickly. There was not even enough time for their bread to rise. They gathered gold and silver from their neighbors as Moses had instructed them. The Israelites remembered to observe the passover sacrifice of God, who had spared their children from the terrible fate of the firstborn sons of Egypt.

MOSES
AS TEACHER

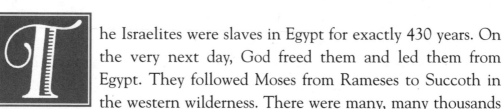

The Israelites were slaves in Egypt for exactly 430 years. On the very next day, God freed them and led them from Egypt. They followed Moses from Rameses to Succoth in the western wilderness. There were many, many thousands of men, women and children on foot. With them, were many flocks and herds of livestock. The Israelites carried the gold and silver and clothes they had received from their Egyptian neighbors. In their cloaks, they had wrapped their kneading bowls containing unleavened dough. After all of the plagues the Egyptians had to endure before Pharaoh released the Israelites, the Egyptians were relieved to see them leave.

The Israelites baked the unleavened dough they took from their homes in Egypt. They had not had time to allow the dough to rise before they left. Because they fled in such a great hurry, they had no other provisions to eat.

To mark the night that they were freed from Egypt, God instructed

Moses to declare a ritual for the observance of passover to his people. The entire congregation of Israel was to celebrate. The meal was to be eaten in each family's house. No part of the animal prepared for the passover meal would be taken outside, nor were any of the animal's bones to be broken. God asked that no foreigner participate in the passover observance.

"Remember this day on which you came out of Egypt, out of the house of slavery," Moses said to his people, "because God brought you out from there by the strength of his hand. No leavened bread shall be eaten. When you have arrived in the land of milk and honey that God promised to us, you shall keep an observance in this month. For seven days, you will eat unleavened bread. On the seventh day, there will be a great festival to God.

"You shall tell your children that you do this because of what God did for the Israelites by freeing them from their Egyptian oppressors. Make a sign on your hand and a reminder on your forehead, so that the teachings of God remain on your lips." The Israelites made small symbols, such as a headband or jewelry and beads as reminders to thank God.

Moses explained to his people the importance of consecrating, or giving special blessings to, the firstborn of all humans and animals. All of the firstborn males of Israelites were to be specially blessed by God, unlike all the firstborn males of the Egyptians whom God's angel struck down. Every firstborn boy and every firstborn male animal belonged to God.

In the future, when your children ask 'What does this mean?' Moses explained, tell them that we are celebrating a very special occasion. "By the strength of his hand, God brought us out of Egypt. He sent many plagues to that country. When Pharaoh would not heed his warnings, ten troubles were visited upon the peoples of Egypt. These included turning their river into blood, destroying their crops with locusts and killing their livestock with disease. Each time, Pharaoh turned his head, and he refused to listen to God.

Finally, God sent a curse so terrible that the Pharaoh could not ignore his power. God struck down all the firstborn male children of Egypt. From the Pharaoh himself to the lowliest slave, everyone lost their firstborn male child to God's wrath. At last Pharaoh listened to God and set our people free."

Moses continued his teachings to his people. "I will sacrifice to God the first pure male offspring of every animal. Every firstborn of my sons, I will promise to God. This special promise will be marked on your hand and your forehead as a reminder of God's goodness. We will always remember, as a people, the fact that God freed us from the Pharaoh."

The people who fled from Egypt listened to what Moses told them. They promised to observe the passover rituals. They acknowledged that their firstborn male children were special in the eyes of God. They had proof of this, because God had killed the firstborn male children of the Pharaoh, yet he had spared the Israelite boys.

The passover ritual is celebrated to this day. Observed for eight days, Passover marks the day that God killed the firstborn of human and animal in Egypt and passed over the homes of the Israelites who had marked their doorways with the blood of a lamb. Today, the first two nights of the holiday are celebrated with festive meals called Seders. The history of the first Passover is told at the Seder. Special food and plates are part of the meal. The plates and utensils used for Passover are not used during any other time of the year. No leavened bread is to be used. Instead, "matzoh," a special kind of bread that does not contain yeast, is eaten. This is a reminder of how the Israelites did not have time to allow their bread dough to rise before they had to leave Egypt.

THE JOURNEY TO THE RED SEA

The story of the exodus of Moses and his people is a very important event in the Bible. It demonstrates the promise, or covenant, between God and the Israelites. After being slaves for hundreds of years, the Hebrews were allowed to leave Egypt. But, difficult times were not over for them.

They followed Moses into the wilderness, in an area that is now in the region of the Sinai Peninsula. There was an easier route to travel to Canaan, the land that God had described to Moses. Yet, God chose to lead the people through the trials of the wilderness in order to complete his plan. He would eventually punish the Egyptians and provide many lessons for the Israelites during their long, difficult journey. During their travels, the people witnessed over and over the power of God.

When Pharaoh let the people depart, God did not lead them by way of the land of the Philistines, for that was too dangerous. If war were to break out, or another catastrophe occur, God feared that the Israelites would return to Egypt. God's route for them was toward the Red Sea.

The Red Sea was called Yam Suph in the Hebrew language. The word "suph" means a woolly kind of seaweed which is found on the shores of the sea. God instructed Moses to take the people back toward Pihahiroth, near the sea. This action would confuse the Pharaoh, who would think that the Israelites were wandering aimlessly through the land.

God said, "I will harden Pharaoh's heart once again. He will pursue the Israelites. Then I will gain glory for myself over Pharaoh and all his army, and the Egyptians will know that I am God."

Moses led the Israelites, carrying the bones of Jacob's son. Before his death, Joseph had instructed the people, "God will surely help you if you carry my bones with you from here."

From the town of Succoth, the Israelites went to Etam, at the edge of the wilderness. There, they made camp. God led them on their long journey by giving them signs to follow. By day, God made a pillar of cloud in the sky which marked the way. In the evening, the pillar glowed like fire, giving the travelers light.

After the Israelites had fled, Pharaoh approached his officials, and asked, "What have we done, letting Israel leave our service?" He ordered that his chariot be brought before him, and that the officers of his army assemble in their chariots. With a strong force, he pursued the Israelites in their flight from Egypt.

The Egyptians caught up with the wandering Israelites at Pihahiroth, in front of Baal-zephon. Pharaoh's army was made up of many horses and chariots and many men on foot. The sight of the army chasing them caused the Israelites to be frightened. Unarmed, having in their possession only those things that they could carry out of Egypt, they cried aloud to God to save them.

The people spoke to Moses, "What have you done to us, bringing us out of Egypt? Is this not the very thing we told you in Egypt when we said to you, 'Let us alone?' It would be better for us to have served the Egyptians and lived, than to die in the wilderness like this."

Moses addressed the fearful crowd: "Do not be afraid, stand firm and see the deliverance that God will accomplish for you today. You will never encounter the Egyptians again. God will fight for you. You need only keep still."

The Israelites struggled to believe Moses's words. The size of the Egyptian army bearing down on them was terrifying.

God spoke to Moses, "Tell the Israelites to go forward. Lift up your staff, and stretch out your hand over the sea. It will be divided and the Israelites will be able to walk on dry ground through the sea. Because the Egyptians are so filled with hatred, they will pursue the people into the divided water. In this way, I will gain glory for myself over Pharaoh and all his army, his chariots and his chariot drivers. The Egyptians will know that I am God."

God sent an angel to the Israelites. The angel went behind the people, and the pillar of cloud was in front of them. The people were thus protected on both sides from the dreadful armies of Pharaoh. At night, the Israelites were protected by the pillar of fire, which lit the sky with its brightness. The Egyptian soldiers did not dare come near the strange glow. Thus, the Israelites found their way safely to the Red Sea under God's protection.

THE
PARTED SEA

s the Israelites approached the Red Sea, they were protected from the armies of Pharaoh by a pillar of cloud (seen at night as a pillar of fire) and an angel of God. With protection that great, the Egyptians in pursuit could not see them from the front or the back.

Then, Moses stretched the staff in his hand over the sea, as God had instructed him. God created a powerful wind from the East that forced the choppy waves away to reveal dry land. The Israelites had never seen such a sight. The divided water formed two great walls on either side of them, and they followed Moses. Miraculously, they were able to walk on the dry land.

Pharaoh's armies, too, were amazed by the sight of the great sea being divided. Why not, they decided, follow the Israelites? Every one of Pharaoh's horses, chariots and men on foot pursued Moses and his people.

God looked down from the pillar of cloud and fire at the Egyptians. The

Egyptians looked up into the pillars of fire and clouds. They were frightened, and struck with a great panic. The wheels of their chariots were unable to turn. The chariots could not move.

"Let us flee from the Israelites," the Egyptians screamed. "God is fighting for them against us."

God spoke to Moses, "Stretch out your staff once more over the sea, so that the water may come back upon the Egyptians, their chariots and drivers."

Moses did as God commanded. When Moses stretched his hand over the sea, the waters returned to their normal depth. The Egyptians tried to escape the rushing water, but they were tossed about in the powerful waves of the moving sea. All of the Egyptians who had followed the Israelites were drowned. Not one of them remained alive. The powerful armies of the Pharaoh were lost in the swirling Red Sea.

God had performed another miracle through the faith and trust of Moses. He had saved the Israelites from the fearful armies of the Pharaoh. The Israelites knew that Moses had been right, and they believed in the power of God.

To thank God for his miracle, the Israelites composed a song to sing to him. It had many verses, which described the great miracle that had happened. The beginning of the song was,

"I will sing to God, for he has triumphed gloriously;
horse and rider he has thrown into the sea.
God is my strength and my might,
and he has become my salvation;
this is my God and I will praise him,
this is my father's God and I will exalt him.
God is a warrior; the Lord is his name."

At the end of the song, the Israelites sang,

"You will bring them in and plant them on the mountain
of your own possession,
the place, O Lord, that you made your abode,
the sanctuary, O Lord, that your hands have established.
The Lord will reign forever and ever."

A prophet named Miriam, who was the sister of Aaron, gathered all the women to dance with her. She took a tambourine and sang loudly in tribute to God's work.

"Sing to the Lord, for he has triumphed gloriously; horse and rider he has thrown into the sea," sang Miriam.

Then, Moses led the people away from the Red Sea. They went into the wilderness of Shur. Soon, they grew fearful of traveling in such a lonely, desolate land. After three days of walking, they could not find any water to drink. The only water available was terribly bitter. The people began to complain again to Moses, "How shall we live if we have nothing to drink?"

God showed Moses a piece of wood and instructed him to throw it into the foul-tasting water. When Moses did this, the water became sweet and cool and was good to drink.

God said to Moses and his people, "If you will listen carefully to my voice, and you do what is right in my sight and give heed to my commandments, I will not bring upon you any of the troubles that I sent to the Pharaoh and the people of Egypt. I am the God that heals you."

The Israelites were comforted by the words of God. They traveled to Elim, where there were twelve springs of water and seventy palm trees. There they camped and rested.

Today, scientists have varying theories about the matter regarding where exactly the Israelites crossed and why the water parted. As many people who dispute the parting as an act of God, there are just as many, perhaps more, who are awestruck by God's power.

GOD'S FOOD IN THE DESERT

wo months after the Israelites left Egypt, they settled in the wilderness of Sin, which is between Elim and Sinai. The people were frightened in the wilderness, and they did not have many provisions. They were hungry, and they complained bitterly to Moses and Aaron.

"If only we had died by the hand of God in Egypt, it would have been better than wandering here in the wilderness, starving to death," they said.

Moses was troubled by the situation. Then, God spoke to him.

"I am going to rain bread from heaven for you. Each day, the people are to go out and gather enough to eat. On the sixth day, they are to gather twice as much as they need, so they can eat on the sabbath. I will test them to see if they follow my instructions," God said.

Moses and Aaron were relieved by God's message. They gathered the people and relayed the words that God had spoken.

"In the evening you shall know that it was God who brought you out of the land of Egypt, for you shall see his glory in the morning. He has heard your angry words and knows that you are hungry. When you complain to us, you are really complaining to God," said Aaron.

"I have heard the bitter doubts of the Israelites. At twilight, you shall eat meat, and in the morning, you shall have your fill of bread. Then, you will know that I am your God," proclaimed God.

That night, a flock of quail rested at the camp of the Israelites on their journey over the Red Sea. In the morning, a layer of dew covered everything in sight. When the sun burned off the dew, a fine flaky substance lay on the ground. It looked like frost. The Israelites asked Moses what it was.

Moses answered, "Here is the bread that God has promised to you. His command is that you shall gather only as much of this bread as you need, no more. Gather enough for those in your tents. None of this bread shall be left over for the next day. On the sixth day, however, you must gather twice as much as you need."

The Israelites began to gather the mysterious bread from heaven, known as "manna," meaning "what is it?" The bread, a white substance that resembled coriander seed was thin and tasted like wafers and honey.

Some of the people took more bread than they needed and stored the extra. This was not what God had asked them to do. The bread they hoarded became infested with worms and grew rotten. Moses was angry with the people, and he reminded them of God's specific instructions. Following his reminder, they followed God's instructions and gathered only the food they needed. On the sixth day, they gathered twice as much food as they required, according to God's wishes.

Moses told them, "This is what God has commanded. Tomorrow is a day of solemn rest, a holy sabbath to God. Cook all that you will need today, for nothing shall be prepared tomorrow."

The word "sabbath" means resting from work. Cooking was forbidden on the sabbath day when the Israelites were settled. It was forbidden, too, while they wandered in the wilderness. On the seventh day, the Israelites went in search of the bread from heaven, but found none, just as Moses had predicted.

Moses said to them, "How long will you refuse to believe in my instructions? God has given you the sabbath; therefore, on the sixth day he gave you enough bread to last for the next day. On the seventh day, you were to do no work, only to rest."

Then, Moses instructed the Israelites to observe God's goodness by measuring the manna. "Take a jar," he told them, "and fill it with manna. Put it before God and keep it throughout the generations. This will be a solemn reminder of God's goodness to you. It will help you remember how God fed you when you were in the wilderness."

The Israelites survived in the wilderness for forty years by eating the manna that God provided. They ate the special bread until they were able to depart from the wilderness into the promised land of Canaan.

THE TEN COMMANDMENTS

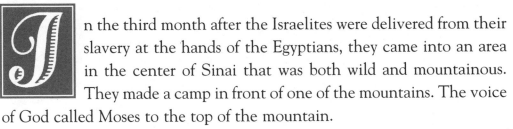

*I*n the third month after the Israelites were delivered from their slavery at the hands of the Egyptians, they came into an area in the center of Sinai that was both wild and mountainous. They made a camp in front of one of the mountains. The voice of God called Moses to the top of the mountain.

When Moses arrived there, God said to him, "You shall say to the house of Jacob and the Israelites, 'You have seen what I did to the Egyptians, and how I carried you on eagle's wings and brought you to myself. If you obey my voice and keep my covenant, you shall be my treasured possession out of all the peoples. Indeed, the whole earth is mine, but you shall be for me a priestly kingdom and a holy nation.' These are the words that you shall speak to the Israelites."

Moses descended from the mountain, gathered the elders of the people and told them what God had said. The people answered him as one, "We will do everything that God asks of us."

Then, God told Moses that he would appear in a dense cloud when he spoke to him so that the Israelites could hear his words. They would know for certain that Moses was to be trusted.

"Go to the people," God instructed him, "and consecrate them today and tomorrow. Have them wash their clothes and prepare for the third day. Because on the third day, I will come down from Mount Sinai so that everyone can see me. Tell the people to observe certain limits when I come. They should be careful not to go up to the mountain or to touch it. Anyone who touches the mountain will be put to death. Only after the blast of a trumpet fashioned from a ram's horn may they approach the mountain."

Moses returned to the people, and he blessed them in the eyes of God. They washed their clothes, and he told them to prepare for the third day.

The morning of the third day began with great lightning and thunder that filled the skies. The sound of a mighty trumpet could be heard by all of the Israelites. They trembled with anticipation. Moses led the Israelites to the foot of Mount Sinai. Within a huge cloud of smoke, God descended on the mountain. The mountain shook as the sound of the trumpet grew louder and louder. Then, God instructed Moses to climb to the peak of Mount Sinai.

When Moses reached the top, God spoke to him, "Go down, Moses," said God in a loud clap of thunder. "Tell the people to keep still."

Moses assured God that he had told the Israelites to keep away from the mountain and not to touch it. God gave the following laws or commandments to Moses:

"I am your God, who brought you out of Egypt, out of the house of slavery. You shall have no other gods before me."

"You shall not make for yourself an idol in the form of anything that is in heaven, or on this earth, or in the water. You shall not worship any idols, for I am your God. I am a jealous God, who will punish those who disobey me, but show steadfast love to the thousandth generation of those who love me and keep my commandments."

"You will not make wrongful use of the name of your God."

"Remember the sabbath day, and keep it holy. Six days shall you labor and do all your work. But the seventh day is a sabbath to God. You shall not do any work—you, your son or your daughter, male or female slave, your livestock or the alien resident in your towns. For in six days I made the heaven and earth and sea and all that is in them, but I rested on the seventh day."

"Honor your father and your mother, so that your days may be long in the land that I am giving you."

"You shall not murder."

"You shall not commit adultery."

"You shall not steal."

"You shall not bear false witness against your neighbor."

"You shall not covet your neighbor's wife, or male or female slave, or ox or donkey, or anything that belongs to your neighbor."

The voice of thunder told Moses to descend from the mountaintop and bring Aaron back. The people heard the words of God through Moses, as lightning and thunder tore through the sky. The trembling mountain was consumed in smoke. The frightened Israelites turned to Moses.

"You speak to us, and we will listen. But do not let God speak to us, because we fear that we will die," they cried.

Moses comforted them, "Do not be afraid. God has come only to test you and to put the fear of him upon you so that you do not commit sin."

Then, Moses returned to the top of the mountain. God said, "You have seen for yourself that I spoke with you from heaven. You shall not make gods of silver or gods of gold. You need to only make an altar for me of earth and sacrifice on it your burnt offerings in every place where I will come to you and bless you."

THE GOLDEN CALF

The voice of God summoned Moses and Joshua to Mount Sinai. The elders and the others of Israel were left behind with Aaron and Hur.

"Wait here for us, until we come down again. God has spoken that he will write his commandments on tablets of stone that I will bring to you. If you have any disputes, go to Aaron and Hur," said Moses to the people.

Moses and Joshua climbed the mountain. For six days, Moses waited for a sign from God. On the seventh day, a great cloud settled over the place. Entering the cloud, Moses remained on the mountain for forty days and forty nights.

The Israelites waiting below the mountain began to ask Aaron if Moses would ever return. The people grew increasingly doubtful.

"Aaron," they said, "come and make gods for us to worship. We are alone in the wilderness. And this man Moses, who helped deliver us from the Egyptians, has been gone for a long time."

Aaron thought for a moment. Then, he replied, "Take off the gold rings that are on your fingers and the gold from your wives' ears and from your sons and your daughters and bring them to me."

The people did as he asked. All their gold jewelry was gathered in a great pile before Aaron. When Aaron saw what they had done, he took the gold, formed it into a mold, and he cast an image of a calf from it.

The Israelites, convinced that Moses would never reappear, were very impressed with the image of the golden calf. Afraid of being in the wilderness without the guidance of their leader, they were eager to pray to something. Aaron built an altar and put the golden calf next to it.

He said, "Tomorrow shall be a festival day to God. We will rise early from our beds, and we will give burnt offerings and sacrifices."

The people ate and drank a great deal. In the morning, as Aaron had said, they rose early. God saw what was happening in the camp of the Israelites.

Angrily, he said to Moses, "Go down at once! The people that I have rescued from the cruel hand of Pharaoh have acted against my instructions! They have cast an idol from gold, and now they worship it and make sacrifices to it. I will punish them severely for what they have done against my word."

At God's words, Moses was afraid. He begged God not to destroy the Israelites.

"God, please do not use your mighty powers against the people that you have rescued from Egypt. Think how the Egyptians will speak of your deed. They will say that you rescued your people only to bring them into the wilderness and kill them. Please, turn against your own wrath and do not destroy your people. Think of the faith of Abraham and Isaac and Israel," he pleaded. It was a plea Moses would have to repeat numerous times over the course of the journey.

Then, Moses reminded God of how he had promised Abraham to give him as many offspring as there were stars in the sky. God took pity on Moses, and he decided not to punish the Israelites for their deed.

Moses descended from the mountaintop with Joshua, carrying the two stone tablets on which the ten commandments were written. The tablets were fashioned by God, and he had written upon them. Moses and Joshua heard a great commotion as they started down Mount Sinai.

Joshua thought it was the sound of war.

Nearing the camp of the Israelites, they saw people dancing and laughing around the golden calf. Moses could not believe his eyes. Enraged with the Israelites, he threw down the sacred tablets he had carried from the mountain, and they broke on the ground. In his anger, Moses rushed to the golden calf and threw it in the fire.

He turned to Aaron, who was in charge of watching over the people and guiding them in his absence. "Why did you do this?" he asked him.

Aaron pleaded with Moses to understand. "The people asked me to make a god for them, because they did not know when or if you would return. I did not know what to do, so I fashioned a calf from their gold for them to worship."

Moses shouted to the crowd who were dancing and running about. "Whoever is with me, let him come and stand by me now!" The sons of Levi immediately gathered around Moses.

"Make war with those in the camp who will not listen," Moses told them. "Take your swords and punish them." Three thousand people were killed by his order.

The next day, Moses said to the Israelites, "You have sinned a great sin. I will try to intercede with God on your behalf." Then he left the camp and returned to the mountain.

Moses called out to God, "These people have sinned a terrible sin in making a god to worship from gold. Please forgive their sins. If you will not, then treat me as one of them. Cast me from you forever."

God replied to Moses, "Whoever has sinned shall be blotted from my book. The sinners will be punished with a plague, but they will not be destroyed. I still wish for you to lead the Israelites to the land I have described to you."

A HOUSE FOR GOD

After God gave the ten commandments to Moses and his people, he asked Moses to return to Mount Sinai to receive instructions for a great tent God wanted constructed in his honor. The tent would be referred to as the "tabernacle."

God told Moses, "Instruct the Israelites to make me an offering. They will give you gold, silver, bronze; blue, purple and crimson yarns, fine linens, goats' hair, tanned rams' skins, fine leather, acacia wood, oil for lamps, jewels and incense. Tell them to build a sanctuary in which I may dwell among them. I will give instructions for building the tabernacle and its furniture."

First, God described the ark of the covenant, a chest to hold the tablets of the commandments. The ark was to be of acacia wood, a strong wood resembling oak, from a tree found on the Sinai peninsula. It would represent the throne of God. The chest would measure about three feet long, 1

$^1/_2$ feet wide and $2^1/_2$ feet high. The measurement used at the time was a "cubit," which was approximately half a meter in length. The ark was to have a cover of pure gold. Two gold-covered wooden poles inserted at its base would be used to carry the ark.

Inside the tabernacle was to be a table to hold the "bread of the Presence," symbolic loaves of bread put before God to thank him for his goodness. The table was also to be constructed of acacia wood and covered with gold. All of the utensils on the table were to be made of gold. This included plates, dishes, pitchers and bowls.

An altar for incense was to be placed in the tabernacle, and an altar for burnt offering in the courtyard outside. A curtain would separate the area of the ark of the covenant from the rest of the interior.

A beautiful lampstand was to reside in the tabernacle. It would have cups to hold burning oil shaped like the blossoms of an almond tree, the first tree to bloom in this region in the spring. Three branches were to be on each side of the lampstand, each one holding a cup of oil, with one in the center making seven cups in all. The gold lampstand would be tended by the people, who would be responsible for keeping the flames lit in the tabernacle through the night.

The tabernacle itself was to be a royal tent for God. It would be fifteen feet wide, by forty-five feet long and fifteen feet high. Over an inner lining of finely embroidered linen, a covering of goat's hair, two layers of leather would rest— one from ramskins and the other from the hides of sea cows.

God asked the Israelites to weave ten curtains of finely twisted yarn for the tabernacle. He chose the royal colors of blue, purple and scarlet yarn. The curtains were to be the same size, forty-two feet long and six feet wide. Two pairs of five curtains would be bound together. There would be fifty loops on the edge of the outermost curtain of each set, with bronze clasps for the loops, so that the tabernacle would be completely covered. Outside, a courtyard would surround the tented area. The north and south ends would be 150 feet in length. The west end of the courtyard would be seventy-five feet in length. The east end would be the same, except that it would be used as the entrance for the tabernacle and would face the sunrise.

After his instructions for the tabernacle, God spoke to Moses and his people: "Set up the tabernacle, the Tent of Meeting, on the first day of the first month. Place the ark of the Testimony (covenant) in it and shield the ark with a curtain. Bring in the table and set upon it what belongs on it. Then bring in the lampstand and set up the lamps. Place the gold altar of incense in front of the ark of the Testimony and put the curtain at the entrance of the tabernacle.

"Place the altar of burnt offering in front of the entrance to the tabernacle. Place a basin of water near the altar. Use the basin to wash your feet and hands when you enter. Set up the courtyard around the tabernacle and put the curtain at the entrance. Take the anointing oil and bless everything in the tabernacle and all its furnishings. Then, it will be holy."

Imagine this beautiful tent in the wilderness! It was here that God had promised to be with the Israelites throughout their travels in the desert. The traveling house of God remained with his people through all their journeys.

MEAT FOR THE ISRAELITES

umbers is the fourth book of the Bible. It begins with a numbering or counting of the Israelites traveling through the wilderness of Sinai. These people of God were again going to be tested. They would nearly forfeit the promised land of Canaan because of their lack of faith.

The Israelites became tired as they moved through the desert wilderness toward their promised home. They complained to Moses about the food.

"When we were in Egypt, we were able to eat delicious fish, cucumbers, melons, leeks, onions and garlic. But, now, we only have manna," they moaned.

The Israelites gathered the manna and ground it in mills, or beat it with mortars. They boiled it and made cakes from it. But the manna still tasted like coriander seed.

God heard the people's complaints to Moses, and he was very angry at their ungratefulness. He created a great fire that burned the outer edges of their camp. Now afraid of the wrath of God, the Israelites cried to Moses to save them. Moses interceded on their behalf to God, and the fire was extinguished. From that day, the place was called "Taberah" which means "burning," because God's fire had visited there.

Moses was tired of hearing the people cry and complain. Many times, he had spoken on their behalf to God.

On one occasion, when he approached God, he said to him, "Why have you treated your servant so badly? Why have I not found favor with you? You lay the burden of these people on me. Did I give birth to them? No. And yet, I carry them the way a nurse carries a suckling child. I am responsible for taking them to the land that you promised to their ancestors. Where am I going to get meat for these people? I am so weary, I would prefer that you put me to death, if I do not find favor in your sight."

God heard Moses's plea for help. He told him, "Gather for me seventy Israelites, whom you know to be the elders of the people and officers over them. Bring them to the Tent of Meeting, the tabernacle, and have them take their place with you. I will come to you and talk to you there. I will put some of the spirit you have received onto them as well, so that the burden of the people's needs is not yours alone.

"Tell the people to prepare themselves, because tomorrow they will have meat to eat. But warn them, that this meat will not be given to them for just a day. They will have enough meat to eat for a whole month, so much meat that they will grow sick of it. This is my punishment to them for complaining against the God that has led them from slavery in Egypt."

Moses was confused by the words. "There are six hundred thousand people among us. How can you possibly find enough meat for all those people to eat for one month? There are not enough flocks and herds to slaughter to feed so many. There are not enough fish in the sea."

God answered Moses. "My power is unlimited. You will see that my words will come true."

Moses approached the begrudging people, and he told them what God had said to him. Then, God came down in a great cloud and spoke to him. Some of the responsibility that God had given to Moses he now spread among the elders of the people.

A great wind stirred in the sky. Migrating quail who were passing over the area fell around the camp, as far as one day's journey from the Israelites. The quail covered the ground everywhere, stacked about waist high. The people could not believe the sight. They worked all day and all night to gather the fallen quail. They brought them back to camp in great numbers. Feasting on the meat, they ate as much as they could.

But, God was not happy with their behavior. He had relieved Moses of some of his responsibilities, because Moses was a good man. Still, most of the Israelites were greedy and complaining. The angered God decided to send a plague to them, to remind them of their promise to him and of his goodness in delivering them from slavery.

Because of God's wrath, the Israelites afterwards called the place where they were Kibroth-hattaavah or "graves of craving," because it symbolized the burial place of those who had died of plague. They were sorry that they had complained so bitterly against God. From Kibroth-hattaavah, they traveled to Hazeroth, which is near the Gulf of Aqaba, a branch of the Red Sea.

THE PROMISED LAND

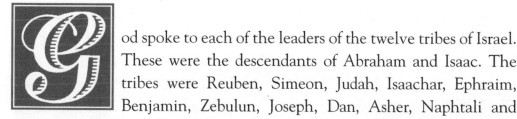

od spoke to each of the leaders of the twelve tribes of Israel. These were the descendants of Abraham and Isaac. The tribes were Reuben, Simeon, Judah, Isaachar, Ephraim, Benjamin, Zebulun, Joseph, Dan, Asher, Naphtali and Gad. He instructed Moses to send some men to travel to the land of Canaan, which he had promised to the Israelites. Moses wanted them to spy out the land.

Moses directed them, "Go explore the land of Canaan. Go to the Negeb, and go up into the hill country and see what the land is like and whether the people who live in it are weak or strong, whether they are few or many, and whether the land they live in is good or bad. We must know if the cities are fortified or unwalled, and whether there are trees. Be brave and bring back to us some of the fruit that grows there. Be sure to include the grapes that should now be ripe."

Twelve leaders from the tribes traveled to Negeb. They arrived in Hebron. From Hebron, they went to the Eshcol Valley, and they cut down a branch with a cluster of grapes on it. The name "Eshcol" means "cluster."

After forty days, they returned to the camp of the Israelites located in the wilderness of Paran at Kadesh. Moses, Aaron and the rest of the Israelite people waited to hear about the land their kinsmen had visited.

"The land we have visited flows with milk and honey," the twelve told them. "The people who live there are strong, and the towns are fortified and very large. Some of the inhabitants are the descendants of Anak. The Amalekites live in the land of Negeb. The Hittites, Jebusites and Amorites live in the hill country. The Canaanites live by the sea and along Jordan."

One of the Israelites, Caleb, spoke out. "Let us go up and occupy this land. Surely, we are able to overcome these people."

But ten others who had been to Canaan said, "No, it is not possible to subdue these people for they are very strong." To convince the rest of the Israelites that this was not a wise thing to do, the group decided to tell stories about the land, which would frighten the people.

"This land which we explored is a land that devours its inhabitants. The people are of great size. When we saw the Anakites that come from Nephilim, we were amazed by their size. Next to them, we are mere grasshoppers." The ten hoped this would discourage the Israelites.

Instead, the people were angry. They complained to Moses and Aaron. They had been traveling in the wilderness for a very long time. They were looking forward to the land that God had promised to them.

"We were better off in Egypt!" they cried. "Let us find a new leader and return to Egypt."

Moses and Aaron were filled with pain for the people. They fell on their faces in front of the crowd. Joshua, the son of Nun, and Caleb, the son of Jephunneh, who both had visited Canaan, tore their clothing, as a sign of their sorrow.

They told the crowd, "The land we have been to is a great land. If God is truly pleased with us, he will bring us there. Do not rebel against God, for the land really is a place of milk and honey. The people are not to be feared as we have said. God is with us."

The Israelites were not comforted by the words of Joshua and Caleb. They threatened to stone them for lying.

Then, God appeared at the Tent of Meeting. He spoke to Moses.

"How long will these people act this way and despise me? They refuse to believe in me despite all I have done for them. I will strike them with pestilence, and I will disinherit them. I will make your descendents into a greater nation than they."

Moses replied to God. "You spoke of a mission to bring these people to Canaan. The Egyptians and our enemies know you have protected them. If you destroy these people, it will be said that you were unable to lead us from this wilderness to the land that you promised to us. You yourself have said, 'The Lord is slow to anger, abounding in steadfast love, and forgiving of iniquity and transgression.'"

Again, God forgave the people as Moses had asked. However, God decided that those who still did not obey his teachings and commandments, despite having seen his glory and good works, would never go to the wonderful new land he had promised.

Joshua
and the River

Imagine how Joshua felt when God commanded him to take the Israelites across the Jordan River into the land that was promised to Moses!

"Everywhere the sole of your foot will tread, I have given to you. From the wilderness and Lebanon as far as the great river, Euphrates, all the land of the Hittites, to the Great Sea in the West shall be yours," said God to Joshua. "Do not be frightened or dismayed, for God is with you wherever you go," God promised.

Joshua told his officers to tell the people in the camp that the crossing was to happen in three days. The people were to prepare to leave with all their provisions by then. They were going to take possession of the land that God gave them. They would leave the desert camp they had set up on the eastern bank of the Jordan River.

In his mind's eye, Joshua saw the new land. Across the river, he glimpsed an image of what they would find in the northern end of the Dead Sea and the southern Jordan Valley. What lay ahead was the western hill country high in the Judean Mountains, where the people would one day build a house of God. Joshua must get the people to Jericho, the only oasis on the western bank in the entire southern half of the Jordan Valley.

Two spies went ahead to Jericho. Although God had given the land to the Israelites, they had to learn something about the inhabitants of the place. During the trip, the spies visited a woman named Rahab. When the king of Jericho heard gossip that two Israelites were visiting, he called for Rahab to bring the men to him. Instead, Rahab hid the spies and lied to the king's men, telling them the Israelites had indeed visited, but had fled. She sent the king's men off in the direction she claimed the Israelites had gone.

Meanwhile, the spies were safe on Rahab's roof with the stalks of flax she had lain out to dry. In return for saving their lives, Rahab asked that they save hers when the time came. She had heard about other battles that the Israelites had fought on the other side of the Jordan and about the God that protected them.

Joshua's men agreed. They told her that when their army marched through her city, she should make certain that her entire family was inside their house. At the window, she should tie a crimson cord to remind them that she lived there. They would be sure that her house was saved from any destruction. Then, the spies escaped by climbing down a rope which she dropped from the window.

Joshua sent his officers with a message for the people in the camp. "When you see the ark of the covenant of God being carried by the priests, then gather up your things and set out," he said. He told them how far behind the ark they were to walk. They should follow in order to know the way to go.

Then, God honored Joshua and gave him a command: "This day I begin to exalt you for all Israel to see. They may know that I will be with you as I was with Moses." Then, he said, "You are the one who shall command the priests who bear the ark of the covenant, saying, 'When you come to the edge of the waters of the Jordan, you shall stand still in the river.'"

So the people set out from their tents. They were ready to cross the Jordan River and were ready to live by God's promise. They followed at a distance behind the ark of the covenant to the Jordan. The waters of the river flowed above the banks, because it was time of the harvest. When the feet of the people carrying the ark touched the water, the river rushed back as if it had been suddenly dammed. The priests indicated that the people should cross to the other side, and the people crossed. Then, with the ark of the covenant held high toward the heavens, the priests supporting it stood still in the middle of the river.

The poeple were so happy to be in the promised land! They prayed and honored God. They talked into the next day about how God had parted the waters for them to cross the river on dry ground. They celebrated this very first Passover ever on the western side of the Jordan River.

Joshua said to them, "God dried up the waters of the Jordan for you until you crossed over, so that all the peoples of the earth may know that the hand of God is mighty, and so that you may fear God forever."

Joshua's army moved toward Jericho. When they were near, God spoke to Joshua. "Remove the sandals from you feet. The place where you stand is holy," instructed God. And Joshua removed his sandals.

When the army came near the city of Jericho, the people there stayed inside their houses. The city was as quiet as if no one lived in it. God spoke to the Israelites.

" I have handed Jericho over to you, along with its king and the soldiers," said God.

According to God's instructions, the Israelites made a circle around the city once a day for six days, with seven priests bearing seven trumpets made of the horns of rams, walking ahead of the ark of the covenant. On the seventh day, they circled Jericho seven times as the priests sounded the trumpets. Finally, each blew a long blast from his trumpet. At the sound, the people summoned a shout so loud it could have filled the whole earth.

"Shout! for God has given you the city," said Joshua.

THE SIGN
OF THE FLEECE

od called Gideon to fight the Midianites. They raided the new promised land of God's people after the Israelites displeased God by not following his commandments. The Midianites stole the Israelites' crops and ruined the land. The Midianites came on camels by the scores and set up encampments. They stole sheep, oxen and donkeys. This went on year after year until the Israelites were living in caves on the brink of starvation.

Something of major importance was needed to stop them. God chose Gideon for the task. But getting Gideon to believe the message took some time, because Gideon made it difficult.

Gideon was the son of Joash, who lived in the village of Ophrah, not far from Shechem. One warm afternoon, Gideon was beating out wheat inside the wine press to hide what he was doing from any spying eyes of the Midianites. An angel of God appeared and spoke to him.

"God is with you, mighty warrior," the angel said.

"But, sir, if God is with us, why has all this hardship happened to us?" asked Gideon.

The angel listened to Gideon's complaints, and told him to rise up and deliver Israel from the Midianites. Gideon protested that his clan was among the weakest and that he was the least significant in his family. Through the angel, God tried to encourage Gideon, explaining that God would be with him as he struck down every last Midianite.

"If now I have found favor in your eyes," said Gideon, not sure that it was God's message he heard, "show me a sign that it is to you that I speak. I will bring an offering from my house and set it before you."

"Do not depart from here until I return," he added, and he entered his house, leaving the messenger to wait outside.

Gideon prepared a young goat for cooking, and he made unleavened cakes from flour. He presented them to the angel, who took a staff in his hand and touched the meat and the cakes. A fire rushed from the rock and consumed Gideon's offering. The angel vanished at the same time.

Realizing he had been indeed talking to an angel, Gideon was momentarily stunned. Gideon cried out to God for protection. The voice of God answered him, saying, "Peace be to you. Do not fear, you shall not die."

Later that night, God spoke to Gideon again. "Take your father's seven-year old bull and go with it to the altar of Baal. Cut down the sacred pole the followers of Baal worship. Next, build an altar to your God on top of the false altar and place the bull as an offering on it. Light the offering with the sacred pole that you cut down."

When the townspeople woke the next morning, they saw that the altar of Baal had been destroyed and that a new altar replaced it. People thought that Gideon, son of Joash, was responsible. The people demanded that

Joash deliver Gideon to them so they could punish him by putting him to death. But the spirit of God took possession of Gideon. He sent messengers so that armies from the various Israelite tribes rose up to follow him.

Gideon said to God, "I must be sure you will deliver Israel by my hand. I will lay a fleece of wool on the threshing floor. If there is dew on the fleece and the ground is dry, I know you will deliver Israel."

The next morning, the fleece was so wet that Gideon had to wring it dry. Enough water dripped from it to fill a bowl. But Gideon needed an unmistakable message from God. He saw that the real test would be if the ground was wet and the fleece was dry! So, he said to God, "Please make a demonstration with the fleece just once more."

And God did what Gideon needed him to do. The next morning, the fleece was bone dry, and the ground was soaked. At last Gideon was ready to command the army against the Midianites. He did not expect to fight the way he finally did. First, God told Gideon his army of 32,000 troops had too many soldiers to battle the Midianites. So Gideon released anyone who was afraid to fight in the coming battle, leaving 10,000 troops. Then, God said to bring the troops down to the river. All the soldiers that stayed on their feet and lapped water from their hands should be separated from those who knelt down to drink. There were 300 troops that lapped water but were ready in case of attack. These were the soldiers that God told Gideon to use to fight the Midianites below in the valley. There were so many of the enemy that the valley looked like it was thick with locusts. Their camels were as countless as sand on the seashore.

At God's command, Gideon and his small army surrounded the Midianite camp. Gideon sounded his trumpet and so did the soldiers, each with a trumpet. They were shouting as they overtook the camp, "For God and for Gideon!" They carried empty water jars in their hands, and at

Gideon's command, smashed them. Inside each jar was a torch. The Midianite soldiers ran around in terror. They thought a great army was attacking them. The Midianites raised their swords against their fellow soldiers as the army fled far across the desert. Gideon's tiny army of trumpeters had won.

SAMSON'S LION

anoah's wife could not get pregnant, nor have children. One day when she was tending to the animals in the pasture, an angel appeared to her in the form of a man. The woman had not seen the man approach. Suddenly, he appeared, but Manoah's wife was not scared.

The man spoke to her softly: "Although you are barren, you shall conceive and bear a son. No razor is to come to his head. He will take special vows to serve God as a Nazirite, and Nazirites never cut their hair. Your son will begin the fight to deliver Israel from the hand of the Philistines who have ruled over the Hebrews for forty years."

The man also told the woman to be careful not to drink wine or any other strong drink. She was not to eat anything unclean, according to the rules of the Hebrews. The woman hurried to find her husband, Manoah.

"A man of God came to me in the pasture. His appearance was awe-inspiring, like an angel's. I did not ask where he came from, and he did not tell me," she said. Then, she explained about the son they were to have.

Manoah prayed to God for another visit from the man of God, who had appeared to his wife. Again when the woman was in the field, she saw the man. This time, she ran to get her husband.

"When your words come true, what is the boy's life going to be like? What is he to do?" asked the anxious father-to-be.

"Let the woman heed what I told her about her diet," said the man of God.

"Can we prepare a young goat to serve you?" the farmer asked the visitor, not fully understanding that he was an angel, who did not to eat the flesh of an animal.

The angel told the man to offer the kid instead to God as a sacrifice.

"What is your name, so that we can remember you?" asked the farmer.

"It is too wonderful," answered the angel, who ascended in a flame from the fire the farmer was beginning to build at the altar.

After Samson grew up, he was strong and determined. He believed in God, and he was confident about what he wanted. His hair was never cut.

"I saw a Philistine woman at Timnah. I want to marry her," he told his parents after returning from a trip alone to the city.

The parents accompanied their son to Timnah. In the vineyards outside the city, Samson rushed ahead of his parents to ask for the hand of the woman he wished to marry. A young lion approached him. The lion roared and Samson moved to protect himself. The young man was filled with the spirit of God. His strong body was invincible. He grabbed the lion and tore it apart with his bare hands until the animal breathed its final breath. Samson's parents never knew about the encounter.

In Timnah, Samson's sweetheart agreed to the marriage, and Samson hurried to tell his eager parents the good news. On the way to the vineyard where he asked them to wait, he passed the dead lion. A swarm of bees had made a hive in the beast's carcass. Samson was delighted to find honey in the animal he had killed. He brought some to his parents, and they ate it.

At the feast to celebrate the wedding, Samson was joined by thirty Philistine guests from the bride's city. He recited a riddle for the thirty guests: Out of the eater came something to eat. Out of the strong came something sweet.

He boasted that he would give them thirty linen garments and thirty garments to wear on feast days if they solved the riddle within seven days. However, if no one was able, they were to give the same prize to Samson.

By the fourth day, the Philistines were angry because they were out of ideas, and none of the ideas was the solution they needed. They coaxed Samson's bride to find out the answer for them, saying she owed them the solution because they were her countrymen. Finally, she agreed.

"You hate me. You have asked a riddle of my people, but I do not even know the answer," she said to Samson.

"I have not even told my mother or my father," he protested.

When the tears filled her eyes, he was moved to tell her. As soon as the thirty Philistines gave him the answer on the seventh day, Samson saw that his wife had duped him. Samson was again filled with the spirit of God. He rushed down to Askleon, killing thirty men for their belongings, amassing enough garments necessary for paying the Philistines' their prizes.

THE HAND
OF A WOMAN

This is a story about a battle that was won by a woman. This story shows irony, because of the surprises. The two women in this story are Deborah and Jael.

Deborah was a judge in Israel. Judges were prohets and military commanders. Deborah liked to deliver her judgments from under a palm tree, of a type called Lappidoth, named in honor of her husband. The palm where she sat as judge was in the hill country between Ramah and Bethel. From here, she spoke to the people of Israel who climbed the hill to request a hearing with her. Often, she summoned people to her to deliver a judgment from God.

One day, Deborah sent for a soldier named Barak. "Go, take position at Mount Tabor with an army of ten thousand men. I will summon the enemy commander Sisera to meet you by the Kishon River with his chariots and troops. Then, I will give his army into your hand in the name of God," she said.

The battleground she described lay at a mountain pass where several mountain streams flowed together to form the Kishon River. The battle was to be fought over control of the northern plains. It was to be the first time that the Israelites from the highlands challenged the people who lived on the plains. The plains were the major trade route, and prosperity belonged to the people that controlled the plains. Barak saw the importance of the battle that Deborah commanded him to fight.

"If you go with me, I will go. If you do not go, I will not," Barak said.

"I will surely go with you. But you realize that the path you are to take will not be a path of glory. God will deliver Sisera into the hand of a woman," said Deborah slyly.

Deborah, Barak and the 10,000 Israelite warriors set off for battle at Mt. Tabor. At the foot of the mountain, the Canaanites gatherd, led by Sisera with his shining chariots and well-bred horses. Barak and Deborah's army was poorly matched by comparison. Then, out of nowhere, a rush of water into the river created a panic that so stirred the horses of the chariots, that the enemy fled before the Israelites. Barak was in hot pursuit. The enemy leader Sisera fled on foot, knowing his army was defeated.

Sisera came upon the tents of a traveling clan. One of the tents belonged to Jael, who was married to Heber, the Kenite. Jael offered Sisera hospitality when he asked. She gave him a rug to cover himself, and she presented a skin of milk for Sisera to drink when he requested water. Then, the commander asked Jael to check through the flap of the tent to see whether anyone had pursued him, and she did as he requested. She told him no one was outside looking for him. Relieved, he relaxed and fell asleep. At that moment, Jael grabbed a tent peg and a mallet. And she plunged the peg into Sisera's temple, killing him immediately.

Barak came by chasing Sisera. Jael went to meet him. She said, "Come and I will show you the man whom you are seeking." In this way, Jael delivered Sisera to the Israelites.

The Song of Deborah is a victory hymn to the events of this story. Here are some of the verses.

"Hear, O kings; give ear, O princes;
to the Lord I will sing,
I will make melody to the Lord,
the God of Israel."

"In the days of Shamgar son of Anath,
in the days of Jael, caravans cease
and travelers kept to the byways.
The peasantry prospered in Israel,
they grew fat on plunder,
because you arose, Deborah,
arose as a mother in Israel."

"Awake, awake, Deborah!
Awake, awake, utter a song!
Arise, Barak, lead away your captives,
O son of Abinoam.
Then marched the remnant of the noble;
the people of the Lord
marched down for him against the mighty.
From Ephraim they set out into the valley,
following you, Benjamin, with your kin;

from Machir marched down the commanders,
and from Zebulun those who bear the marshal's staff;
the chiefs of Issachar came with Deborah,
and Issachar faithful to Barak;
into the valley they rushed out at his heels."

"Most blessed of women be Jael,
the wife of Heber the Kenite,
of tent-dwelling women most blessed.
He asked water and she gave him milk,
she brought him curds in a lordly bowl.
She put her hand to the tent peg
and her right hand to the workmen's mallet;
she struck Sisera a blow,
she crushed his head,
she shattered and pierced his temple.
He sank, he fell
he lay still at her feet;
at her feet he sank,
where he sank, there he fell dead."

THE LOYALTY OF RUTH AND NAOMI

In the time when the judges ruled, a famine raged through the land. Elimelech took his wife Naomi and their two sons, Mahlon and Chilion, from Bethlehem in the land of Judah to live in the country of Moab, where the conditions were better. They were in Moab only a short time when Elimelech died. This unfortunate event left Naomi alone to raise her two sons.

When it was right to marry, both boys took Moabite wives. One man married Oprah. The other son married Ruth. In less than ten years, both sons died. Now Naomi was alone with two daughters-in-law.

Naomi had heard that God had forgiven the people of Judah and that the famine was over. Eager to return to her birthplace of Bethlehem, she set out with her daughters-in-law for the land of Judah. Shortly into the journey, Naomi asked to stop.

"Go back to your mother's houses. May God deal as kindly with you as you have dealt with my sons and me," said Naomi to her sons' wives.

She kissed the young women, and they wept loudly. They both protested that they intended to return to Bethlehem with Naomi.

But Naomi insisted. "Turn back now, my daughters. Why do you want to go with me? I have no more sons to give you. Start a new life, for your husbands are gone. It has been far more bitter for me, because I see God has turned his back on me."

All three were very sad. It was a while before their tears abated. Orpah kissed Naomi good-bye. But, Ruth clung to her mother-in-law.

"Go," Naomi commanded her. "Return with your sister-in-law to your people. I will return to mine."

But Ruth said, "Do not force me to leave. Where you go, I will go. Where you lodge, I will lodge. Your people shall be my people. Your God shall be my God."

Naomi saw that Ruth was determined, so she said no more. When they came to Bethlehem, the whole town stirred with excitement. They had heard that the two women were moving to the town. Word spread that Naomi was returning with an unknown foreign woman, younger than herself.

"Is it you, Naomi?" said one of the residents in the group, who dared to speak.

"Do not call me Naomi," she answered. "Call me Mara, because God has dealt bitterly with me."

It was the beginning of the barley harvest. Since Naomi had no fields planted, she asked Ruth to go glean, or gather up, barley left in the fields of Boaz, a rich relative of her dead husband. As it happened, Ruth was gleaning behind the reapers in the same field where Boaz was supervising the operation. He had just arrived from the town of Bethlehem.

"Who is that young woman?" Boaz asked his servant who was in charge of the reapers.

"She is the Moabite who came back with Naomi from the country of Moab," explained the servant.

Boaz went over to where Ruth was gathering barley. "I have ordered the young men not to bother you. If you get thirsty, go to the vessels from which they drink under my protection."

"Why have I found favor with you when I am a foreigner?" Ruth asked Boaz.

"I heard about your kindness to your mother-in-law since the death of your husband. May God reward you for your deeds," said Boaz.

When the meal was served, Boaz invited Ruth to eat some of his bread. He invited her to dip a morsel in the sour wine on his table. Out of earshot of Ruth, Boaz instructed the men who worked for him to pull out handfuls of barley from the standing sheaves for her to gather.

At the end of the day, Ruth weighed what she had gleaned. She brought it to town and showed Naomi how much she had gathered, and they divided it between them. As they did so, Ruth spoke about Boaz, who was very good to her. She related her pleasant dealings with him. Naomi threw her hands up joyfully and blessed the name of God.

"I need to seek security for you. Who better than our kinsman Boaz? Tonight he will be winnowing barley at the threshing floor. Go there," said Naomi. The threshing floor was an elevated space where the kernels of grain were separated from the chaff. Winnowing was done in the evening when the wind picked up, by beating the grain and tossing it into the air so the chaff was carried away.

As Naomi advised, Ruth first bathed and anointed herself with oil. She put on her best clothing and set out to find Boaz, who was happy that she had chosen to meet him.

"May God bless you," he said to her. "You have not gone after young men, but you have chosen me. But, I understand that there is a man who is closer to you in kinship than myself. If he does not claim your hand before morning, I would be honored marry you."

Boaz did not want people to talk about Ruth, because she met him at the threshing floor. He was careful not to spoil her reputation. So he weighed out six measures of barley and put it on her back, then sent her home to Naomi. Ruth was disturbed when she told her mother-in-law about the closer kinship of someone else. But, Naomi advised her to worry. She was certain that Boaz would solve the matter before the sun set the following day.

Now it happened that Naomi owned a parcel of land that had belonged to her husband Elimelech. As a landowner and a close kinsman, Boaz went to the marketplace to represent Naomi's interests. He offered the parcel to the next-of-kin in question, explaining that the land belonged to Elimelech and his sons, all of whom were deceased. With the purchase of the land went everything that belonged with that land, meaning Ruth. If Ruth had then had a son, the land would belong to him and the man's investment would be lost. The man Boaz spoke to refused to marry Ruth because he had already had sons, and did not want to risk their rights if he had another son with Ruth.

So Boaz said he would buy the parcel, and, accordingly, marry Ruth the Moabite.

Ruth and Boaz were very happy together. They had a son named Obed, who became the father of Jesse, who was the father of David. Thus, they continued the line of heritage that otherwise would have died with Naomi's sons.

GOD'S CONVERSATION WITH SAMUEL

amuel's mother knew before his birth that he would be a prophet. Like Samson's mother, she never cut her son's hair nor permitted him to drink wine or other intoxicants, because he would become a Nazirite who served God. Samuel's mother and Samson's mother at first were childless. When God heard their prayers, both gave birth. When the time was right, they gave their sons to the priests.

This is the story of Samuel and how he came to be a prophet. Samuel's father was called Elkanah. Elkanah had two wives, as was the custom during his time. One wife was called Hannah. The other's name was Peninnah. Hannah was childless, and Peninnah had many sons and daughters. While Elkanah loved both of his wives, he preferred Hannah to Peninnah, even though Hannah had not borne him any children.

Every year, Elkanah and his family made a pilgrimage through the mountains to Shiloh, which was about twenty miles north of Jerusalem. On the day when Elkanah offered his animal in sacrifice to God, he shared portions of the meat with his wives and children. Peninnah and the children got one portion each. But Hannah, the favorite, received two. Peninnah retaliated by provoking Hannah with remarks about how God had punished her by closing up her womb and making her childless. One night Hannah could stand it no more.

"Hannah, why do you weep?" asked Elkanah in concern.

"It is because my womb is closed," said Hannah.

She was so sad that she wasn't hungry. Instead, she left the others to dine and drink wine, and went to pray at the Shiloh temple. She asked God for help and vowed that if she conceived a male child, she would dedicate him to a life of temple service. After the prayer, Hannah felt at peace. She joined her husband where he dined, because she was no longer sad.

In due time, Hannah conceived and gave birth to a son. She named him Samuel, which means "he who is from God" in Hebrew.

"I have asked for him from God," she said.

That year when Elkanah and his household went to Shiloh to sacrifice and pray, Hannah remained at home with Samuel. She explained to her husband that she would not go to the temple while she was nursing Samuel. As soon as their son was weaned, however, she intended to return to the temple. On that trip, she would leave Samuel there to begin his training. And that is what happened.

The temple at Shiloh was under the care of the priest, Eli, who directed Samuel's training. Eli was a worthy priest in his duties, but his sons were nothing but scoundrels. Whenever anyone offered a sacrifice at Shiloh, the sons took whatever cuts of meat they wanted—even God's share. Eli knew of their behavior and told them to stop, but he took no action against them. So they continued.

God sent a prophet to speak with Eli about the situation. The man spoke the words of God: "I revealed myself to Moses, your ancestor in Egypt. I promised that your family and the family of your ancestor would have the privilege of serving at the temple. But now I say to you that the time is coming when I will cut off your strength and the strength of your ancestor's family, so that that privilege will be taken away, and no one in your family will live to an old age."

Eli knew the word of God was true, and he listened. He had done wrong by allowing the evil deeds of his sons. He repented and continued to be the priest at the temple. Meanwhile, Samuel was becoming closer to God through his training.

One night when Eli and Samuel were on their cots, Samuel thought he heard Eli call him.

"Samuel! Samuel!" he heard.

"Here I am!" he answered. He went over to the priest's cot to inquire what he wanted. "Here I am, for you called me."

"I did not call, my son. Lie down again," said the groggy priest.

The same thing happened again. And a third time. Only this time, a very groggy Eli finally realized what was going on.

"If it happens again, you say, 'Speak, God, for I am listening,'" Eli said to Samuel.

When Samuel heard his name again, he did as Eli had instructed. God told the young man about his plan to punish Eli and his house. The next morning, Samuel was still disturbed by the message, and he tried to avoid Eli. But the priest would not let Samuel hide what he had heard. Samuel told Eli everything.

This was the first time that God spoke to Samuel. The message signified that Samuel, from that moment, was a prophet of God.

DAVID AND THE GIANT, GOLIATH

he town called Socoh was on the border between Judah and the land called Philistia. Socoh belonged to Judah, but the residents of Philistia, called the Philistines, claimed that the town was theirs. The Philistine army challenged the army of King Saul and Judah. They gathered in a fierce group on a mountain in the high Judean range. The army of King Saul assembled on another mountain facing them. In between was a plush, green valley.

A giant named Goliath who stood threateningly at over nine feet tall emerged from the Philstine army. He had earned a reputation in the region, and some claimed Goliath was even ten feet tall. He wore a bronze helmet and a coat of scaled armor that protected his massive body. His legs were covered in plated bronze, and he slung a javelin of bronze on his back. He challenged the army of King Saul, which was huddled together, frightened at his enormity.

"Choose a man for yourselves," said Goliath. "If he is able to kill me, then we will be your servants. Otherwise, you shall be our servants and serve us."

David was the youngest son of eight boys whose father was Jesse. The three eldest sons were in King Saul's army. Too young to join the army, David went back and forth from Saul's army camp to Bethlehem to feed his father's sheep and to bring his brothers and the army a supply of grain, loaves of bread and freshly made cheese. One day when David arrived at the camp with the food, the war cry of the Israelites resounded in the Judean Mountains.

Then Goliath began to start shouting back. "Who is this Philistine that he should challenge the army of the living God?" asked David, bravely. "No one should be afraid of him. Your servant will go and fight with this Philistine," David said to King Saul.

Saul answered him, "You are not able to fight the Philistine. You are young and inexperienced, and the giant has been a warrior from his youth."

"Whenever a lion or a bear came and took a lamb from my father's flock, I went after it and struck it down. If it turned against me, I would catch it by its hair, strike it down and kill it. God, who saved me from the paw of the lion and from the paw of the bear, will save me from the hand of this Philistine," responded David without a trace of fear.

"Go and may the Lord be with you!" commanded Saul to the boy.

Then Saul put his own bronze helmet on David's head. The king's royal coat of armor was put on. David, the shepherd warrior, strapped Saul's sword between his shoulders. Then, he tried to walk. Unaccustomed to the heavy weight of the armor David was unable to move even a few steps. David lifted off the bulky helmet, laid the armor respectfully on the ground and unstrapped the sword. With his own staff in his hand, he selected five smooth stones and deposited them into his pouch. He held his shepherd's sling in his other hand, then went to meet the Philistine in the once peaceful valley below the two armies on the cliffs.

"Am I a dog that you come to me with sticks?" ridiculed the giant.

David answered calmly. "You come to me with your sword and spear and javelin. But I come to you in the name of the God of the armies of Israel. This very day the Lord will deliver you into my hand, and I will strike you down and cut off your head."

Without speaking another word, David rushed to the battle line to meet Goliath. David slipped his hand into his bag and took out a stone. Making certain the stone was secure in his sling, he aimed at the giant's forehead. The only spot on the huge forehead that was unprotected by Goliath's helmet was David's target. The stone made contact just where David intended.

Goliath instantly toppled face down to the ground. Then, David stood over the Philistine he had killed. He removed the giant's sword from the sheath around his wide waist, hoisted it as high as he could and brought it down to cut off Goliath's head.

Seeing their champion dead, the warring Philistines fled. A deafening shout rose from the camp of the army of Israel. David brought the head of the giant to Saul.

"I am the son of your servant, Jesse, from Bethlehem," David said.

Saul recognized David's importance, although he was still young. The relationship between the mighty king and the soon-to-be famous warrior boy was to be a long one.

DAVID
AND JONATHAN

Saul's son was named Jonathan, and he was about the same age as David. From the moment that the shepherd hero spoke to the king after his defeat of Goliath, Jonathan felt a close bond. That was how devoted the king's son was to David. Then, Jonathan made a covenant with David to show his love. He took off his robe and gave it to David. He did the same thing with his armor, sword, bow and belt. David was very moved by his friend's gesture. David didn't know then that Jonathan's loyalty would protect him from Saul's jealousy in the future.

After his victory over Goliath, David was a well-known hero. Word of the battle had reached everywhere the army went. In town after town throughout Israel, the women came out to meet the king's army, dancing and singing. They sang, "Saul has killed his thousands, and David, his ten thousands." The king began to watch David very closely, and he decided not to let him return to his father's house.

One day, when David was playing his lyre in the king's house, Saul said out loud, "I will pin David to the wall," and he threw his spear at David, but he missed. In spite of his jealousy, Saul knew God was with David, so Saul made him a commander in the army. David had more success in battle than all of Saul's commanders. Every day, David became more famous.

Jonathan knew of his father's increasing hatred and jealousy of David. He overheard Saul speaking with his servants about killing his friend.

"My father Saul is trying to kill you. Be on guard tomorrow morning. Stay in a secret place and hide yourself. I will go out and stand beside my father in the field. If I learn anything, I will tell you," Jonathan confided to David.

To his father, Jonathan said, "How can you kill David without a reason?"

Saul paid attention to his son's words and swore, "As the Lord lives, he shall not be put to death."

David returned to Saul's presence as before. There was another war with the Philistines, and David won that battle as he had the first. Saul again was jealous, and again he planned to kill David. David fled to the prophet Samuel for protection. But Saul's messengers found him. When they came upon Samuel, they were filled with the spirit of God. Three times, Saul sent his messengers after David, and three times they were overcome with the spirit of God before they could harm the boy. Finally, Saul sought out Samuel and David, and he, too, was unable to take David because of the power of God.

David left the protection of Samuel. Jonathan, son of Saul, understood his father's intention to kill David. He knew of David's hiding, and Jonathan went to find him.

A little boy accompanied Jonathan, and Jonathan tricked him.

"Run and find the arrows I shoot," said the king's son to the boy. The boy ran, and Jonathan kept shooting arrows in front of him. He commanded the boy to find them all. Once he had, Jonathan told him to run ahead and bring the arrows to the city and wait.

Upon seeing Jonathan, David bowed to his friend. The two young men kissed each other and wept, knowing that David must flee run for his life.

Jonathan said, "Go in peace. The Lord shall honor the agreement between me and you and between my descendants and your descendants forever."

David fled, and Jonathan returned to his home. But Saul tried many more times to kill David, and, each time he failed, because God protected David. Several times, David spared Saul's life.

The last time that David could have killed Saul, David had learned that Saul was, in fact, looking to ambush him in the wilderness. So, David learned from his spies where Saul was camped with his large army.

When Saul saw David, he said, "Is this your voice, my son David?"

David said, "Why does my lord pursue his servant? What have I done? What guilt is on my hands? If it is God that has stirred you up against me, may he accept an offering. If it is mortals, may they be cursed before God, because they have driven me out from my share of the heritage of God, to worship God in Israel."

Saul replied, "I have done wrong," Saul said, "Come back, my son David, for I will never harm you again. My life was precious in your sight today. I have been a fool and have made a great mistake."

David answered. "As I valued your life, may my life be valued by God."

Then David went away and Saul returned to his home.

ABIGAIL'S GENEROSITY

abal was a man who lived in the area of Maon. He had property in the green sloping country around Mount Carmel, not so far from his village, but far enough away that he could not visit every day to see to his affairs there. The sheep on the land that Nabal owned near Mount Carmel were recently sheared. Although Nabal had ordered the clipping of their wool, he had not supervised. He left the job instead to the shepherds who worked for him. Nabal's name means "fool" in Hebrew. In this story he showed why this name was appropriate.

Nabal was as mean and foolish as his wife , Abigail was clever and beautiful. One day, David sent ten young men from his army to pay a visit to Nabal. Nabal met them on his land. Abigail knew nothing about the visit until after the men returned to David.

One of the men greeted Nabal in David's name, as David had instructed him to do.

He said, "Peace be to you, and peace be to your house. Peace be to all that you have. The shepherds that did your shearing have been camping with us, and we did them no harm. They missed no sheep on our account. We protected them. Ask them and they will tell you. Therefore, look with favor on my young men on this feast day. Please give whatever you can spare to them, your servants, and to David, son of Jesse."

Nabal answered the hungry men very rudely. "Who is David? Who is Jesse? Shall I take my bread and my water and the meat that I have butchered for my shearers and give it to some men who come from I do not know where?"

When David's men returned and told him of Nabal's treatment, David prepared to retaliate against the man's rudeness. David assembled four hundred of his soldiers, and he instructed them to strap on their swords. He told the remaining two hundred men in his army to stay at the camp and guard their provisions. David wanted to make sure that no traveling bands stole anything they dearly needed. Then, David strapped his sword between his shoulders.

In the meantime, one of Nabal's shepherds described to Abigail how poorly Nabal had treated David's messengers. The shepherd told her also of David's honorable treatment of them at Mount Carmel and how David's army had not threatened to take even one of Nabal's sheep. He said that he felt evil had been done to David by his master Nabal and that evil would be returned to Nabal's household.

Abigail hurriedly gathered up two hundred loaves of bread, two skins of wine, five sheep dressed for cooking, five measures of grain, one hundred clusters of raisins and two hundred fig cakes. Her gifts were loaded on donkeys, and she instructed her servants to ride with them ahead of her to

David's camp. Upon their arrival, they were to tell David she followed.

At the same time, David began to make his way down the mountain in the direction of Nabal's house. When Abigail encountered David and his army, she bowed and spoke to him.

"Upon me alone, my lord, be the guilt. Do not take seriously this ill-natured, fellow, Nabal. For as his name is, so is he. Folly is with him. I, your servant, did not see the young men you sent," said Abigail. David stopped to listen. His army waited.

She continued. "God has restrained you from spilling Nabal's blood and has spared you the guilt of taking vengeance with your own hand. Let your enemies and those who seek to do evil to you be like Nabal, a fool."

David said, "Blessed be the God of Israel who sent you to meet me today! Blessed be your good sense and blessed be you, who have kept me today from avenging myself by own hand!"

David accepted Abigail's gifts. He shared the hospitality of his rough camp with the travelers. Abigail returned with the servants and the donkeys to her home. When they arrived, Nabal was celebrating the feast day in the house. She did not share with him what happened. The following day, when the wine of merriment was out of his head, she told him what she had done. As she recounted the event and her misgivings over how he had treated David's men, his heart ached within him, and he suffered a stroke. Ten days later, God struck him dead.

When David heard of Nabal's death, he blessed God for his justice and for keeping him from murder. So touched was David by Abigail's goodness that he set off from his camp to woo her. Shortly afterward, David and Abigail were married.

DAVID'S OFFERING AT JERUSALEM

od promised David that he would be king after Saul. While he was king, Saul had displeased God. One day, God visited the prophet Samuel, who was mourning Saul as though he were dead.

"How long will you grieve over Saul?" God inquired of Samuel. "I have rejected him from being king over Israel. Fill your horn with oil and set out to the household of Jesse of Bethlehem."

Samuel did as God instructed. He took a heifer, that is a young cow that had not yet given birth. In Bethlehem in the land of Judea, he greeted Jesse and invited him to share in the sacrifice he was to offer. He told Jesse that God had told him what to do. Samuel's duty was to anoint one of Jesse's children to be the next king.

At the sacrifice, Samuel looked over Jesse's sons. The first to appear was the firstborn, who was named Eliab. Samuel thought that surely this fine young man was the son he was to anoint in God's name.

But God interrupted Samuel's thoughts. "Do not look upon his appearance or his height, because I have rejected him. God does not see as mortals see. I look into the heart," said God.

Next, Jesse called his son Abinadab to pass before Samuel.

"Neither have I chosen this one," said God.

One by one, Jesse sent his sons to present themselves to Samuel. Each time, God answered the same way, "Neither have I chosen this one." Finally, the last son passed before Samuel, and God had not chosen any.

"Are all your sons here?" asked Samuel.

"All but the youngest, but he is keeping the sheep," answered Jesse.

Samuel ordered Jesse to send for his youngest son. The boy was ruddy in complexion from the hours he spent outdoors with the sheep. He had beautiful, pure eyes. His disposition was gentle.

"Anoint him. This is the one," said God.

Samuel took the horn of oil he had brought for this purpose, and he anointed the youngest son of Jesse in the presence of his brothers. The boy's name was David.

When David became king, he made Jerusalem the capital of his kingdom. He brought the sacred ark of the covenant to the city with the chosen men of Israel. God promised David that he would establish the throne of David's kingdom forever. David's offspring would build a house for God's name.

On one occasion, God had become angry at Israel. David sent messengers throughout the land to count the number of men whom he could call upon to fill his army. When counts were made in those days, each person counted had to pay a tax to the temple. David thought that all of this temple money would influence God to bless them and forget about his anger. But David's thinking only made God angrier.

"I have done wrong by the counting," David prayed.

God spoke to David through a prophet named Gad. He said, "Three punishments I offer you. Choose one of the three, and I will do it to you. Here is the first. Shall three years of famine come to you on your land? Or will you flee three months as your foes pursue you? Or shall there be three days' plague in your land?"

David chose the last of God's punishments, three days of plague. From the morning of the first day until the evening of the third day, God brought disease in the land. From one end of Israel to the other, people became sick with an illness that spared no one it attacked. In all, seventy thousand people died. Then, God's angel stretched out a hand toward Jerusalem to destroy it on the evening of the last day. God took mercy and told the angel that enough harm had been done.

God spoke to David, "Go and build an altar in Jerusalem, at the place where the angel stopped."

David did as God commanded him. He went to Araunah, the owner of the property.

"Why has the king come to his servant?" asked Araunah.

"I choose to buy your land to build an altar to God. I do this because God has spared the people from the plague," answered King David.

"Take and offer up what seems good to you. Here are the oxen for the burnt offering. And the threshing equipment and the yokes of the oxen for the wood. All this I give to the king," said Araunah.

But David refused the generous offer. "No, but I will buy them from you for a price. I will not offer a burnt offering to God that cost me nothing."

David paid Araunah with fifty pieces of silver from the belt at his waist. He built an altar to God at that location. On the altar, David sacrificed Araunah's oxen to God as a sign of repentance for what he had done.

David was king for forty years. He reigned thirty-three of those years in

Jerusalem. Before his death, David confided in his son Solomon about many things. He spoke about the loyalty and treachery of individual Israelites. He told his son about the reason God told him to build the altar. He appealed to Solomon to be a wise ruler.

KING SOLOMON'S WISDOM

God appeared to Solomon in a dream.

"Ask what I should give you," said God.

Solomon answered. "You have shown great and steadfast love to your servant, my father David. And now you have made me king. Give your servant, therefore, an understanding mind to govern the people and to tell the difference between good and evil."

What Solomon asked pleased God.

"Because you have asked this, and have not asked for a long life or one full of riches, nor death to your enemies, I will give you what you ask. I give you a wise mind. No one like you has come before, and no one like you shall come after," said God.

God also promised King Solomon many riches and much honor if Solomon would steadfastly follow the commandments. When Solomon awoke, he realized he had been dreaming. He went to Jerusalem and gave up burnt offerings for God. Then, he provided a feast for all in his court.

Soon afterward, two women came to Solomon. They were very troubled.

"Please, my lord, this woman and I live in the same house. I gave birth to my son. Three days later, she gave birth to her son. No one else was in the house with us. During the night, this woman's son died, because she accidentally lay on top of him. She got up from bed in the middle of the night, and she took my son from beside me while I slept. Then, she laid him at her breast to suckle. She put her dead son at my breast. When I rose in the morning to nurse my son, I saw that he was dead. But, when I looked at him closely, he was not the son that I had borne. He was her dead son."

The second woman protested. "No, the living son is mine. The dead son is hers."

And the two continued to argue before King Solomon. Finally, he spoke.

"The one says, 'This is my son that is alive, and your son is dead.' At the same time, the other says, 'Not so! Your son is dead, and my son is the living one,'" said the king.

Without a moment's hesitation, he instructed his servant to fetch him a sword. The servant returned promptly with it.

"Divide the living boy in two," said Solomon to the servant. "Give half to the one woman and half to the other."

The mother whose son was alive burned with compassion for her child.

"Please, my lord, give the living boy to her. Certainly do not kill him," said the real mother.

The pretend mother snapped, "He shall be neither mine nor yours. Go ahead and divide the baby," she said to the king's servant.

The king interrupted the servant. "Give the first woman the living boy. Do not kill him. She is the real mother."

All of Israel heard the story of the king's judgment. They stood in awe of Solomon, because they saw his wisdom. They recognized the hand of God in the king's rendering of justice.

Solomon was wiser than anyone else alive. People came from all over the world, from the lands of all the kings on earth, to hear him speak his wisdom. He wrote three thousand proverbs, and he composed over one thousand songs. He spoke of everything, from the cedar that grew in Lebanon to the hyssop that grew on the wall of the palace. He was acquainted with all kinds of animals, including birds, reptiles and fish.

God asked Solomon to build a temple to honor him. Because of Solomon's importance, people in other lands heard of God's desire. King Hiram of Tyre, an old friend of King David, heard, too. He sent word to Solomon through a messenger.

"I can supply the cedar and cypress timber. My servants will transport it to the sea from Lebanon. They will construct rafts from the timber to travel by sea to the place you indicate. There, I will have them broken up for you to take away. Your payment will provide food for my household," spoke the messenger from Hiram.

Hiram was true to his offer. Solomon gave Hiram 280,000 bushels of wheat and about 1,000 gallons of olive oil. Into the hills formed by the Judean Mountains, Solomon set 80,000 stonecutters to work, and they quarried out great stones for the foundation. Hiram's builders helped prepare the timber. In the fourth year of Solomon's reign over Israel, the king started to build the house of God in gratitude for all of his riches.

SOLOMON'S TEMPLE TO GOD

hen God asked King Solomon to build him a house, a temple, Solomon began the work immediately. The king oversaw the construction himself. The house of God had to be more beautiful than all other houses. The temple had to be the grandest, most glorious building in Israel.

From the floor to the rafters of the ceiling, boards of cypress lined the building. Gourds and open flowers were carved in cedar on the walls. Pure gold glistened from the inner sanctuary that sheltered the ark of the covenant. Chains of gold formed a door to the ark. Two cherubs made of olive wood with wings half their length spread their wings to the fullest. The wing from one cherub touched the far wall; the other's wing reached the opposite wall. The center of the sanctuary sat under the ceiling formed from their inner wings. The cherubs were overlaid with gold so they shone like the sun.

The floor of the house was also overlaid with gold in both the inner sanctuary and the other rooms. Two doors of olive wood separated the sanctuary from the outer chambers. Carvings of cherubs, palm trees and open flowers decorated the doors. Gold leaf adorned the cherubs and palm trees.

The house was three stories high. It had a vestibule, framed windows all around the building and side chambers throughout its length. Outside, the stone was perfectly finished. This had been done at the quarry so that no noise from an ax or an iron tool would disturb the peace of building the temple. The entrance to the middle story was on the south side of the house. One climbed winding stairs to that story, and then went from the middle story to the third as the stairs continued to wind upward. The roof was built of cedar beams and planks.

King Hiram of Tyre, who supplied the cypress and cedar for the temple, cast two pillars of bronze for the front of the temple, one on either side of the entrance stairs to the first floor. Carvings of four hundred pomegranates in two rows each decorated the tops of the pillars, called the capitals. Hiram also made ten huge basins of bronze. Five basins sat regally on the south of the house, and five basins sat on the north side. The stands had borders from which lions, oxen and cherubs seemed to spring alive. Each basin had four bronze wheels with bronze axles. The supports were decorated with wreaths. Solomon made a cast bronze vessel of enormous size and called it the sea of bronze. Surrounding the "sea" were panels with rows of cherubs, lions, palm trees and wreaths. The brim of the large vessel was made like a lily in the form of a large cup.

The house of God was finished in seven years. King Solomon brought into the temple the items that his father King David had dedicated to God. Solomon stored them in the treasuries. He assembled the elders of Israel and the leaders of the tribes and ancestral houses of the Israelites. A glorious festival to celebrate the new temple began with the sacrifice of many sheep and oxen. The ark of the covenant was carried in on such long poles that the ends protruded from the holy place in front of the inner sanctuary. Inside the ark were the two tablets of stone that Moses put there at Horeb when God made the covenant with the Israelites that allowed them to come out of Egypt.

Solomon prayed to God in the wondrous new temple.

"Let your word be confirmed, which you promised to your servant, my father David," Solomon prayed. His prayer was long, because the occasion was a sacred one. Some of his words were, "If someone sins against a neighbor and swears before your altar in this house, hear in heaven and judge your servant. Condemn the guilty by having them experience their own conduct. Reward the righteous according to their own goodness."

King Solomon also asked God to forgive the people of Israel for turning against him in the future, once they asked for forgiveness. Solomon prayed for God's help in times of famine and war. He sought protection from foreign enemies and asked God to hear the prayers of foreigners who might come to pray in the new temple.

The festival lasted for seven days. On the eighth day, King Solomon sent the Israelites away. They left in good spirits because of the goodness God had shown to Israel. God appeared for the second time to Solomon. He told Solomon he had heard his prayers and had blessed the new temple, which would celebrate his name forever. Then, he spoke of his promise to King David.

"If you walk before me, as David walked, with purity of heart according to my commandments, then I will establish your royal throne over Israel forever. There will always be a successor on the throne of Israel. If you turn aside from following me, you or your children, I will cast you out of my sight. Israel will then become a proverb among all peoples."

Three times each year, Solomon gave burnt offerings of sacrifice before God in the temple he had built.

THE QUEEN OF SHEBA

olomon was the wisest and richest man alive during his reign. Others were wise. Still others were rich. But no one compared with Solomon in terms of the two qualities of wisdom and wealth.

The amount of gold that came into Solomon's house in one year was 666 talents, and one talent weighed about seventy-five pounds! The gold came from traders and merchants, from the kings of Arabia and the governors of Israel. All the gold that arrived was put to use in the kingdom. King Solomon had three hundred shields of beaten gold. He sat on a great ivory throne overlaid with fine gold. The throne had six steps. A golden lion stood on each end of every step. The top of the throne was rounded in the back, and armrests resembling lions were on either side of the seat.

The king's drinking vessels were made of gold. Garments, weaponry, spices, horses, mules, apes and baboons were brought as gifts to Solomon from visitors who came to hear his wisdom. Although most were truly interested in hearing Solomon speak, many came to test his wisdom. Still others came to see for themselves the wealth of Solomon's court.

The Queen of Sheba heard of Solomon's fame and how God had blessed him with a just mind. She came with many riddles for Solomon to solve. The queen spoke with Solomon for a whole day. In riddle after riddle, the king passed her test.

At the end of the day of riddles, the queen gave Solomon the customary gift expected of a visitor to the throne. Only the queen's gift was tremendous. Scores of camels carried spices from Arabia. She also brought gold and precious stones from all over the world to the wisest king on earth!

Afterward, the Queen of Sheba dined at Solomon's table. She noted with detail the presentation of the food on the table, the seating of Solomon's officials and how carefully the attendants met his needs. She studied the attendants' clothing, and how the valets handled themselves before the king. She observed as Solomon lit burnt offerings in the temple. Whatever resistance she had felt to Solomon's esteemed reputation melted away like rain in the sunshine.

"The report that I heard in my land of your accomplishments and your wisdom was true. But I did not believe it until I came and saw for myself. Now I know that not even half had been told to me. Because God loves Israel, he has made you a just and righteous king," said the Queen of Sheba.

Never again did such spices come to Solomon's kingdom as those brought by the Queen of Sheba.

Solomon, however, like his father before him, displeased God. His habit of loving women from all the nations of the world made God worry. The God of Israel knew that the women in Solomon's life worshipped other gods. He did not want Solomon to become distracted by these other influences.

God spoke to Solomon. "You shall not enter into marriage with any woman from any other nation of the world. Neither shall they enter into marriage with you. For they will surely move your heart to follow their gods."

And that is what happened. Shortly after the visit from the Queen of Sheba, Solomon did indeed marry many wives, as was the custom of the time. He selected foreign women, and he distracted himself with their gods. Solomon followed Astarte, the goddess of the Sidonians. He prayed to Milcom, god of the Ammonites. He built a temple for Chemosh of Moab, and one for Molech of the Ammonites. He did the same for all of the gods of his foreign wives. He offered incense and sacrifices to them.

God was angry with Solomon for his unfaithfulness. Still, God was loyal to his promise to Solomon's father King David. God spoke to Solomon.

"Since you have not done what I commanded you, I will tear the kingdom from you and give it to your servant. For the sake of your father David, I will not do it in your lifetime. I will tear it out of the hand of your son. I will not, however, tear away the entire kingdom. I will give one tribe to your son for the sake of my servant David and for the sake of Jerusalem, which I have chosen."

Solomon ruled the kingdom of Israel for forty years. He was buried in the city of his father David. His son Rehoboam succeeded him as king.

THE PROPHET ELISHA

lisha was a holy man of God. As a prophet, he spent much of his time traveling, accompanied by his servant Gehazi. Here are several stories about Elisha, one where he helps a woman whose husband has not paid his debts, another in which he answers the plea of a woman who wants a child and a few in which he feeds hungry people.

Once a woman cried out to Elisha, "You know that my husband feared God, but he died. And now the debt collector will take my two children as slaves."

"What shall I do for you?" inquired Elisha, knowing he could not directly fight the debt collector, who was obeying the law. Then he said, "Tell me what you have in the house."

"Your servant has nothing in the house except a jar of oil," said the woman.

Elisha answered, "Go outside, borrow vessels from all of your neighbors. Collect many vessels."

The woman followed Elisha's instructions.

When she returned, the prophet said, "Shut the door to the house and go inside and pour oil into all the vessels."

Soon, all the vessels were full, and there were no more vessels to be found. Then, the oil stopped flowing.

Elisha spoke softly to the woman. "Go sell the oil and pay your debts. Now you and your children can live in peace."

Some time ago, Elisha was passing through a village called Shunem. A wealthy woman urged him to come in and have a meal with her and her husband, who was much older than she was. Elisha accepted the hospitality and thanked them. Now, whenever the prophet went through the village, he stopped to dine with the couple. One day, the wife spoke to her husband about Elisha.

"I am sure that the man who regularly passes our way is a holy man of God. Let us make a small chamber for him with a bed, a table, a chair and a lamp, so that he can stay there whenever he comes to us," said the wife to her husband, and he agreed.

So, whenever Elisha visited, he stayed in the chamber with his servant Gehazi. One day, Elisha asked his servant to speak to the woman for him.

Gehazi delivered Elisha's message in Elisha's own words: "Since you have taken all this trouble for us, what may be done for you?"

The woman sent a message back to Elisha through Gehazi.

"She said she has no son, and her husband is old," Gehazi told the prophet.

Elisha asked Gehazi to summon the woman. The woman stood outside Elisha's door.

"At this season, in due time, you shall have a son," said Elisha.

The woman was very grateful. And she hoped the prophet had not told her false words.

But, as Elisha predicted, she bore a son in due time. When the child was older, he went to his father one day in the field as he was reaping.

"My head! my head!" cried the boy.

The father brought the boy to his mother. The child sat on her lap until noon. Then, he died. The poor mother did not know what to do, so she went to the prophet's room and laid the child on Elisha's bed. Next, she set out on a donkey with a servant for Mount Carmel to find Elisha. She found him at the foot of a mountain praying. Gehazi tried to push her away.

"Let her alone, for she is in bitter distress," corrected Elisha.

"Did I not ask my lord for a son? Did I not say, 'Do not mislead me?'" pleaded the woman.

Gehazi went on ahead to the woman's village and laid the staff of Elisha on the child's face. But nothing changed. When Elisha arrived at the house, he saw the child lying dead on his bed. He closed the door to his room, leaving Gehazi and the mother outside. He prayed to God. Then, he lay upon the child, put his mouth upon the boy's mouth, his eyes on the boy's eyes and his hands on the boy's hands. The flesh of the child began to grow warm. He sneezed seven times, then he opened his eyes. Elisha summoned Gehazi and the boy's mother.

"Take your son," said the prophet.

In the land of Gilgal, there was a famine. Elisha decided to feed the people in God's name. He instructed Gehazi to put a large pot on the fire. Herbs were gathered for the stew. He found a wild vine and took from it a lapful of wild gourds, not knowing what they were. Wild gourds were thrown into the pot. The first to eat tasted the stew in the large pot.

"O man of God, there is death in the pot!" they cried.

"Then bring some flour," said Elisha.

Once he threw the flour into the stew, Elisha told the people to eat. They did, and there was nothing harmful in the pot.

Another day, a man came from a nearby field and brought food from the earth to Elisha. He carried twenty loaves of barley and fresh ears of grain in his sack.

"Give it to the people and let them eat," said Elisha.

"How can I set this before one hundred people?" demanded Gehazi.

"Give it to the people and let them eat. For thus says God, 'They shall eat and have some left,'" corrected Elisha.

Gehazi set the food down before the crowd. They ate. And there was some left.

THE PROPHET ELIJAH AND KING AHAB

ing Ahab, son of Omri, did evil in the sight of God. He erected an altar to the god Baal, the Canaanite storm god. By so doing, he elevated the worship of Baal to official status in Israel. He and his wife Jezebel, daughter of King Ethbaal of the Sidonians, served Baal and worshipped him. Ahab did more to provoke the anger of God than had all the kings of Israel who had gone before him.

Elijah, a holy man of God, said to Ahab, "As the God of Israel lives, there shall be neither dew nor rain these years, except when I speak to end the drought."

Then God sent Elijah to live east of the Jordan River and far from Ahab's capital. The ravens brought him bread and meat in the morning and bread and meat in the evening. He drank from a wadi, a stream bed that contains water only in the rainy season. After a while, even the wadi dried up, because there was no rain in the land. Next, God instructed Elijah to go live in Sidon in the village of Zarephath. At the gate of the town, he saw a widow and spoke to her.

"Bring me a little water in a vessel, so that I may drink," asked Elijah.

The woman left to do as he asked, and when she returned, Elijah spoke again.

"Bring me a morsel of bread in your hand," he added.

She said, "As your God lives, I have nothing baked, only a handful of meal in a jar. I have only a little oil in a jug. I am now gathering a couple of sticks, so that I may go home and prepare the meal for myself and my son so that we will not die."

"Do not be afraid," said Elijah to the woman. "Go and do as you have said, but first make me a little cake and bring it to me. Afterwards, make something for yourself and your son."

When the woman looked confused, Elijah went on. "Thus says the God of Israel: The jar of meal will not be emptied and the jug of oil will not fail until the day that God sends rain on the earth."

The woman did as Elijah requested. She and her household ate for many days, as did Elijah. The jar of meal was not emptied, nor did the jug of oil run dry.

After many days, God again sent word to Elijah. It was the third year of the drought.

"Go, present yourself to Ahab. Say that I will send rain on the earth," instructed God to Elijah.

A man named Obadiah saw Elijah coming, recognized him and fell to the ground to honor him.

"Is it you, my lord Elijah?" Obadiah asked.

"It is I. Go, tell your lord that Elijah is here," said Elijah.

Obadiah was shocked. "How have I sinned, that you would hand me over to Ahab to kill me? There is no nation to which my lord Ahab has not sent messengers to find you to end the drought. When they would say, 'He is not here,' Ahab would require an oath of the nation that you were not there. Now you say, 'Go, tell your lord that Elijah is here.' As soon as I have gone from you, the spirit of God will carry you I know not where. And, when Ahab cannot find you, he will kill me."

"As God lives, I will surely show myself to Ahab today," promised Elijah.

So, Obadiah delivered the message to Ahab. When Ahab saw Elijah, he was angry.

"Is it you, you who have caused such trouble throughout Israel?" asked Ahab.

Elijah protested. "I have not troubled Israel," he said. "But you have, and you have troubled your father's house. Have all of Israel assemble at Mount Carmel. Also bring the 450 prophets of Baal and the 450 prophets of Asherah, who eat at your wife Jezebel's table."

Ahab did as Elijah instructed. Elijah spoke to all who assembled at Mount Carmel.

"How long will you limp in two different directions? If God is God, follow him. If Baal, then follow Baal," shouted Elijah.

No one said a word. No one moved at all. Elijah spoke to them again.

"I, even I, am a single prophet of God. But Baal's prophets number 450. Let two bulls be brought to us. Let Baal's prophets choose one bull, cut it in pieces, lay it on the wood and put no fire to it. I will prepare the other bull in the same fashion. Then, they will call upon the name of Baal, and I, upon the name of God. The one who answers by fire is indeed God," said Elijah to the crowd.

The prophets of Baal were certain of victory. They went first and chose their bull. Then, they prepared the animal. From early morning until noon, they wailed.

"O Baal, answer us!" cried Baal's prophets.

Nothing happened. Finally, they limped around the altar they had made. Elijah mocked them, saying Baal was probably meditating. Perhaps Baal had wandered away, Elijah teased, or maybe he was merely sleeping. As was their custom, the worshippers of Baal cried aloud. They cut themselves with swords and lances until blood gushed over them. Still, Baal did not make fire.

Elijah spoke to all the people there. "Come closer to me," he said.

He took twelve stones, according to the number of the tribes of the sons of Jacob. Then, he made a trench around the altar of God, large enough to hold two measures of seed. He put his wood in order on the altar, and he cut the bull in pieces. He laid it on the wood.

"Fill four jars with water and pour it on the burnt offering and on the wood," he ordered.

He commanded that they do this three times. After the water was poured for the third time, it ran around the altar and filled the trench. He entreated God to let his power be known to all on that day. Then, the fire of God consumed the burnt offering, the wood, the stones, the dust and even the water in the trench. When the people witnessed it, they fell to the ground to honor God.

Elijah ordered that the prophets of Baal be punished by death. Then, he spoke to Ahab.

"Go eat and drink. For there is a sound of rushing rain," said Elijah.

Ahab immediately did as Elijah instructed. With his servant, Elijah climbed Mount Carmel.

"Go look toward the sea," Elijah commanded the servant.

"There is nothing," reported the servant.

Seven times, this was repeated.

After the seventh, the servant said, "Look, a little cloud no bigger than a person's hand is rising out of the sea."

He told the servant to bring a message to Ahab to harness his chariot and leave before the rain stopped him from leaving. Ahab harnessed his chariot and fled for his life. But God went ahead of Ahab to the entrance of the house where he would find Jezebel.

When Ahab told Jezebel what had happened at Mount Carmel, she was furious. She sent a messenger to Elijah to speak in her name.

"So may the gods do to me, and more also, if I do not make your life like the life of one of them by this time tomorrow," she threatened.

Elijah set out from Mount Carmel to escape. On the journey, he found Elisha, plowing. Twelve yoke of oxen were ahead of Elisha, and he was with the twelfth. Elijah threw his cape over Elisha and made Elisha his disciple.

GOD'S ANSWER TO HEZEKIAH'S PRAYER

ezekiah was a good king, faithful to God's commandments. He was a descendant of David, to whom God had promised an eternal dynasty in the city of Jerusalem, in the land of Judah. Hezekiah was twenty-five years old when he began to rule Judah, and he was king of that land for twenty-nine years. During his reign, King Hezekiah stopped the worship of other gods by royal decree. The only legitimate temple of worship was the house of God in Jerusalem.

What Hezekiah did was right in the eyes of God, just as what David had done before him was right with God. Hezekiah removed the false places of worship in the land. He cut down the sacred pole of the Canaanite goddess Asherah. He broke into pieces the bronze serpent of Moses, which had started to be used in pagan rituals.

King Hezekiah prospered under God's protection. In spite of the attacks of the king of Assyria in many lands, King Hezekiah of Judah retaliated against Assyria. Hezekiah tried to expand the borders of Judah into Gaza. In the fourteenth year of Hezekiah's rule, the forces of King Sennacherib of Assyria attacked and captured the cities of Judah. The Assyrian king's hostility toward Judah demonstrated to Hezekiah the hostility of his own actions against the land of Gaza.

Hezekiah sent a messenger to Sennacherib, saying, "I have done wrong. Withdraw from Judah. Whatever payment you impose on me, I will honor."

The Assyrian King demanded huge payment. Hezekiah gave him all the silver in the house of God and in the treasuries of the kingdom. He stripped the gold from the doors of the temple and from all of the doorposts in the land of Judah. But King Sennacherib of Assyria was not satisfied in his aggression against the kingdom of Hezekiah. Instead, the Assyrian army marched directly to Jerusalem. The army stood its ground near an important pipeline to the city's water supply. Hezekiah sent out the palace officers to speak to the Assyrian forces.

The leader of the enemy army spoke to Hezekiah's officers in the name of the king of Assyria. They mocked Hezekiah, saying, "Your God said to me, 'Go up against this land and destroy it.'"

Then, in a loud voice spoken in the language of Judah, the enemy leader shouted additional insults to the people of Jerusalem, "Hear the word of the great king, the king of Assyria! Thus says the king, 'Do not let Hezekiah deceive you, because he will not be able to deliver you out of my hand. Do not listen to Hezekiah when he misleads you by saying, "God will deliver us."'"

But, the people of Jerusalem remained silent as King Hezekiah commanded them to do. Hezekiah retired to his quarters. He tore his clothes and covered himself with sackcloth. Then, he entered the house of God to pray. He sent his servants, also in sackcloth, to the prophet Isaiah.

Isaiah said to Hezekiah's servants, "Thus says God: 'Do not be afraid because of the words you have heard from the servants of the king of Assyria. I will put a spirit in him. He shall hear a rumor and return to his own land. I will cause him to fall by the sword in his own land.'"

In the temple, Hezekiah prayed to God. "Save us, O God, from the hand of the king of Assyria so that all the kingdoms of earth may know that you are God alone."

God heard Hezekiah. He gave his answer in a message to Hezekiah, which he sent to the king through Isaiah. The answer spoke to the king at great length about the aggression of the king of Assyria. Hezekiah learned that God would turn the Assyrians back the way they came. God said to Hezekiah, "And this shall be the sign for you. This year you shall eat what grows. In the second year, eat what springs from that. Then, in the third year, sow, reap, plant vineyards and eat their fruit."

Isaiah's prophecy told the king that the people of Judah would not be immediately delivered from the aggression of the Assyrians. Several years would pass before they were masters of their land again, but Jerusalem would not fall to the invaders.

God spoke this truth to Hezekiah through Isaiah, "The survivors of the house of Judah shall again take root downward and bear fruit upward. Concerning the king of Assyria, he shall not come into this city. For I will defend this city to save it, for my own sake and for the sake of my servant David."

This was how God kept his promise to David and how God rewarded Hezekiah for his faithfulness.

JOASH
AND THE PROPHET

 oash became King of Israel when he was only seven years old. For forty years, he ruled the country. He tried to follow the rules of God. Like many before him, he fell into worshipping the false gods of neighboring countries.

Joash's reign was easy when his actions were pure. When Joash turned away from God, his reign was in turmoil. God saved Joash's life when he was an infant. By this act, God saw that the House of David again ruled Israel. He also saw that the House of Ahab, because of its worship of false gods, lost its rule.

As an infant, Joash hid with his nurse in the home of King Joram's daughter, King Ahaziah's sister. The sister was named Jehosheba. Jehosheba hid the baby heir away from Athaliah, King Ahaziah's mother. Athaliah was angry that King Ahaziah had been murdered, so she tried to murder the young heirs to the throne. All the heirs to the House of David died except Joash.

Athaliah was from the blood line of King Ahab. During the first seven years of Joash's life, while he was in hiding in the house of Jehosheba, Athaliah ruled Israel.

When the time was right, Athaliah was killed and Joash became king. Sometime later King Joash decided to repair the temple in Jerusalem. All the priests gathered before Joash in the temple, set high in the Judean Mountains.

Joash spoke to his priests. "When there is money left over from what you collect in taxes, use it for the repairs," but no repairs were made. Finally, Joash ordered that a collection chest be placed outside the altar in the temple for donations from the people of Israel. Day after day, the leaders and residents of Israel put money into the chest. When it was full, the chest was brought before the king's officers and emptied. Then it was returned to the gate outside the altar, and the people refilled it. Each time it was emptied, the priests were surprised by the wealth that the chest contained.

King Joash hired masons and carpenters, workers of iron and bronze molders for the temple. They labored long and arduously on the repairs. Soon the temple was restored to its former splendor. Leftover money paid for new vessels of gold and silver and fine utensils to be used for the burnt offerings. Joash celebrated the repair of the temple, and his people praised God.

But, as he aged, Joash thought less and less about the Temple of God. He was swayed by the habits of others. Like others of his ancestors who ignored God's teaching to turn away from other gods of the region, Joash disobeyed, too.

Joash began to worship the sacred poles and idols that his neighbors used to honor the goddess Asherah. Joash's subjects did the same. The sparkling temple was abandoned.

Then God sent the prophet Zechariah to Joash and the people of Israel.

"Why do you disobey God's teachings? You cannot prosper as a people if you disobey," said Zechariah.

The people shouted down Zechariah, so that his words were lost to their uproar. Still, the prophet tried to communicate the word of God. No one listened. The mountains resounded with the noise of their refusal to hear. At the king's command, the crowd moved toward Zechariah. They stoned him to death, right in the courtyard of the newly repaired temple.

"May God see what you have done and avenge it!" were Zechariah's last words.

God immediately punished Joash and Israel. Before the year was over, an army was sent against Jerusalem by the king of Damascus.

The enemy army was tiny compared to the army of Israel, but they easily won their battle against Israel. The enemy army killed the king's officials and sent many treasures from Jerusalem to their king in Damascus. Before they left the city, they severely wounded Joash.

Instead of giving helping their wounded king, the officials killed him in his bed. Because the prophet Zechariah had been killed, Joash was now murdered.

Joash's son Amaziah, reigned next. Amaziah was king for twenty-five years. Amaziah killed the servants who had killed his father, but he spared the lives of the servants' children.

Amaziah interpreted the words of God as given to Moses. The words said, "The parents shall not be put to death for the children. Or the children be put to death for the parents. But all shall be put to death for their own sins."

Like his father before him, Amaziah later turned against the advice of a prophet, who told him to not wage war against other countries. He went to battle, against the prophet's words. He was defeated, and the northern wall of Jerusalem was torn down.

NEHEMIAH AND THE WALL OF JERUSALEM

 ehemiah was employed by a Persian king named Artaxerxes. Nehemiah rebuilt the wall of Jerusalem. After the wall was finished, he increased the number of people who lived in Jerusalem. He brought to the city the Jews in exile and their children.

This is Nehemiah's story. In the twentieth year of the reign of King Artaxerxes, Nehemiah brought the king wine. It was no different from any other time that Nehemiah had brought wine. Except that on this day Nehemiah was sad.

"Why do you look so sad?" inquired the king.

"Why should my face not be sad, when the city of my ancestors' graves lies in waste with its gates destroyed," answered Nehemiah.

"What do you request?" asked the king.

"I ask that you send me to Judah so that I may rebuild Jerusalem," said

Nehemiah, bravely, for this was a powerful king in a distant land, and Nehemiah was only a servant.

The king and the queen, who sat beside him in the elaborate dining hall, exchanged looks. The other servants stared at Nehemiah. No one dared to move. Then, the king granted Nehemiah's request.

Nehemiah set a date for his departure from the kingdom. He asked the king to give him letters for the governors of the various lands through which he must pass on the trip to Judah. These included a letter to Asaph, the keeper of the king's forest, from whom Nehemiah had to procure timber for the beams of the gates of the city. Although the governors of the various lands were not pleased to be disturbed by Nehemiah, they nonetheless let him pass. It was not looked upon with favor at the time that one would set out on a mission to improve the fate of the people of Israel. But God had put the idea in Nehemiah's heart, so his mission was blessed and he arrived in Jerusalem safely.

The only animal that Nehemiah took was the one he rode. He went out by night and inspected the Valley Gate in the western wall of Jerusalem. He passed the Dragon's Spring and rode north to the Dung Gate. He rode to the Fountain Gate at the southern tip of the city and to the King's Pool that was fed from the Gihon spring farther up the lush valley. The elaborate rock terraces on the eastern slope of the city set in the Judean Mountains had collapsed. The valley floor was a tumble of stones, and Nehemiah's horse could not find footing. The damage was clear to Nehemiah, and he returned by the Valley Gate.

When the rulers of the other lands saw what Nehemiah intended to do, they claimed his act was a revolt against his king. So Nehemiah had to muster a great force of Hebrews for the work. They came from many surrounding nations. Half of the them stood guard by night with their servants. By day, they worked with their weapons in sight.

At this time, there was famine in the land. Nehemiah called a great assembly of Jewish nobility. They were seizing lands from their own people in return for food. Families had to barter their fields, vineyards and houses to get grain for themselves and their children.

"You are taking interest from your people," he accused the nobles. A rumbling of voices stirred from the assembly.

Nehemiah continued. "We have brought back our kin who were sold to other nations. Now you are selling them yourselves," he said.

The nobles were silent. Nehemiah ordered them to restore to the people their fields, vineyards and houses. In addition, he told the nobles to give back the interest they had earned during the famine.

The wall was completed in what is now known as October, less than two months after it was begun. The rival nations saw the hand of God in the tremendous effort. Many sent letters to intimidate Nehemiah, but he remained steadfast to his mission to make Jerusalem a safe city.

By the seventh month, the people of Israel were settled in the newly walled Jerusalem. Nehemiah called together the nobles. He named the priests and appointed officers. He placed his brother Hanani in charge of the city. Then he turned to the book of his ancestors and named the names of the Jews who had been in captivity. Next, the Jews who had never suffered captivity were named. In all, 42,360 people were named, in addition to over 7,000 male and female slaves. Horses, mules, camels and donkeys were safe also in the restored city. Nehemiah never charged the people any tax, nor did he take food or wine from them as the previous governors had done.

QUEEN ESTHER

his is the story of how Queen Esther saved herself, Mordecai and the other Jews living within the Persian Empire from death. What makes this story different from many others in the Bible was that Esther was a very powerful woman. She was a Hebrew queen married to a Persian king. She reigned in the land of Persia where Hebrews were forced to live against their will. God's protection of the Hebrew people, including Esther, is very strong.

The story begins before Esther was Queen of Persia. The queen's name at the time was Vashti. The king's name was Ahasuerus. The story takes place in the city of Susa, the place where the Persian rulers lived in the winter. During the other seasons, the throne was in the capital city of Persepolis.

The king ordered a banquet held in the winter residence. For 180 days, the nobles and governors throughout the kingdom were delighted with the wealth and generosity of their king. By the seventh day, King Ahasuerus was lightheaded from wine. He commanded his servants to bring Queen Vashti to him. But the queen refused to come.

The king was so indignant that Vashti disobeyed his order, that he consulted every wise man in the kingdom and discussed the matter with every one of his officials. The king asked each of them the same question.

"According to the law, what is to be done to Queen Vashti for refusing the command of the king?" asked King Ahasuerus.

The wise men and officials saw the problem that the queen's actions created for the king. Maybe even more so, they recognized the problem in their own lives.

"This deed of the queen will become known among all women, causing them to look with contempt on their husbands. They will ignore us," said one official.

"They will justify their actions, saying, 'King Ahasuerus commanded Queen Vashti to be brought before him, and she did not come,'" echoed another.

Then one of the sages spoke, "If it pleases the king, let a royal order go out. Let it be written among our laws, and may it not be changed for all time, that Vashti is never again to appear before King Ahasuerus. Let the king give her royal position to a better woman."

The king liked the idea. Immediately, his letters arrived in all the royal provinces. Every man should be master in his own house; that was the message of the king's decree as it was carried throughout the kingdom. The men rejoiced that they had not lost any of their superior position to women.

Although the king banished Vashti, he wanted a wife. Under the counsel of his officials, he decreed that beautiful young virgins be gathered by special commissioners in all the provinces of the kingdom. The virgin who most pleased the king would replace Vashti as queen.

In the city of Susa, a Jewish man named Mordecai lived with his young cousin, Esther. They were descendants of those had come to Persia from Jerusalem when they were captured by the forces of the king of Babylonia. Esther was like a daughter to Mordecai. When news of the king's decree spread throughout the kingdom, Mordecai knew Esther would be taken with the other young women. He told her to keep secret the fact that she was a Hebrew. Every day, Mordecai walked to the king's residence to try to learn of Esther's fate among the other virgins brought to the king.

Esther won the favor of Hegai, who was in charge of the virgins assembled in the palace. Esther was treated well and remained under Hegai's supervision for twelve months. Finally, each girl went before King Ahasuerus. When Esther presented herself, she spoke only as Hegai had advised. The king preferred Esther to the other virgins, and he declared that she would be the new queen. No one knew of her heritage, because Esther had listened to Mordecai.

Mordecai earned the position of a lesser official in the king's court. Two other officials became angry with the king, and they plotted to kill King Ahasuerus. Mordecai uncovered their plot, and he told Queen Esther what he knew. When Esther told the king, the men were hanged. Then she told the king it was Mordecai that had saved his life.

Haman was a high official of the king's, but Mordecai did not respect his judgment. Mordecai did not bow before Haman to show respect as was expected of the lesser officials. Day after day, Mordecai's peers asked him why he did not bow before Haman. Finally, in an attempt to distance themselves from Mordecai's behavior, the other lower officials spoke to Haman. They said that Mordecai was a Hebrew. They knew this, because Mordecai had shared his secret.

Haman was already furious with Mordecai for his behavior, and this new information about the disrespectful lower official gave Haman a way to retaliate. Haman spoke to the king about the Hebrews in his realm. He filled Ahasuerus's mind with ideas about how the laws of the Hebrew people were different from the king's laws. Haman's story was so detailed and vicious, that the king believed it wholeheartedly. Immediately, King Ahasuerus removed his signet ring and put it on Haman's finger. He gave the royal order that plans be made to kill the Hebrew people in Persia.

This news deeply distressed Queen Esther. The queen sent her servant to alert Mordecai about what was to occur. Mordecai offered a copy of the decree to his cousin, asking her to intervene with the king to reverse the evil doings of Haman. After three days Esther had a plan.

Esther dressed in her best robes to appear before the king. She stood in the inner court of the king's palace. As soon as the king saw Esther he was anxious to hear what she had come for. She invited him to attend a banquet she was planning for the following evening. When the king agreed, she asked that he bring Haman, too. The king quickly and readily agreed.

The day before the banquet, Haman passed the king's gate and saw Mordecai. Still, Mordecai did not bow in respect. Haman decided to order a gallow be made, intended for Mordecai. When the king was in good spirits at Esther's banquet, Haman planned tell him to have Mordecai hanged on it.

That evening, the king was having trouble sleeping. To occupy his time he went over some daily records and acounts which reminded him of Mordecai's noble deed. He recalled how Mordecai had saved his life during the plot by the two officials. The next morning, wanting to reward Mordecai, Ahaseurus instructed Haman to honor Mordecai with a robe and a horse for what he had done. This was the beginning of Haman's fall from importance.

Haman was frustrated that the king decided to make Mordecai the focus of his honors. Haman, however, still attended the banquet with the king at Queen Esther's request.

The following day, at another banquet, Esther petitioned Ahasuerus to reverse the decree he granted to kill the Hebrews. She said that she had kept quiet about her heritage while slavery was the only condition they had to endure. The killing, however, of herself and her people, because of Haman's counsel, was too much to silence her any longer.

King Ahasuerus granted Queen Esther's request. In addition, he gave to her all of the riches of Haman's household. Haman was hanged from the gallows he had ordered for Mordecai. The king gave Mordecai the signet ring from his own finger. Queen Esther put Mordecai in charge of what had been the household of Haman.

The Hebrews in Persia were saved by Esther's courage. Today, their freedom from Haman's wicked plan is celebrated by the Jewish people as the feast of Purim.

JOB'S LESSON

There once was a man in the land of Uz whose name was Job. He was blameless and upright. He feared God, and he turned away from evil. Job had seven sons and three daughters. He was a rich landowner with 7,000 sheep, 3,000 camels, 500 yoke of oxen, 500 donkeys and many servants. Job's sons held feasts in one another's houses and invited their sisters to attend. At the end of the festivals, Job offered burnt sacrifices at dawn the next morning in case his children had sinned and had turned their hearts away from God.

One day Satan appeared before God. God asked Satan where he had been.

"Going to and fro on the earth," answered Satan.

"Have you observed my servant Job? There is no one as blameless and upright as Job on the earth," said God.

"Does Job fear God for nothing?" asked Satan. "Have you not put a fence around him and all that he has on every side? Stretch out your hand and touch what he has. Watch him curse you to your face."

God answered Satan's wager: "Very well. All that he has is in your power. Only, do not stretch out your hand against his person!"

Satan left God's presence. Soon, a messenger came to Job. Then, a second messenger came. Then, a third. The message from the first was that an army from Arabia had stolen Job's herds while they were grazing and carried them off. The army had killed the servants with their swords. The second messenger told Job that the fire of God had come from heaven and had burned up the flocks and Job's servants. The third messenger reported that a great wind had come from across the desert and had struck the four corners of the house where Job's sons and daughters were eating. The three messengers claimed to be the only ones to have survived.

Job tore his robe and shaved his head in sorrow. Then, he fell on the ground and prayed, "I came naked from my mother's womb. And naked shall I return. God gave and God has taken away. Blessed be his name."

Again, Satan appeared before God. And, again, God asked about Job. God boasted to Satan that Job still was blameless and upright, even though Satan had destroyed his possessions.

"Stretch out your hand and touch his bone and his flesh. Then, he will curse you to your face," taunted Satan.

"Very well. He is in your power. Only spare his life," said God.

So Satan inflicted loathsome sores on Job from the soles of the man's feet to the crown of his head. When Job's wife questioned him about his continued faith, Job did not curse God. Instead, he told her she was speaking foolishly and explained why he was not angry.

"Shall we receive the good at the hand of God and not receive the bad?" Job corrected his wife.

For seven days, Job sat in misery in the company of three friends. They sat day and night on the hard ground. Then Job cursed the day he was born.

One friend answered him, "How happy is the one whom God corrects. Do not despise the discipline of the Almighty. For he wounds, but he binds up. He strikes, but his hands heal."

"Oh, that I might have my request and that it would please God to crush me. Teach me, and I will be silent. Make me understand how I have gone wrong," pleaded Job.

Job's friends prodded him. What indeed had Job done wrong against God? Still, Job did not curse God.

Job prayed instead. "Grant two things to me," he said. "How many are my sins? Make me know what I did against you."

He continued his prayer, and it was beautiful. The words were poetry. Here is some of what he said: "There is hope for a tree if it is cut down, that it will sprout again. ... As waters fail from a lake and a river wastes away and dries up, so mortals lie down and do not rise again until the heavens are no more. ... The waters wear away the stones, the torrents wash away the soil of the earth, so do you destroy the hope of mortals."

Job tried then to console himself with his faith in God's goodness. "I know my witness is in heaven. And he that knows me is on high," he said.

Job talked to his friends of his good deeds. The friends did not respond, because they saw that Job had spoken of his value before God in spite of what they saw as God's punishment. A holy man named Elihu happened by, and he was angry with Job's friends for blaming Job. After he corrected the friends, Elihu corrected Job for making excuses for himself before God. He told Job to listen and learn wisdom.

Elihu spoke these words to Job. "You say, 'I am in the right before God.' Look at the heavens. Observe the clouds, which are higher than you. Will your cry keep you from suffering? Stop and consider the wondrous works of

God. Can you, like him, spread out the skies, hard as a molten mirror?" And Job listened.

Then, God spoke to Job. "Gird up your loins like a man," God began. Then, one after another, God asked Job questions about the majesty of life. "Is it by your wisdom that the hawk soars and spreads its wings toward the south? Is it at your command that the eagle mounts up and makes its nest on high?" questioned God.

"I have spoken once, and then twice, but no more," said Job to God.

"Will you put me in the wrong? Will you condemn me so that you may be justified?" demanded God.

Job answered God correctly. "I have uttered what I did not understand. I repent before you."

God directed Job and his friends to offer a sacrifice of seven bulls and seven rams. He restored Job's fortune when Job prayed for his friends. Twice as much wealth as he originally possessed was his. Job lived among his children 140 years, their children and two more generations of children. He died full of the richness of having lived many years appreciating the wonder of God.

DANIEL IN BABYLONIA

This is the story of Daniel, who served as a wise man in the court of the King of Babylonia.

During the third year of the reign of King Jehoiakim of Judah, King Nebuchadnezzar of Babylonia attacked Jerusalem and destroyed it. The people of Judah became the slaves of Babylon, and the king of Babylonia ordered his palace master to bring to him the top Hebrews in the land. He wanted young, handsome men without any physical defects. They were to be chosen from those with royal blood and from among the nobility. The young men selected were taught to be wise men, Babylonian style. For three years, they learned the language and literature of the new land.

In return, the young, handsome and royal Hebrew wise men received large rations of food and wine each day, the same food the king ate in his palace. Daniel would not eat the food, because he followed the diet given to his people by God. He had eaten this way all of his short life. Fortunately, the palace master understood Daniel's predicament. But, he feared for his life if Daniel were to be become ill for not eating the king's generous portions.

Daniel had an idea. "Why not try a test for ten days? Give your Babylonian servants their present diet. As for the Israelites, let us be given vegetables to eat and water to drink. At the end of that time, you can compare their appearance with our appearance. If we look in better health, we can eat our diet."

The palace master agreed. At the end of ten days, the Israelites looked healthier than the young men who had eaten the royal rations. The guard withdrew the royal rations and wine from the diets of the young Hebrews.

Daniel became a wise man in the king's court after three years. Like his countrymen, Daniel was counted as wiser than the wise men from the king's country. In the second year of Nebuchadnezzar's reign, the king had a disquieting dream. He called upon the magicians, enchanters, sorcerers and Babylonian wise men to explain the meaning of his dream. But he told them nothing about the dream.

"Oh, king, live forever! Tell your servants the dream, and we will reveal the interpretation," said one of the kings' wise men.

"This is a public decree," answered the king, who was not very good humor. "If you do not tell me both the dream itself and its meaning, you will be torn limb from limb. Your houses will be laid to ruin."

A second sage spoke. "Let the king first tell his servants the dream. Then we can give its interpretation," said the sage.

"I know for certain that you are trying to gain more time now that I have made the decree," said the king.

"There is no one on earth who can reveal what the king demands! In fact, no king, however great or powerful, has ever asked such a thing of any magician or enchanter or wise man. No one can reveal it except the gods, who do not dwell among human beings," said an outspoken wise man from Babylonia.

Daniel asked for an audience with the king. He requested that Nebuchadnezzar grant him some time interpret the king's dream. Then, Daniel went to his home and told the other Hebrew wise men the mystery. Afterwards, he went to bed and prayed. A vision in the night revealed the meaning of the dream. "Blessed be the name of God from age to age, for wisdom and power are his," Daniel prayed.

Daniel returned to the king and asked a stay on the lives of the wise men the king had sentenced to death.

"Are you able to tell me the dream that I have seen and its interpretation?" demanded the king.

Daniel answered Nebuchadnezzar. "No wise men, enchanters, magicians or diviners can show the king the mystery that the king is asking. But, there is a God in heaven who reveals mysteries. He has disclosed to me the meaning that you ask."

Daniel told the king that what God had shown in the dream was the end of Nebuchadnezzar's days. He explained that Nebuchadnezzar's concerns after the dream were of the hereafter.

"You were looking, O King, and lo! there was a great statue. This statue was huge, its brilliance extraordinary. It was standing before you, and its appearance was frightening. The head of that statue was of fine gold, its chest and arms were of silver, its middle and thighs of bronze, its legs of iron, its feet partly of iron and partly of clay," said Daniel as Nebuchadnezzar listened.

Daniel continued. "Then, the iron, the clay, the bronze, the silver and the gold were all broken in pieces. They became like the chaff of the summer threshing floors. The wind carried them away, so that not a trace of them was found. The stone that struck the statue became a great mountain and filled the whole earth."

To satisfy the second request of the king, Daniel interpreted the dream. Nebuchadnezzar was the statue's head of the gold. The silver chest, bronze middle and iron legs symbolized the kingdoms to follow after Nebuchadnezzar's rule. These kingdoms would be partly strong and partly brittle as seen in the feet and toes of the statue. They would mix with one another in marriage, but the union would not last, just as iron does not mix with clay. In the days of those same kings, the God of heaven would set up a different kingdom that could never be destroyed or left to another people. This kingdom would crush all of the other kingdoms.

King Nebuchadnezzar thanked Daniel and honored him with many gifts. He made Daniel his chief sage.

This story of Daniel is called an apocalypse, because God used Daniel, a person, to reveal his message about the future.

DANIEL
AND THE LIONS

irst Daniel served as a wise man in the court of King Nebuchadnezzar of Babylonia. Then David served his son Belshazzar at a festival. King Belshazzar called upon Daniel for an interpretation of some mysterious writing.

King Belshazzar hosted a great festival for 1,000 of his lords, the queen and the court. The gathering was celebrated with enormous amounts of wine. Under the brew's influence, the king ordered the servants to bring in the gold and silver that his father, Nebuchadnezzar, had taken from the temple of Jerusalem and brought to Babylonia. He commanded the servants to hand out the precious vessels among the lords and the ladies at the feast. They drank the wine and started to sing to the gods of their beliefs.

Soon they gasped in horror, for they saw the fingers of a human hand start to write on the plaster of the palace wall. The king turned pale, his limbs collapsed and his knees buckled. Everyone waited silently, terrified, for the king to speak.

"Whoever can read this writing and tell me its interpretation shall be clothed in purple, have a chain of gold around his neck and rank third in the kingdom after myself and the queen," the king proclaimed.

Not one of his entourage of sages at the festival could interpret the writing. The queen suggested that Daniel be brought before the king.

Said Daniel to the king, "Keep your gifts or give them to someone else! Nevertheless, I will read the writing to the kings and interpret it."

The writing had to do with Belshazzar and his father Nebuchadnezzar. Daniel spoke of the doings of Belshazzar's father when he was king. He told Belshazzar that Nebuchadnezzar had been majestic and powerful. But, because his spirit and heart had hardened, he was deposed from his throne and lived his last years without glory while Belshazzar ruled. Daniel said that now Belshazzar's heart had hardened, too, even though he knew what had become of his father for the same thing. The writing, he explained, said that God had numbered the days of Belshazzar's kingdom. At that very moment, the kingdom was being divided. Daniel's interpretation of the writing was correct. That night, Belshazzar was killed, and Babylon fell.

Under the new Prussian Empire, Darius ruled in Babylon. Darius held Daniel in such high regard that he appointed him governor of the whole kingdom. Soon the jealous presidents and commissioners throughout the land sought to discredit the Hebrew wise man. But they could not find any evidence that Daniel had done wrong as governor. So, they decided among themselves that the only way to complain against Daniel was in connection with the law of his God.

"Oh, King Darius, live forever! All the presidents and commissioners of the kingdom are agreed that the king should decree that no one in the

kingdom shall pray to anyone but you for thirty days. Disobedient subjects and slaves will be thrown into a den of lions," said the spokesman of the disgruntled group to the king.

Daniel knew of the decree by Darius, but he prayed to God as always. In fact, he prayed before an open window, because he was not afraid. The conspirators spied on him and told the king what they witnessed. Distressed at having to punish Daniel, the king nonetheless gave his approval to have him brought to the den of lions in order to honor the ill-conceived decree.

"May your God, whom you faithfully serve, deliver you!" the king said to Daniel before he was taken away to the lions.

A giant stone was laid at the mouth of the den with Daniel and the lions inside. The king sealed it with his own signet ring. Then Darius returned to the palace and spent the night fasting, unable to sleep. At day-break, Darius returned to the den. Daniel was untouched by even a single lion. Not one scratch nor one drop of blood marred him. The lions were tame, despite their hunger and the human in their midst. When Darius saw Daniel alive, he rejoiced.

Daniel was released from the den, and the conspirators were thrown to the lions. Only this time, the lions did not stand back as they had done for Daniel. King Darius decreed that within his dominion, people should trem-ble and fear before the God of Daniel. He wrote his decree to all the peo-ple of the world in their own languages.

"For he is the living God, enduring forever. His kingdom shall never be destroyed, and his dominion has no end. He delivers and rescues, he works signs and wonders in heaven and on earth. For he has saved Daniel from the power of the lions," decreed the king.

JONAH AND THE BIG FISH

 onah ran. He ran away from God's command to go to Nineveh in Babylonia and tell the people there that God was displeased with them. Jonah was supposed to preach that unless the people of Ninevah changed, God would punish them. Ninevah was a great enemy of Jonah's people.

Jonah ran down the mountains and as far away from Jerusalem as he could. He fled to the Mediterranean and the seaport. He found a ship bound for Tarshish, and he paid his fare. Below deck, in the hold of the ship, Jonah believed he was finally far enough away from God. He fell asleep.

While he slept, a great wind came upon the sea. Such a mighty storm followed that the ship threatened to break up. The sailors prayed to their gods. They threw the ship's cargo into the sea to lighten the boat. Jonah slept peacefully through the rocking of the waves and the howling of the wind. He slept until the captain awakened him.

"What are you doing sound asleep? Get up and call on your God," commanded the captain.

By now, the troubled sailors had decided to cast lots to determine who was the cause of the disaster. In those days, the custom was for sailors to throw sticks on to the deck when they cast lots. The sticks fell into a "no" pattern for each sailor, saying that he was not the cause of the squall. When Jonah approached the deck from below, they handed him the sticks and told him to throw. Jonah's lot said "yes."

"What is your occupation? Where do you come from? And of what people are you?" They screamed their questions at him.

"I am a Hebrew," answered Jonah.

"Tell us why this calamity has come upon us," shouted the sailors.

"Pick me up and throw me into the sea," yelled Jonah over the sound of the crashing waves. "I know it is my fault that the sea is so stormy."

But the men rowed harder to bring the ship back to land. Still, the sea grew more and more stormy. So they picked Jonah up and tossed him into the Mediterranean. No sooner had they done so than the waters quieted.

A big fish swam to Jonah. The fish saved him from drowning by swallowing him from the frightful water. For three days and three nights, the fish housed Jonah in its belly, where he was forced to live with the digestion that went on there. Then the fish vomited him onto dry land.

God spoke to Jonah a second time. God told him to take the message to Nineveh. This time, Jonah traveled to the foreign city. He told the people of Ninevah that in forty days God would see to it that their city was overpowered.

When word of this prophecy reached the king, he rose from the throne. He removed his robe and covered himself with a sackcloth. He sat in ashes and made himself humble. Then, he ordered his subjects to cover both themselves and their animals with sackcloth, and to abstain from eating and drinking. They were to cry out mightily to God and ask forgiveness. God was moved by their reaction, and he reversed the plan to punish the people of Nineveh.

Jonah was furious with God for changing his mind. Was this not unfair? If God punished the Hebrew people for what they did, what about these Assyrians? Jonah ran away from God again. He sat outside Nineveh to witness what he feebly hoped would be God's punishment on the city. Nothing happened. God made a vine grow next to Jonah and gave him shade, and Jonah's mood brightened. By dawn the next day, God had a worm attack the bush so that the bush withered. At sunrise, a sultry, hot east wind picked up and the sun pounded Jonah's head until he felt faint, and he asked God to let him die. God spoke to Jonah again.

"Is it right for you to be angry about the bush?" asked God.

"Angry enough to die," answered Jonah.

"You are concerned about the bush, for which you did not labor and which you did not grow. It came into being in a night and perished in a night. Should I not be concerned about the great city of Nineveh, where more than 120,000 people reside along with many, many animals?" said God.

This was God's lesson for Jonah. Some people think this story was told as a satire. Jonah's responses to God were funny. At the same time, Jonah recognized the serious point. A satire is intended to make the rest of us laugh, too, and then stop and think.

THE NEW
TESTAMENT

THE
ANGEL'S NEWS

This is the story of the news that the angel Gabriel brought from God. First, Gabriel visited Elizabeth's husband Zechariah. Six months later, Gabriel appeared to Mary, who was engaged to Joseph. The story starts with Zechariah in the days when King Herod ruled Judea for the Romans. Zechariah was an elderly priest, who was married to Elizabeth, the descendent of Aaron, who was the ancestor of a line of Israel's priests. The priestly couple were childless.

One day, Zechariah won when the priests in the temple cast lots. That meant that he was to be the priest from the group to enter the sanctuary and offer incense to God. Outside the sanctuary, the other priests and the assembly of worshippers prayed in the chamber while Zechariah made his offering of incense.

At the right side of the altar in the sanctuary, an angel waited for

Zechariah to approach. Zechariah was terrified by the vision. But the angel tried to calm him.

"Do not be afraid, Zechariah, for your prayer has been heard. Your wife Elizabeth will give birth to a son, and you will name him John. You will have joy and gladness, and many others will also rejoice over this birth. Like the other prophets, John must never drink wine or strong drink, for he will be great in the sight of God. Even before his birth, he will be filled with the Holy Spirit. He will turn many people of Israel back to God."

Zechariah was still frightened of the angel who appeared at the altar. "How will I know that this is so?" he asked the angel. "After all, I am an old man, and my wife is getting on in years."

"I am Gabriel, messenger of God. I have been sent to bring you good news. Because you did not believe my words, you will become mute until the day they come true," spoke the angel.

The people outside the sanctuary wondered what had happened to Zechariah. Surely, offering the incense did not take this long. They were used to waiting for the priests who took turns with the incense. They began to suspect the hand of God in the unusual delay.

When Zechariah appeared at the door to the assembly, he confirmed the people's instincts. He motioned to them, wildly at first, and they real- ized that he could not speak. His muteness must be related to a vision they were sure he had in the sanctuary. Zechariah served for the rest of the day in the temple, then he went home to Elizabeth, unable to tell her what had happened.

In a short period of time, Elizabeth conceived a baby. As soon as she recognized the signs of pregnancy, she prayed.

"God has done this for me. He looked favorably upon me and took away the disgrace of being childless," said Elizabeth.

In the sixth month of Elizabeth's pregnancy, God sent the angel Gabriel to the town in Galilee called Nazareth. Nazareth was watered by mountain streams. Its green olive groves, orchards and grasses welcomed the angel.

Mary saw the angel. She was a virgin who was engaged to a local carpenter. His name was Joseph and he was from the house of David.

Gabriel spoke to Mary. "Greetings, favored one! God is with you," he said.

Mary thought the greeting to be strange, and the angel understood her thoughts.

"Do not be afraid, Mary, for you have found favor with God. Now you will conceive and bear a son, and you will name him Jesus. He will be great, and he will be called the Son of the Most High. God will give him the throne of his ancestor David. He will reign over the house of Jacob forever, and of his kingdom there will be no end," proclaimed the angel.

Mary said, "How can this be, since I am a virgin?"

"The Holy Spirit will come upon you, and the power of the Most High will shield you from harm. The child to be born will be holy. He will be called Son of God," responded the angel.

Gabriel told Mary about her relative Elizabeth, who, in her old age, had also conceived a son. He told her it was Elizabeth's sixth month of pregancy, and Mary praised God. She knew Elizabeth had thought she would die childless.

Mary accepted what the angel told her. "Here I am, the servant of God. Let it be with me according to your word," she said. The angel returned to God.

Mary hurried to the hill country of Judea. She was eager to visit Elizabeth and to share the recent events with her. When Elizabeth heard Mary approach, she felt the child she carried leap within her womb. Elizabeth was filled with the Holy Spirit, and she embraced Mary.

"Blessed are you among women, and blessed is the fruit of your womb," cried Elizabeth.

Mary answered her, "My soul magnifies the Lord, and my spirit rejoices in God my Savior." Mary was ready to be the mother of the Son of God.

THE BABY IN THE FEEDBOX

This is the story of the birth of Jesus. It begins with an account of the baby's genealogy. Jesus was a descendant of David, and David was a descendant of Abraham, to whom God made the promise of a long line of descendants. About fifty generations came between Abraham and Jesus. And there were fourteen more generations from the exile to the birth of Jesus. Even as a young man, Jesus grew to be called the Messiah, or Christ.

The angel Gabriel told a virgin named Mary that she had conceived and would give birth to a baby she was to call Jesus. What the angel announced and Mary accepted as the hand of God came to be evident when Mary became pregnant. But Mary was engaged to a righteous man named Joseph, of the bloodline of David. Mary's father had promised her to Joseph in marriage. When Joseph saw that Mary was pregnant, he could no longer honor their engagement. He had respected Mary like the virgin he believed her to be, so he knew the child was not his. Still, Joseph did not want to disgrace her publicly, although what he thought Mary had done gave reasons for a divorce, if not execution. Joseph planned to send Mary away quietly. But while Joseph slept, an angel appeared to him in a dream.

The angel spoke. "Joseph, son of David, do not be afraid to take Mary as your wife. The child she conceived is from the Holy Spirit. She will bear a son, and you are to name him Jesus, for he will save his people from their sins."

The man who tells this story, Matthew, explains this with the words of the prophet that said, "Look, the virgin shall conceive and bear a son, and they shall name him Emmanuel, which means, 'God is with us.'" The details of what the angel spoke in the dream became clearer to Joseph. He now believed that the child Mary was carrying was a child from God. Joseph blessed the pregnancy. He did not become intimate with his wife until after she gave birth to Jesus.

In the final months of Mary's pregnancy, Emperor Augustus of Rome made a decree. All of the people within the Roman world were to register so the emperor could more efficiently collect taxes and enlist men for the army. The registration, or census as it was also called, was to occur in the town of birth of every head of a household in the Roman Empire. At that time, the lands of Galilee and Judea were governed by rulers appointed by Rome. Joseph and Mary traveled from the village of Nazareth in Galilee to the city of Judea and the city of David, called Bethlehem, in Judea. They had to make the trip, because Joseph was descended from the family of David.

They followed the roads from the Upper Galilee hills south into Judea. They passed near the mountain city of Jerusalem. A few miles south down the mountainous terrain was the city of Bethlehem. Joseph and his pregnant wife could not find any place to stay in the city. The inns were filled beyond capacity, and they could house fewer than half of the thousands of people who came to register for the emperor's census. Soon, it was time for Mary to give birth. Joseph and Mary had no shelter for the night, even after Joseph pleaded with the innkeepers because Mary was ready to give birth. Eveywhere the answer was the same. All the beds were occupied in Bethlehem.

The desperate travelers went in search of a cave for shelter while Mary gave birth. They found such a cave, in Bethlehem, being used as a stable, and there Mary's time came. She brought a baby boy into the world, and Joseph called him Jesus. Mary wrapped the baby in bands of cloth she had prepared and which she had brought from Nazareth. Joseph placed the newborn baby into the manger, or animal feedbox, that he had cleaned for this purpose. The family slept that night with the smell of the animals.

Jesus was born in Bethlehem during the rule of king Herod. Soon, Herod would hear of the birth of Jesus. He too would become threatened by the power he feared in the baby. The parents of Jesus would have to avoid Herod's fear.

THE SHEPHERDS' VISIT

any shepherds grazed their flocks in the rocky pastures around Bethlehem,. At night, the shepherds watched the animals to be sure they were safe. Teams of shepherds took shifts of watch while the others slept.

One night, an angel startled the shepherds on watch. The angel stood before them resplendent in gold light, and the shepherds knew the light came from God. Frightened, the shepherds huddled closer as they overlooked the sheep. Not one dared to stand nor address the angel.

The angel comforted them, "Do not be afraid. You see, I am bringing you good news of great joy for all the people. To you is born this day in the city of David, a Savior, who is the Messiah, the Christ. This will be a sign for you. You will find a child wrapped in bands of cloth and lying in a manger."

Suddenly, surrounding the angel was the heavenly host. They were the armies of heaven, which came to give testament to the blessedness of the birth that the angel described to the shepherds.

"Glory to God in the highest heaven, and peace and goodwill among those on whom God's favor rests."

The song of the angels was beautiful. It was the purest sound the shepherds had ever heard, and it filled the hills and plains in all directions. The shepards delighted in the melody and were at peace. Then, the angel and the heavenly host left the shepherds to watch over the flock as they had found them. But the shepherds were very excited by the apparitions, and they could not return to their watch and ignore what they had heard and seen.

"Let us go now to Bethlehem. Let us see this thing that has taken place," said one of the shepherds.

"Yes, let us witness what God has made known to us," said another.

The shepherds hurried to the city of David, which was Bethlehem, as the angel had instructed them. They traveled until they came upon the barn where Mary had given birth to Jesus. Respectfully, the shepherds approached the barn. Inside the cattle feedbox was a newborn, a healthy child. The child was wrapped in bands of cloth, as the angel had described to them.

The shepherds dropped to the ground and honored God. They introduced themselves to Mary and Joseph and paid their respects to the baby Jesus. They told Mary and Joseph about the angel's message and the chorus of the heavenly army. Mary treasured the message of the shepherds. She kept the words of the heavenly chorus in her heart to ponder their meaning. After a brief visit, the shepherds returned to their flocks, glorifying and praising God as they traveled back to the pasture.

After eight days passed, the baby Jesus was taken to the temple. The boy was to be presented to the priests in Jerusalem according to the religious law of the Israelites. At the temple was a righteous and devout man called Simeon. Simeon had been guided by the Holy Spirit to visit the temple in Jerusalem that day. Upon seeing the baby Jesus, Simeon took the child into his arms and praised God.

"Master, my eyes have seen your salvation," prayed Simeon, because he knew he held the Son of God in his arms.

Mary and Joseph were amazed by the words Simeon spoke about their son. Simeon blessed both parents. Then, he spoke directly to Mary.

"This child is destined for the falling and the rising of many in Israel. He will be a sign from God, a sign that humans will oppose. The inner thoughts of many people will be revealed, and a sword will pierce your own soul," said Simeon about the future of the child.

In the temple at the time was also the widow Anna, who was eighty-four years old. She worshipped there night and day. Anna, too, spoke of the child, and she introduced him to the people in the temple as the redemption of Jerusalem.

Mary and Joseph praised God and offered a sacrifice to honor him. When they had followed all the laws, they returned from Jerusalem. After a stay in Egypt they returned to the land of Galilee and the town of Nazareth. In Nazareth, the child Jesus grew to be strong, and he was filled with wisdom beyond his years. It was clear to those people who believed, that the favor of God was with Jesus.

THE GIFTS
OF THE WISE MEN

hen Joseph traveled with Mary from Nazareth to
Bethlehem for the census taking, King Herod the
Great ruled the lands of Galilee and Judea for the
emperor of Rome. All of the emperor's subjects had to
return to the place where the head of the household was born. In
Bethlehem, Mary knew it was time to give birth. But the innkeepers all
said the same thing, "No more beds." Baby Jesus opened his eyes for the
first time in a stable. His bed was a feedbox that belonged to the animals.
His parents met the visit of the shepherds from the barn that was the only
shelter available for them in Bethlehem.

Three wise men lived in a land in the East. They were schooled in
astrology, the study of the stars and planets in relation to human affairs.
These men were most interested in a different star that shone vividly in the
sky to the west. It was part of no constellation or cluster of stars that

belonged to the winter sky of the northern hemisphere in their location. And it pointed to something wonderful, an event they had studied through the stars. They set off with their camels to follow the path of the bright light in the sky.

Months later, they came to Jerusalem in the land of Judea. Their visit was an event, even in the city where Jews from many places came each year to worship in the Temple. The wise men wore exotic robes. They were seated upon camels on handwoven, colorful blankets. Strapped to the camels' sides were gifts from the East. People stared at the foreigners and tried to discover why the men had come to Jerusalem. The foreigners were excited about their special search.

"Where is the child who has been born king of the Jews?" asked one of the wise men.

Before the people could respond to the strange question, another of the wise men spoke: "We have observed his star since its rising."

"We have come to pay our respect to the baby," said the third wise man.

The king heard the news of the wise men from several of his officers. They had details of the travelers who were passing through town on their camels in search of the king of the Jews who had just been born. Herod did not want someone to challenge his kingship, particularly from such a special king, whose birth was announced by an extraordinary star. Besides, the emperor had named him, Herod the Great, King of the Jews. The king called an assembly of his chief priests and scribes, or scholars.

"Where is this Messiah to be born?" he demanded.

"In Bethlehem of Judea, according to prophecy," answered one of the priests.

"The prophet has said, 'And you, Bethlehem, in the land of Judah, from you shall come a ruler to rule my people Israel,'" said one of the scribes.

Herod dismissed the priests and scribes. Once they were gone, he called for the wise men from the East.

"Tell me the exact time when the star appeared," ordered King Herod the Great.

The wise men told him all they knew of the star. When they finished, King Herod pretended to be interested in the event. Herod tried to trick them to return so he could learn more about this child who had been born.

"Go and search diligently for the child. When you have found him, bring me word so that I, too, can go and pay him respect," said the king.

The wise men said their farewells to the king and set out to follow the star to its destination. It led them to the town of Bethlehem. A house in the distance was lit by the star. The wise men were overcome with joy as they neared the place. They removed from the camels the gifts they had brought from the East. Entering the house, they saw the child Jesus in the arms of his mother. They bowed in greeting to Joseph. Then, they approached Mary and Jesus with their heads low in respect. They marveled in wonder at the child. They offered their gifts. One brought gold. Another offered frankincense. The third left myrrh, a resin that was used for anointing and balming.

The wise men followed the stars and the planets back to their land. They ignored King Herod's request that they revisit Jerusalem with news of the young king of the Jews. A dream had warned them of Herod's real interest in the newborn. Herod's motives were evil. He had no intention of paying respect to the baby.

THE BOYHOOD OF JESUS

 fter he was presented as a newborn at the temple in Jerusalem, the city of David and the city of birth of his father, the boy Jesus lived in the town of Nazareth with his parents. For the most part, his boyhood was quiet and secluded. Nazareth was not a major town in Galilee. The town lay fifteen miles to the west of the Sea of Galilee. The Upper Galilee hills framed the town. Farms, pastures and the day-to-day doings of town life occupied the young Jesus.

However, life around Jesus was not all peaceful from the start. At the time of his birth, his parents had worried about where they would stay on the night that he was ready to come into the world. Once the wise men passed through Bethlehem with gifts to honor the baby, King Herod was threatened by the acclaimed kingship of Jesus. When the wise men failed to return to Jerusalem to tell the king the whereabouts of the recently born king of the Jews, Herod vowed to kill the child.

God watched out for Jesus and his parents. An angel appeared to Joseph in a dream when the wise men departed for the East.

"Get up, take the child and his mother and flee to Egypt. Remain there until I tell you. Herod is about to search for the child in order to destroy him," said the angel to Joseph.

Like Jacob's son Joseph, Moses and the people of Israel had done before him, Jesus's family escaped to neighboring Egypt. Just like the Pharaoh had ordered at the birth of Moses, King Herod of Judea decreed the death of the newborn boys living under his rule. Cries came from every house and farm where the laughter of young children had been heard just that morning. Every boy younger than two years was murdered by the king's men in Bethlehem. The people of the town screamed and mourned.

The words of the prophet Jeremiah had written centuries earlier, "A voice was heard in Ramah, wailing and loud lamentation, Rachel weeping for her children; she refused to be consoled, because they are no more." What the prophet had spoken long ago came to be executed at the order of King Herod.

After the mean king died, his kingdom was divided among his three sons, Archelaus, Herod Antipas and Philip. Archelaus inherited the lands of Judea, Samaria and Idumea. Herod Antipas governed Galilee and Perea. To Philip went the land northeast of the Sea of Galilee. Nazareth, where Joseph had lived when he became engaged to Mary, was in Galilee, the land governed by Herod Antipas.

The angel of God reappeared to Joseph in another dream. At Herod's death, Joseph and his family were still living in the country of Egypt.

The angel said, "Get up, take the child and his mother and go to the land of Israel. For those who were seeking the child's life are dead."

When he awoke, Joseph remembered the angel's words. Joseph also remembered the writings of the prophet that said, "Out of Egypt I have called my son." That day, he and his family departed the country of Egypt.

When Joseph learned that Archelaus was ruling over Judea, where Bethlehem was located, he was afraid to return. The news was that Archelaus was as mean as Herod. The second son, Herod Antipas, who governed Galilee, was a more just ruler than Archelaus. So, Joseph returned to Nazareth with Mary and the baby Jesus.

JESUS IN THE TEMPLE AT JERUSALEM

very year, Jesus's parents celebrated the Passover holiday in Jerusalem. The feast honored the freeing of the Israelites from their slavery in Egypt. It observed the passing over the desert by the Israelites who were led by Moses and guided by God. For the Israelites years ago and for the Jewish people, Passover is a time spent with family and friends. Then, as now, the Israelites shared special Passover food, and they recited special Passover prayers. An important part of the celebration of Passover were the prayers that people said together in the temple.

When Jesus was twelve years old, he traveled with Mary and Joseph to Jerusalem for Passover. In the holy city high in the Judean Mountains, Passover was celebrated by the Israelites as a glorious festival each year. Many people traveled great distances to attend the festivities. Children played until late in the day with cousins from other parts of the land. Their parents reminisced about other Passovers until the dawn announced the new day. They told stories and sang songs about what was new since the last Passover. Families visited each other and brought gifts of food and wine. The travelers slept in the houses of relatives.

Now that Jesus was older, he spent less time playing with the children. He talked with his cousins about life in their towns and the exciting things that had happened as they each journeyed to the festival. They told tales of the king and the emperor. They talked about the good sweets to be found in the homes of some of the relatives. They spoke, too, about the teachings they heard in the temple.

On the last day of the Passover festival, all of the visitors began to leave. They said their good-byes and promised to return the following year. They bid their friends from distant places a safe journey. Then, they loaded their donkeys for the trip home. A caravan wove down the mountain. Donkeys swayed from side to side with the gifts their owners were given to bring home with them and the personal items the owners had brought with them. Although everyone brought gifts from home and had shared what they brought, somehow the donkeys always seemed to carry more baggage on the return trip.

People on foot were tired from the festival and lack of sleep while they were there. The terrain was rugged on the journey across the mountains. People were also preoccupied with the work they had to do when they got home. They worried about their animals, their farms and their business affairs. The old and the infirm and the very youngest demanded a certain amount of care, and at times, the caravan had to stop for them to rest or to address someone's discomfort.

It was no wonder, then, that neither Jesus's parents nor anyone else who knew him noticed that Jesus had not left Jerusalem with the others making their way north across the mountains to Galilee. He was a young man on the verge of becoming an adult. Surely, he knew the way to safety cross the hills of Jerusalem with the others. If anyone did stop to look for him and could not find him, it could easily have been assumed that Jesus was walking with his cousins and friends as young people do. He was strong enough to catch up with the others. He was wise enough to not take any action that would cause himself harm.

A full day passed before Mary and Joseph questioned why Jesus was not among their party of travelers. At first, they calmly looked for him with friends and family camped a distance away. But no one had seen the young man since they all left Jerusalem. Mary and Joseph said goodbye to the other travelers. They had no choice but to return across the rugged hills they had just passed through in order to search for their son. Not everyone had left the city of Jerusalem when they returned. The residents of the city were still busy after the recent festival. Much activity was taking place there.

Mary and Joseph searched for three days before they found Jesus. They located him in the temple, sitting among the teachers of the law of the Israelites. They saw him listening to the teachers' interpretations as if he were much older. Jesus understood what they taught even though he had not yet begun formal study of the law God gave to the Israelites. The teachers knew he understood by the questions he asked. Not only were his parents amazed at the depth of the boy's understanding, but, so too, were the priests.

Mary interrupted her son and the teachers. Her concerns were those of a mother who thought she had lost her child.

"Child, why have you treated us like this? Your father and I have been very worried," said Mary to Jesus.

He answered, "Why were you searching for me? Did you not know that I must be in my Father's house?"

Jesus left the temple with his earthly parents and returned with them to Nazareth in the land of Galilee. There he was obedient to their ways as he increased in wisdom far beyond his years.

JOHN, THE BAPTIST

John was born according to the message the angel Gabriel gave his father Zechariah at the incense altar. Zechariah was mute as the angel said he would be, because he doubted the message. When John was born, Elizabeth's relatives and neighbors rejoiced, because they knew God had shown his mercy. When John was eight days old, his parents presented him at the temple, as was the custom. The priests and the people present were going to name the boy Zechariah after his father. But Elizabeth protested.

"No, he is to be called John," said John's mother, since this was the name the angel Gabriel had already given the child.

"But none of your relatives has this name," they said.

The people commented on how unusual it was that Elizabeth was calling her only child John. They knew this child to be a gift of God, and they expected no others to follow. Finally, someone motioned to Zechariah for his opinion. Zechariah wrote on a tablet, "His name is John." And the people were amazed.

To their additional surprise, Zechariah began to speak. The people saw this as an act of God. They felt the same kind of fear they had on the day the angel caused Zechariah' muteness.

"What will this child become?" said one person after another.

Zechariah was filled with the Holy Spirit. He answered the people in a long, beautiful prayer. In part of it, he prayed, "And you, child, will be called the prophet of the Most High; for you will go before God to prepare his way, to give the knowledge of salvation to his people through the forgiveness of their sins." This is how Zechariah told the people his son's purpose.

During this period, Tiberius was the emperor of Rome, and Pontius Pilate was the governor of Judea. Until he reached manhood, John lived alone in the sparse hill country of Judea. When John was called by God to begin his work, he traveled to the Jordan River. Word of his call reached the people in the area, and they spread the word even farther. The people clamored to be baptized, because they understood from John's preaching that he could perform the baptism for the forgiveness of sins. The prophet Isaiah had spoken of John as "The voice of one crying out in the wilderness: 'Prepare the way of God, make his paths straight.'" Everyone in the crowd wanted to be baptized by John. He was dressed in cloth made from the hair of camels, which he secured around his waist with a wide leather belt. He ate wild honey and locusts, which were like grasshoppers.

John reprimanded them. "You brood of vipers!" he accused. "Do not begin to say to yourselves, 'We have Abraham as our ancestor.' God is able to raise up children even from these stones. You must bear fruits worthy of repentance. Every tree that does not bear good fruit is cut down by the ax and thrown into the fire."

"What, then, should we do?" the people asked John.

"Whoever has two coats must share with anyone who has none. And whoever has food must do likewise," he answered.

Even tax collectors came to be baptized. They asked, "Teacher, what should we do?"

"Collect no more than the taxes owed," John told the tax collectors.

There were soldiers, too, in the crowd. "And, we, what should we do?" they asked one of them.

"Do not threaten or falsely accuse anyone for money. Be satisfied with your own wages," said John to the soldiers.

The people wondered among themselves whether John was the Messiah, Israel's divine king of the house of David. John corrected this thinking, too.

"I baptize you with water. But one more powerful than I is coming. I am not worthy to untie the thong of his sandals. He will baptize you with the Holy Spirit and with fire. With a winnowing fork in his hand, he will separate the grain. He will gather the wheat into his granary, but he will burn the chaff with unquenchable fire," said John.

And the people asked John, "What then? Are you Elijah?"

"I am not," he answered.

"Who are you?" they demanded.

One of the priests sent by the Jews to witness John's actions spoke out. "Let us have an answer for those who sent us. What do you say about yourself?" yelled the priest.

"I am the voice of one crying out in the wilderness: 'Make straight the way of the Lord,' as the prophet Isaiah said," answered John.

THE BAPTISM OF JESUS

ohn the Baptist honored his call by God to baptize people who were sorry for their sins with the water of the Jordan River. People asked John if he was the Messiah. John answered that one more powerful than himself was coming, one whose sandals he was not worthy to tie. The news made the hearts of many people joyous, and they sang the praises of God. The excitement that the Son of God had been born and was living in Galilee spread through the land.

John acted with the power and spirit of Elijah, as the angel Gabriel had told John's father Zechariah that he would. John softened the hearts of parents toward their children, and he showed the wisdom of honoring God to those who had disobeyed him. As Gabriel had foretold, John prepared the people to once again follow God.

One day, God directed his son to be baptized. Jesus left the home of his parents. He traveled from Nazereth to the land of Galilee to the Jordan River. A crowd was assembled. John, Jesus's relative, was baptizing people in the river. When John saw Jesus approach, he began to protest.

"I need to be baptized by you. Why do you come to me to be baptized?" John asked Jesus. The crowd quieted and waited for the young man from Nazareth to speak.

"Let it be so," answered Jesus. "For we act according to God's will as revealed in scripture."

Jesus waded into the water of the River Jordan and stood waist-high. Everyone watched as John supported his head, and the waters covered him. As the head of Jesus surfaced in the river, the heavens opened. John marveled at what he saw. But, the crowd of thousands was frightened. What they saw was the Holy Spirit descending as a beautiful light that shone in the shape of a dove above the head of Jesus. The people dropped to their knees, and a voice spoke to them from above them.

"This is my beloved Son, with whom I am well pleased," said the voice of God.

John addressed the crowd, which was no longer fearful. "The one who sent me to baptize with water said to me, 'He over whose head the Holy Spirit rests is the one who baptizes with the power of the Holy Spirit.'"

A great murmur arose from among the people assembled in the desert on the bank of the Jordan River.

"This is the Messiah," said some.

"This is the Son of God," agreed others.

"Surely, this is the king of the Jews," proclaimed others in the crowd.

Still, there were some assembled who did not believe.

John said, "I myself have seen, and I testify that this is the Son of God."

After his baptism, Jesus went to pray in the wilderness of the desert. The King of Judea, Herod Antipas, son of King Herod the Great, was angry with John. He ordered his men to capture John because John had preached against Herod's wickedness. And they led him off to prison.

When Jesus heard of John's imprisonment, he returned to Galilee. Jesus settled in Capernaum on the Sea of Galilee to set up his ministry. Capernaum was located in the territory of Zebulun and Naphtali. This fulfilled the words of the prophet Isaiah.

Isaiah had proclaimed, "In the land of Zebulun, land of Naphtali, on the road by the sea, across the Jordan, the people who sat in darkness have seen a great light. And for those who sat in the region and shadow of death, light has dawned."

From Capernaum, Jesus gave his message to the people. He said, "Repent, for the kingdom of heaven is at hand."

Confusion by some over the importance of John the Baptist and Jesus continued. On one occasion, Jesus traveled to the land of Judea with his disciples and went deep into the countryside. They spent some time there baptizing people. John was nearby, baptizing at Aenon near Salim, because water was abundant at that location. This was before John was put into prison.

A discussion arose between the disciples of John and some of the Jews who were present. When they were unable to agree, one of the Jews brought the matter to John to solve.

"Rabbi, the one who was with you across the Jordan is baptizing close to here, and all are going to him."

John answered, "No one can receive anything except what has been given from heaven. You yourselves are witnesses that I have said, 'I am not the Messiah, but I have been sent ahead of him.' He who has the bride (God's people) is the bridegroom. The friend of the bridegroom, the best man who stands and hears him, rejoices greatly at the bridegroom's voice. For this reason, my joy has been fulfilled. He must increase, but I must decrease."

29

SATAN'S TEMPTATION AND JESUS AT NAZARETH

After his baptism in the Jordan River, Jesus was led by the Holy Spirit into the desert wilderness. The land was arid. Poisonous snakes and scorpions made it their home. Jesus remained unfrightened in this wilderness for forty days and forty nights, as Moses and Elijah had done before him. Jesus fasted and prayed. He cared not about his hunger, because he knew that God had always provided for those who believed in him. When his ancestors wandered in the desert, God had supplied manna for them. He had satisfied their thirst and protected them. So, Jesus placed himself in God's care.

At the end of forty days and forty nights, Jesus was starving for food. His body was weak from such a long period in the wilderness. The devil appeared before him, apparently believing that Jesus's weakness would allow him to be tempted and, thus, encourage him to act against God.

"If you are the Son of God," said the devil to Jesus, "command this stone to become a loaf of bread."

Jesus was not fooled by the devil. He remembered the words of God to his ancestors, "Remember the long way that God has led you these forty years in the wilderness in order to humble you. He humbled you by letting you hunger, and then he fed you with manna. The clothes on your back did not wear out, and your feet did not swell these forty years. Therefore, keep the commandments of God by walking in his ways and by fearing him."

Jesus answered the devil, according to God's teachings. "One does not live by bread alone," he said.

The devil tempted Jesus again. He led Jesus up the mountain to the holy city of Jerusalem. Once in the city, he brought Jesus to the pinnacle of the temple. At this height, the devil said:

"If you are the Son of God, throw yourself down from here. For it is written in the psalm, 'He will command his angels concerning you. On their hands they will bear you up, so that you will not dash your foot against even a stone,'" proclaimed the devil.

But Jesus corrected the devil. "It is also written," he said, "'Do not put God to the test.'"

The devil tried once more to turn Jesus against God's teachings. Jesus and the devil traveled to the peak of a very high mountain. From there, they looked down upon the kingdoms of the world in their glorious splendor. Again, the devil spoke.

" I will give you all of these if you will fall down and worship me," said the slimy devil.

Jesus was strong before the devil's treachery. He no longer felt hungry or exhausted from his forty days and forty nights in the wilderness. Jesus replied:

"Away with you, Satan! For it is written also, 'Worship God and serve him only,'" quoted Jesus.

The miserable devil departed, because he saw his efforts were thwarted by the righteousness of Jesus. No sooner did the devil disappear than God sent his angels to tend to Jesus. They came and fed him, as they had come for Elijah when he was starving from his time of prayer in the wilderness.

After his contest with the devil, Jesus was filled with the Holy Spirit. He returned to Galilee from the land of Judea. Word of his coming spread throughout the towns where he passed on his journey. In the various towns and villages, he preached in the synagogues. His teachings were received with praise.

At last, Jesus reached the town of his childhood. He entered Nazareth on the sabbath and went to the synagogue as was customary. When he stood up to read the word of God, the scroll of the prophet Isaiah was handed to him by an attendant.

Jesus read, "The spirit of God is upon me, because he has anointed me to bring good news to the poor. He has sent me to proclaim release to the captives and recovery of sight to the blind. He told me to free the oppressed and to proclaim the year of God's favor."

Jesus rolled up the scroll once more. He gave it back to the attendant, and he sat down. Everyone in the assembly waited to hear what Jesus would say next. It was the custom in the synagogues to stand to read from scripture and to sit in order to teach.

"Today this scripture has taken place in your hearing," Jesus taught.

The people embraced the gracious words that he had spoken.

"Is this not Joseph's son?" they said among themselves, grateful that he was from their community.

Jesus knew what they were thinking. He said, "You will say, 'Do here in your hometown the things that we have heard that you did at Capernaum.'"

The people of Nazareth wanted Jesus to do a miracle. Jesus knew they didn't really believe in him. He reminded them that Elijah and Elisha didn't do miracles for everyone. The people were so angry they pushed Jesus to the edge of a steep hill, planning to throw him off the cliff. But Jesus walked right past his angry neighbors and left the town.

THE VISIT
BY NICODEMUS

esus was in the city of Jerusalem for the feast of Passover, a trip he had made every year since childhood. He entered the temple to pray as he always did for the Passover. Perhaps he had in his mind the memories of his trip to Jerusalem when he was twelve years old, the year that his parents, Mary and Joseph unknowingly left the city without him. That was the year that he first spoke with the Jewish teachers about the law and when they first recognized his wisdom.

On this Passover occasion, when Jesus entered the temple, he was shocked. In the outer area, he found people selling cattle, sheep and doves. Money changers converted foreign money into the local coins. Jesus drove the animals out the temple. He overturned the tables of coins so that a racket of silver resounded inside the walls.

"Stop making my father's house a marketplace!" he ordered.

The Jews assembled in the temple responded to his outrage. "What sign can you show us for doing this?" they demanded of Jesus.

"Destroy this temple, and in three days I will raise it up," he said to them.

Unknown to the confused assembly, Jesus was really describing the temple of his body. After he was raised from the dead, his disciples would remember what he said. They would understand then the words that Jesus spoke on this day in the temple.

One of the leaders of the Jews came to Jesus at night. His name was Nicodemus. Nicodemus was a Pharisee, a Jewish teacher.

"Rabbi, we know that you are a teacher who has come from God," said Nicodemus to Jesus. "No one can perform the signs that you do without the presence of God."

Jesus answered Nicodemus. "Very truly, I tell you, no one can see the kingdom of God without being born again."

"How can anyone be born again after having grown old? Can we re-enter the wombs of our mothers and be born a second time?" asked Nicodemus.

"No one can enter the kingdom of God without being born of water and the Spirit," said Jesus. Jesus was referring to baptism.

"How can these things be?" asked Nicodemus.

"What is born of the flesh is flesh, and what is born of the Spirit is spirit. The wind blows where it chooses and you hear the sound of it. But you do not know where it comes from or where it goes. So it is with everyone who is born of the Spirit," said Jesus.

Jesus spoke of the wind as a symbol of the Holy Spirit. Still Nicodemus did not understand. Nor did he think about what took place the day that Jesus was baptized. On that day, thousands of people had been frightened by what they saw when the head of Jesus resurfaced from its baptism in the Jordan River. They saw the Holy Spirit descend as a beautiful light, shining above the head of Jesus in the form of a dove. The people had dropped to their knees. Then, the voice of God spoke to them from the heavens, 'This is my beloved Son, with whom I am well pleased.'

"Are you a teacher of Israel, but you do not understand these things?" asked Jesus. "If I have told you about earthly things and you do not believe, how can you believe if I tell you about heavenly things?"

Nicodemus listened and thought about the meaning of Jesus's words.

"For God so loved the world that he gave his only Son. Everyone who believes in him will not perish but, instead, will have eternal life," explained Jesus.

Nicodemus did not respond, so Jesus continued. He knew what was in Nicodemus's heart, just as he knew what was in everyone's heart. He knew this because he was the Son of God.

"And this is the judgment. The light came into the world, and people loved darkness rather than light, because their deeds were evil. But those who do what is true come to the light, so that it may be clearly seen that their deeds have been done according to God's will," said Jesus.

Perhaps Nicodemus remembered the words of the prophet Isaiah. "In the land of Zebulun, land of Naphtali, on the road by the sea, across the Jordan, the people who sat in darkness have seen a great light. And for those who sat in the region and shadow of death, light has dawned."

Nicodemus asked no further questions. By his teaching, Jesus showed that faith in God should not be based on signs. The way to reach God's kingdom was to believe in God's son. Even Jesus was baptized, and he was God's Son. He did not intend to allow the Jewish people to be distracted by his signs. His duty was to lead them to God according to how he lived his life and by his teaching that they must ask God's forgiveness and repent. In this way, they would be born anew. Nicodemus finally understood the answer to the question he asked Jesus.

THE WOMAN AT THE WELL

ohn the Baptist heard the news from some of his followers:

"Jesus is baptizing more disciples than John," said the rumor mongers.

"He has made more disciples for himself than John," they said.

Now, Jesus himself was not baptizing people. Instead the baptizing was being done by his disciples, including John the Baptist. Jesus was the teacher, and his message to the people was how to return to the Father. He knew that God had called upon John to baptize with water. The people needed to see this so they would believe that God forgave them. In order to explain the truth, he decided to speak to the people himself.

He set off from the land of Judea for Galilee, the land of his parents and the land where he spent his youth. The most direct route to Galilee was through Samaria. The Samaritans were non-Jewish descendants who had lived in the Holy Land for centuries. They practiced a similar religion. But a long-standing hostility existed between the two related peoples.

Jesus stopped in Samaria in the city of Sychar. In the time of Jacob, Sychar was called Shechem, and it was here that Jacob had sent Joseph to look for his brothers and their flocks. When Jesus came to Sychar, it was noon. He stopped at Jacob's well, as it was called. He was tired from the journey, and he sat at the side of the well to rest. His disciples continued into the city to purchase food, since they had depleted their supply during the trip. A Samaritan woman came with her water jar to draw water from the well.

"Please, give me a drink," Jesus asked the woman.

"How is it that you, a Jew, ask a drink of me, a woman of Samaria?" questioned the woman, for it was not customary for Jews and Samaritans to share food and drink.

Jesus answered her. "If you knew the gift of God, who it is that asks you for a drink, you would ask him instead. And he would give you water of life."

"Sir, you have no bucket, and the well is deep. Where do you intend to get the water of life? Are you saying you are greater than our ancestor Jacob, who gave us the well? And who drank from it with his sons and his flocks?" asked the woman.

"Whoever drinks of the water from this well will be thirsty again. But those who drink of the water that I will give them will never be thirsty. The water I give will become in them a spring of water gushing up to eternal life," answered Jesus.

"Sir, give me this water, so that I may never be thirsty or have to come here again to draw water," said the woman.

Jesus told the woman to get her husband and to bring him back.

"I have no husband," she said.

"You are right in saying you have no husband," replied Jesus.

"Sir, I see that you are a prophet. But, our people worship on this mountain," she said, pointing to Mount Gerizim, the mountain that the Samaritans believed God identified for worship. "And your people say that the place for worship is Jerusalem," referring to the city in the Judean Mountains where the Jews believed God told them to worship.

Jesus corrected her. "Woman," he said, "the hour is coming when you will worship the Father neither on your mountain nor in Jerusalem. The hour is coming, and is now here, when the true worshippers will worship the Father in spirit and truth. God is spirit, and those who worship him must do so in spirit and truth."

"I know the Messiah, the Christ, is coming. When he comes, he will proclaim all things to us," she said.

"I am he, the Messiah, who is speaking to you," responded Jesus.

Just then, the disciples returned from shopping for food. They were surprised to see Jesus conversing with the Samaritan woman, but they did not question him. The woman left her water jar on the side of the well, and she returned to her neighborhood. When she got there, she was brimming with the news of the man she had met at Jacob's well.

"Come and see the man who told me everything about myself. Can he be the Messiah?" she asked her neighbors.

They rushed back to the well with her, because she aroused their interest. Surely, if the Messiah was in their city, they wanted to meet him!

Meanwhile, the disciples urged Jesus to eat some of the food they had bought, but he refused.

"I have food to eat that you do not know about," he protested.

The disciples spoke among themselves. "Did one of the Samaritans bring him food? How strange!" they said.

"My food is to do the will of the one who sent me, and to complete his work. Look around you and see how the fields are ripe for harvesting. The reaper is already receiving wages and is gathering fruit for eternal life," said Jesus, meaning that the time of the harvest had already come, and people needed to be "gathered" for God.

The Samaritans who had come to meet Jesus believed in him, because they heard his message. They asked him to stay with them, and he remained in Sychar to teach for two more days.

The neighbors of the Samaritan woman whom Jesus met at the well said, "It is no longer because of what you said that we believe. We have heard for ourselves, and we know that this is truly the Savior of the world."

JESUS
IN CANA

he little village of Cana in central Galilee was situated close to Nazareth. It was the hometown of Nathanael, the follower that Jesus found under the fig tree. Jesus was invited to a wedding in Cana. His mother was also invited. The disciples were guests at the wedding, too. As was customary at weddings of the time, the guests anticipated a week of festivities.

On one of the wedding days, Mary, the mother of Jesus, searched out her son. "They have no wine," she informed Jesus.

"What concern is that of yours and mine?" asked Jesus, wondering why the hosts had not prepared better to entertain their guests.

Then, he added, "My hour has not yet come." This time, Jesus was speaking of the hour of his death when he would be joined with his heavenly father, who made all things.

But, Mary spoke to the servants of the wedding hosts. "Do whatever he tells you."

Jesus told the servants to take six stone water jars. The vessels were used for the Jewish purification rites of washing hands and vessels. He told them to fill the jars with water. The servants obeyed.

"Now draw some water out of each jar. Take what you draw to the chief steward," Jesus instructed them.

The servants who did as Jesus had asked left the water they drew in new vessels for the steward. When the steward tasted the water, it had turned into wine. Only the servants who had drawn the water from the purification jars knew what had happened. But they said nothing to the steward about what had happened. Then, the steward called for the bridegroom.

"Everyone serves the good wine first. Afterwards, when the guests have become drunk, that is the time to serve inferior wine. Why have you kept the good wine until now?" the steward asked the bridegroom.

This was the first of the signs that Jesus gave to the people. To many Jews, the sign revealed the glory of God. The disciples of Jesus believed he was the Son of God.

After the wedding, Jesus traveled first to Capernaum. Word had reached Capernaum about the wine at the wedding in Cana. More and more people gathered to observe Jesus along the way, and many waited for another sign. Jesus left Capernaum after a few days. From the land of Galilee, he traveled to the land of Judea. It was Passover, and Jesus joined the hundreds of thousands who celebrated Passover in Jerusalem. From Jerusalem, he passed through Samaria on his return trip to Galilee. It was then he had the conversation with the woman at the well. He set out again after a few days to finish his trip.

When Jesus arrived in Galilee from Judea, he was met by a crowd of people. They knew how he had cleared the market of animals and that he disrupted the business of the money changers at the temple at Jerusalem. The crowd welcomed Jesus back to Galilee, because they, too, had been in Jerusalem for Passover. They had seen through their own eyes what took place in the temple.

An official rushed to find Jesus. The official's son lingered on the brink of death. The official begged Jesus to travel to Capernaum, where the boy was lying hopelessly ill in bed.

"Unless you see signs and wonders, you will not believe," said Jesus calmly.

"Sir, come down before my little boy dies," pleaded the official.

Jesus answered, "Go home, your son will live."

The man believed what Jesus told him and started on the road to Capernaum. As he neared his house, his servants met him.

"The boy is alive!" cried one.

"He is no longer sick!" shouted another. The servant's face was flushed with excitement.

"At what hour did my son recover?" the official asked them.

"Yesterday at one in the afternoon, his fever left him," reported the first servant.

The king's official knew that one in the afternoon was exactly the time when Jesus told him his son would live. The official believed in the message of Jesus. He taught his son to believe, too. After the servants told and retold the story to the rest of the official's household, everyone in the household believed what Jesus had to say.

THE CALL OF THE TWELVE APOSTLES

The crowd wanted to hear Jesus speak the word of God. At the shore of the lake of Gennesaret, as the local people called the Sea of Galilee, the mob pressed tighter together. There were so many people, it was hard for them to keep a steady footing. The pushing and shoving made it difficult for people to hear. Two rowboats were in the lake not far away. Jesus motioned to a fisherman washing his net over the side of one of the boats.

When the boat belonging to Simon, who was also called Peter, came close to shore, Jesus waded into the water and got on board. He asked Peter to row a short distance away from the crowd. Then, he sat down and taught the assembly, in the same way as the rabbis sat to teach in the synagogues. Afterwards, he requested that Peter row into deeper water.

"Let down your nets for a catch," he told the fisherman.

"Master, we have worked all night long, and we have caught nothing.

But, if you say so, I will let down the nets," answered Peter respectfully, because he recognized that Jesus was the Son of God.

So many fish swam into the net that the little craft started to sink. The nets were beginning to break. Peter called urgently to his partners in the other boat. Their names were James and John, and they were the sons of Zebedee. James and John helped Peter pull the swollen net from the lake. The three fishermen filled Peter's boat to capacity with fish. Then, they hoisted the still swollen net and its contents into the rowboat of James and John. Soon, the second boat held as many fish as the first boat. Peter thought both were going to sink.

"Do not be afraid," Jesus told him. "From now on, you will be catching people."

The fishermen rowed to shore. James and John said good-bye to their father Zebedee. The three fishermen left their boats and everything they owned in order to follow Jesus.

Jesus began a tour of preaching to crowds in the land of Galilee, and his three disciples went with him. Very early one morning, while it was still dark, Jesus rose to pray in a a deserted place. When Peter, James and John awoke, the sun was up. They set out to locate Jesus.

"Everyone is searching for you," they told him. They referred to the officials who found fault with what Jesus taught, as well as to the crowd that did not want Jesus to leave their town.

Jesus answered. "Let us go now to the neighboring towns so that I may proclaim the message there also. For that is what I came to do," he said.

They went with him throughout Galilee. Jesus spoke in the synagogues, too. When he found evil there, he spoke against it. People brought to him the sick, including those with incurable diseases, pain, epilepsy and paralysis, and Jesus cured them. Great crowds began to follow him and his disciples.

The day came that Jesus had selected twelve disciples, whom he also called apostles. He assembled a crowd in the hill country of Galilee. There, he named the apostles. They were Simon, whom Jesus named Peter; Peter's brother Andrew; James and John, the sons of Zebedee; Philip; Bartholomew; Matthew; Thomas; James, the son of Alphaeus; Simon, who was also called the Zealot; Judas, son of James; and Judas Iscariot, who became a traitor.

Then, Jesus spoke one of his parables, which were like a proverb or a riddle that made his listeners see things in a new way.

Jesus said, "A farmer went out to sow seed. As he sowed, some seed fell on the path, and the birds came and ate it. Other seed fell on rocky ground where there was not much soil. The seed sprang up quickly, but, because it had no roots, it was scorched when the sun came out. Still other seed fell among thorns. But when the thorns grew, they choked it. Finally, seed fell into good soil and brought forth grain, which grew and increased one-hundredfold."

The disciples were puzzled by the parable. Jesus asked them how they would understand the other parables he intended to deliver to the crowds that gathered to hear his words. When they had no answers for him, Jesus explained the meaning.

"The sower sows the word. When people on the path where the word is sown hear, Satan comes immediately to take away the word. When those on rocky ground hear the word, they are instantly joyous. But they have no root. When trouble arises, they fall away from the word. When others hear among the thorns, they listen. But the cares of the world and the lure of wealth choke the word for them. Only when the word is heard by people on the good soil will it bear fruit for them."

The apostles listened to the explanation, and they understood what Jesus meant.

THROUGH THE ROOF

esus and his disciples crossed the Sea of Galilee after traveling and speaking in the land of Gadara to the southeast. Back in Galilee, where Jesus made his home, he began to teach once more. An audience of listeners was assembled from many villages in Galilee and Judea, including the city of Jerusalem. In their midst were many Pharisees, the recognized authorities on the Jewish law and how to observe its practices.

Some men arrived at the house in Capernaum where Jesus was teaching. They carried a paralyzed man on a bed, each supporting one corner of the bed on his shoulder. They came to present the man on the bed to Jesus, hoping that the Son of God would heal him. The crowd around the house where Jesus sat teaching was very thick. Every attempt that the four men made to find an opening in which to enter the house was thwarted by too many people in the way. Finally, they had no choice but to try to go up to the roof. Two of them climbed onto the roof, and the other two hoisted the man and his bed above the crowds. Then the first two lifted the paralyzed man up to where they stood on the rooftop, and the second two men joined them.

The four men carefully removed pieces of roof until they had made a hole big enough. Through the hole, they lowered their paralyzed friend on his bed at the feet of the Messiah. When Jesus saw them, he was very moved by their faith.

"Friend, your sins are forgiven," he said.

The Pharisees were outraged by the words Jesus had spoken. "Who can forgive sins except God alone? Who are you, daring to speak for God?" they demanded of Jesus.

Jesus answered them with questions. "Why do you ask such questions as these in your hearts? Which is easier to say, 'Your sins are forgiven?' Or, 'Stand up and walk?' My Father has given me authority to forgive sins."

Jesus turned to the paralyzed man. He said, "Stand up and take up your bed and go home."

To the amazement of the crowd, the man did as Jesus instructed. They glorified God, and they were struck with awe. They spoke among themselves of the strange things they had seen that day.

Jesus displeased the Pharisees on other occasions, too. Sometimes, the argument was about the sabbath. That was the day when prayer was the only accepted activity, according to the law of the Jewish people. One sabbath, Jesus entered the synagogue to teach. Before him sat a man with a withered right hand. The Pharisees watched Jesus closely to see whether he would disobey the law and heal on this day.

Even though Jesus knew what they were thinking, he called the man to him. "Come and stand here," said Jesus.

The man with the withered hand got up and stood before Jesus, as he had been instructed. Jesus spoke to the Pharisees in the synagogue.

"I ask you, is it lawful to do good or harm on the sabbath? Lawful to save life or destroy it?" demanded Jesus.

The eyes of Jesus met the eyes of the Pharisees in the room. Then, he spoke again to the man.

"Stretch out your hand," Jesus said to the man with the withered right hand.

When the man did as Jesus asked, his hand became perfect. The man fell to his knees and thanked God. The Pharisees were furious, and they discussed among themselves what they should do about Jesus.

On another sabbath, Jesus was in Jerusalem to attend a festival. Near the Sheep Gate, along the wall of Jerusalem closest to the temple, lay the Bethesda pool. Its waters were said to be healing waters. Five porticos, areas protected from the elements by a roof, surrounded the pool. Inside each portico were many invalids, including people who were blind, lame and paralyzed. One of the invalids had been ill for thirty-eight years. Jesus was moved to compassion when he saw the poor man who was lying by the pool, but who was unable to enter the water by himself.

"Do you want to be made well?" Jesus asked the invalid.

"Sir, I have no one to put me into the pool. Whenever I make my way, someone else steps down into it ahead of me," answered the man.

"Stand, take up the mat upon which you lie and walk," instructed Jesus.

At once, the man was well, and he began to walk. When the Pharisees, who had not witnessed what happened, saw him with his mat in his hand, they chastised him.

"It is the Sabbath. It is unlawful for you to carry your mat," they scolded.

"But the man who made me well said to take up my mat and walk," said the cured man.

"Who is the man who spoke this to you?" they demanded.

By this time, Jesus had left the pool. The man saw him in the temple. He heard others speak of him as Jesus.

Jesus addressed him, "See, you have been made well! Do not sin anymore, so that nothing worse happens to you."

When the man told the Pharisees that it was Jesus who had cured him, they were furious. The Pharisees were so angry, they began to think about how they would kill Jesus. Jesus' next words made them even more angry because Jesus made himself equal with God.

"My Father is still working. I, too, am working," said Jesus to the Pharisees.

THE KINGDOM OF HEAVEN

His disciples asked Jesus a question. "Why do you speak to the crowds in parables?" they inquired.

Parables were brief stories that Jesus told when he taught. The stories, much like riddles, teased the imagination of the people that heard them. They told of things that people knew from their everyday lives in order to make them think in a new way, from God's viewpoint.

"You have been given the secrets of the kingdom of heaven. These crowds have not been given the same secrets," Jesus replied to the disciples.

He continued his explanation, "The reason I speak to them in parables is that when they see, they do not see clearly, and when they hear, they do not listen or understand. Blessed are your eyes, for they see, and blessed are your ears, for they hear."

Many people gathered to hear Jesus's parables. There were so many people, that once again he had to teach them from the sea. Seated in a boat he found at the edge of the Sea of Galilee, Jesus taught. The crowd listened from the shore as Jesus taught the parable of the weeds among the wheat:

"The kingdom of heaven is like someone who sowed good seed in his field," said Jesus to the crowd. "But, while everybody was asleep, an enemy came and planted weeds among the wheat seeds. Then, the enemy went away. When the plants sprouted and began to bear grain, the weeds also sprouted. The farmers' workers came to him about the problem.

"'Master, did you sow good seed in your fields?' they asked the farmer. 'If you did,' inquired the farm hands, 'where did these weeds come from?' 'An enemy has done this to me,' answered the farmer.

"When the workers asked him if he wished them to go and pull up the troublesome weeds from the fields, he told them no. To do so would mean that they would pull up the wheat as well.

"'Let both of them grow together until the harvest. At harvest time, I will tell the reapers to collect the weeds first and bind them into bundles to be burned. Afterwards, they will gather the wheat and store it in my barn,' said the farmer to his workers."

When Jesus finished the parable about the weeds and the wheat, he rowed back to shore, and left the crowd in order to find some time alone. After a short time, his disciples discovered him. They asked for an explanation of the parable he had just taught.

"The one who sows the good seed is the Son of God," said Jesus.

The field was the world, he explained. The children who would inherit the kingdom of heaven were the good seed. The children of Satan were the weeds that grew alongside the wheat. Satan was the enemy that sowed the seeds that became weeds. The harvest in the parable stood for the judgment at the end of time. The angels were the reapers who collected the good seed at the time of the harvest.

Jesus assured them, "Just as the weeds are collected and burned up with fire, so it will be at the end of the time. The Son of God will send his angels, and they will separate and keep out of his kingdom all the causes of sin and all the evildoers. They will throw the evildoers into the furnace of fire. There will be weeping and the gnashing of teeth at the judgment harvest. Those who did good will shine then like the sun in the kingdom of their Father."

Jesus gave the crowds and his disciples other short parables to think about. One was the parable of the mustard seed, a story about small beginnings and great endings. The parable he taught was this.

"The kingdom of heaven is like a mustard seed that someone took and sowed in his field. It is the smallest of all seeds, this mustard seed, yet, when it is full-grown, it is the greatest of shrubs. The birds of the air flock to its branches and in them, they make their nests," said Jesus.

Then, he spoke another parable. It was the parable of the yeast, the story about how a small amount of yeast allowed dough to rise and expand.

"The kingdom of heaven is like yeast that a woman took and mixed with three measures of flour until all of it rose into dough for bread," taught Jesus.

He gave three more parables about the kingdom of heaven, or god's loving rule in our lives. This is what he said:

"The kingdom of heaven is like a treasure hidden in a field by the person who found it. In his joy, this person sells every possession in order to buy that field," Jesus taught in the first parable.

Then, he gave the second parable. "The kingdom of heaven is like a merchant in search of fine pearls. Upon finding one pearl of great value, the merchant sells everything in order to buy the beautiful pearl."

Finally, Jesus taught the third parable, which was similar to the parable about the weeds among the wheat. "The kingdom of heaven is like a net, which, when thrown into the sea, catches fish of every kind. The fishermen pull the heavy net ashore. They put the good fish into baskets for safe keeping, and they toss the bad fish back into the water."

The parables Jesus gave to the crowds proved the words of the prophet Isaiah, which said, "I will open my mouth to speak in parables; I will proclaim what has been hidden from the world."

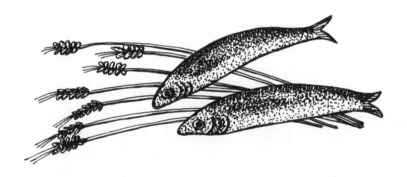

THE TEACHINGS FROM THE MOUNTAIN

he crowds that came together to hear Jesus teach grew larger and larger. On both sides of the Jordan River, they formed in masses to listen to him. In Galilee and Judea people by the thousands pushed closer to hear.

On one occasion, Jesus addressed a large crowd of followers. As Moses had done before him, he ascended a nearby mountain. Like a rabbi, he sat down to teach. These are some of his teachings from that day. Many of them are part of our everyday vocabulary today. If we listen closely, we'll recognize some things that we've often heard.

"Blessed are the poor in spirit, for theirs is the kingdom of heaven.

"Blessed are they who mourn, for they will be comforted.

"Blessed are the meek, for they will inherit the earth.

"Blessed are they who hunger and thirst for righteousness, for they will be filled.

"Blessed are the merciful, for they will receive mercy.

"Blessed are the pure of heart, for they will see God.

"Blessed are they who make peace, for they will be called the children of God.

"Blessed are they who others persecute for their righteousness. Theirs is the kingdom of heaven.

"Blessed are you when people speak ill of you and accuse you falsely on my account. Be glad, because your reward is in heaven like the prophets that came before you."

These teachings are called the Beatitudes. After Jesus taught the Beatitudes, he continued to speak about many things. Next, he gave two short parables, or stories, to his listeners as his way of teaching them how to behave according to God's laws.

This is the first parable. "You are the salt of the earth. But, if salt has lost its taste, how can it become salty again? It is no longer any good, so it is thrown out and trampled underfoot."

Jesus gave the second parable. "You are the light of the world, in whose reflection a whole city is unable to hide. No one puts a lighted lamp under a bushel basket. Instead, the lamp on the table gives light to the whole house. What you must do is let your light shine so others can see it. When they see your good works, they will give glory to God."

Then, Jesus made clear to his followers that he believed in the law and the prophets. In particular, he spoke to those followers who wanted to question his authority and to those that were outright jealous or that wanted to cause him difficulty. Jesus said that he had come not to destroy the law, but to see that its teachings came to pass. He taught, "Whoever breaks one of the least of the commandments and teaches other people to do the same thing, will be called the least in the kingdom of heaven. Whoever follows the commandments and teaches them will be called great in the king-dom of heaven."

But, he told the people not to judge each other. If they did, they them-selves would be judged. To illustrate his point he asked them, "Why do you see the speck in your neighbor's eye, but you do not notice the log in your own eye?"

Jesus spoke about the ancient law against murder. From his seat on the mountain, he told his followers that even when they were angry with another person, they would be judged. If they insulted someone, for exam-ple, if they said, "you fool," they would also be judged. He told the crowd that if someone wronged them, the best thing to do was to come to an agreement quickly with that person.

Instead of "an eye for an eye and a tooth for a tooth," which gave the person who was wronged the opportunity to hurt the bully in the same fashion, Jesus taught another way. "If anyone strikes you on the right cheek, turn the other also. If anyone wants to take your coat, give your cloak, as well as your coat. If anyone forces you to carry a load for one mile, go the second mile also."

Instead of following the practice to "Love your neighbor and hate your enemy," Jesus told them to "Love your enemies and pray for the people who persecute you." He explained that God made the sun rise on evil and on good people.

"The eye is the lamp of the body. If your eye is healthy, your whole body will be full of light. If your eye is unhealthy, your whole body will be full of darkness. If the light in you is darkness, how great is the size of that dark-ness!" said Jesus, helping the crowd to look at things in a new way. If they had spiritually healthy eyes, they would see according to his teachings.

"Do not worry about your life, what you will eat or what you will drink.

Do not worry about your body, what you will wear. Look at the birds of the air. They neither sow seeds nor reap the harvest nor gather the grain into barns. Yet the heavenly Father feeds them," explained Jesus, teaching the crowd about believing in God's goodness. He asked, "Are you not of more value than the birds to God?"

"Consider the lilies of the field and how they grow. The lilies do not toil in the fields nor spin yarn. But even Solomon in his glory was not dressed like one of these lilies!" said Jesus.

"Do not worry about tomorrow, because tomorrow will bring worries of its own. Today's trouble is enough for today," Jesus told the crowd.

THE COMPASSION OF JESUS

esus traveled throughout the land, from village to town, across the Upper Galilee hills and down to the green marshes of the Jordan River, preaching the word of God and the way to heaven. His disciples and a large crowd of followers accompanied him to every place he visited. The village of Nain was in the land of Galilee, near Nazareth.

When they arrived at the village gate of the village, Jesus and his followers were met by a funeral procession. A young man had died, they were told, who was his mother's only son. The woman was a widow, and her sorrow was great. She was accompanied by many villagers who shared in her grief over her son's untimely death. Jesus felt the woman's heartbreak, and compassion for her filled his heart.

"Do not weep," said Jesus to the poor woman.

She was so surprised by his words that she momentarily stopped crying.

Jesus walked to the open coffin of the young man and touched it. He ordered the funeral bearers to halt the procession.

"Young man, I say to you, rise!" Jesus instructed the dead man.

As soon as he said the words, the young man sat up. He began to speak to his mother. The villagers became frightened by what they saw.

"A great prophet is among us!" said some.

"God has looked with favor on his people," said others.

The mother and her son were filled with joy. The funeral bearers embraced them, and their neighbors were overcome with happiness for them. Word of what happened spread throughout the surrounding country and neighboring Judea.

Jesus continued to travel the countryside and teach the people the word of God. On his journey, he came to the house of Simm, a Pharisee, a Jewish scholar. The Pharisee asked the traveler to dine with him, and Jesus accepted the invitation. When word of the visit to the Pharisee's house spread through the village, a woman who was a sinner rushed to the house. With her, she brought an expensive alabaster jar filled with perfumed oil.

The woman positioned herself near Jesus and stood weeping. Her tears washed the feet of Jesus. Kneeling, she dried his feet with her hair. Then, she anointed them with the perfumed oil she had brought. The Pharisee whose house it was became confused.

"If this man were a prophet, he would know who and what kind of woman he has allowed to touch him. This woman is a sinner!" proclaimed the Pharisee.

The Pharisee was horrified, because even to be touched by a sinner was forbidden by Jewish law. The common fear was that the sin would wear off on the innocent person the sinner touched.

"Simon, I have something to say to you," Jesus said.

"Teacher," Simm answered as though addressing a rabbi, "speak."

Jesus answered with a parable. "A certain money lender had two debtors. One owed five hundred denarii. The other owed fifty." In that time, the denarius was the day's wage for a laborer, so the debtors owed a substantial amount of money.

"When the debtors could not pay, the lender canceled both debts. Which of them will love the lender more?" asked Jesus.

Simon responded, "I suppose the one with the greater debt."

"You have judged correctly," said Jesus.

He explained the parable to the Pharisee who had questioned why he allowed the woman to touch him when she was a sinner.

"I entered your house. You gave me no water for my feet. But she bathed my feet with her tears. She dried them with the hair on her head. You did not anoint my head, but she anointed my feet with her oil. Her sins, which were many, have been forgiven. But the one for whom little is forgiven also loves little," corrected Jesus.

Then, he said to the woman, "Your sins are forgiven."

The other people in the Pharisee's house who had witnessed what took place murmured among themselves.

"Who is this that forgives sins?" they grumbled.

"Only God forgives," they protested.

Jesus ignored their protests. He turned to the woman who had anointed his feet. "Your faith has saved you. Go in peace," he said to her.

Jesus left the village of the Pharisee and went with his disciples and the growing crowd of followers throughout the land. His message was, as always, the good news of the kingdom of God. An increasingly large group of women followed. Many had been cured by Jesus of evil spirits. He cured still others of many infirmities, including disease, plague, blindness and leprosy. The women's names were Mary, called Magdalene, Joanna, the wife of King Herod's steward Chuza, Susanna and many others.

THE DAUGHTER OF JAIRUS

The leader of the synagogue rushed to speak to Jesus when he returned to the shore of the Sea of Galilee. Jesus had been teaching from his boat. The leader was an important man in the community. His job was to preside over meetings of worship. Upkeep of the synagogue building was his responsibility, too. Jesus knew the man when he saw him. The man's name was Jairus.

Jairus had an only daughter, who was twelve years old. The girl had suddenly become very sick. Poor Jairus was distraught over his daughter's serious illness. He threw himself at the feet of Jesus. He implored Jesus for help.

"My little daughter is at the point of death! Come and lay your hands on her. Make her well so she will live," Jairus begged Jesus.

Jesus followed Jairus to his house. A huge crowd accompanied them.

Someone in the crowd touched the fringe on Jesus's robe. Jewish law required that men wear tassels on their robes, and Jesus dressed according to that tradition.

"If I but touch his clothes, I will be made well," said the woman who touched Jesus.

Her touch was against the custom dictated by the purity laws of the Jewish religion. But the woman had heard about the power of Jesus to heal the sick and unfortunate. For twelve years, she had suffered from hemorrhages that made it impossible for her to live a normal life. Many physicians had treated the severe bleeding that afflicted her, but they were unsuccessful. With each treatment, the woman's condition had only worsened. She had spent everything she had on the unsatisfactory care the doctors had given her. The woman was desperate to be well.

Immediately when she touched Jesus's robe, she felt better than she had for the twelve long years of her illness. She was healed at that moment. For his part, Jesus was aware that someone touched him. He could feel that someone had set his healing power in motion.

"Who is it that touched my robe?" asked Jesus. He spoke directly into the crowd.

"You see the crowd pressing in on you," said one of the disciples, incredulous that Jesus expected to find whoever it was that had touched him.

"How can you ask who touched you?" responded another disciple.

The woman trembled with fear, because she was aware that she had been healed. Falling at the feet of Jesus, she confessed that she was the one. Tears of gratitude replaced her earlier tears of fright.

Jesus comforted the woman. "Daughter, your faith has made you well. Go in peace. Be healed of your disease."

As Jesus was dismissing the healed woman, some people from the house of the synagogue leader found Jairus in the crowd.

"Your daughter is dead," they told him. "Why trouble the teacher any further?" they asked, speaking of Jesus.

Jesus overheard. "Do not fear, only believe," he told Jairus.

He instructed the crowd not to come any farther. Only Peter, James and John, the brother of James, were allowed to accompany him and Jairus to the synagogue leader's house. Jesus had earlier singled out these three apostles to witness special events. They were among the first disciples he had named. When the small party arrived at the house of Jairus, they saw the flute players who were hired for funerals. Mourners had also gathered upon receiving word of the girl's death. Outside on the grounds and inside the rooms great commotion of weeping and wailing surrounded the house.

"Why make a commotion and weep? This child is not dead, only sleeping," said Jesus, interrupting the display of mourning.

The mourners laughed at his words. How ridiculous to speak like this when they had seen with their own eyes that the girl was dead! Wasn't her own mother inside with her when she died? Ignoring the ridicule, Jesus entered the house with Jairus and the three disciples. He cleared the building of everyone but the girl's mother. At the child's bed, he took her hand.

"Talitha cum," said Jesus to her. The words meant, "Little girl, get up!" in Aramic, a language like Hebrew which Jesus spoke.

Just as though waking from sleep, the girl rose. She stood and began to walk. She asked her parents for something to eat. Jesus ordered the astounded parents to tell no one what had occurred. Then, he told them to give their daughter something to eat.

Good Over Evil

Jesus showed that he had great power over evil. In the first example in this story, he proved that his authority was more powerful than evil by calming a raging storm. On the two other occasions, he demonstrated his power by performing miracles that healed people. In all three stories, Jesus fought the evil and triumphed. He criticized it sharply, and he commanded it to be gone.

Here is the first story. One evening, Jesus said to his disciples, "Let us go across the sea to the other side."

They left the crowd on the shore of the Sea of Galilee, and the disciples in Jesus's boat began to row. Other boats of disciples set out to accompany them on the trip across the sea. They had not traveled far when the pleasant weather conditions turned very bad. A howling wind brought with it a furious storm. Giant waves spilled over the sides of the boats. The disciples feared they might sink with the rolling waves. As the dangerous elements attacked the little fleet, Jesus slept undisturbed on one of the seat cushions. Nothing bothered his sleep, neither the raging wind nor the savage water. Certain that they would drown without intervention, the disciples in his boat woke Jesus.

"Teacher," yelled one of them into the powerful noises of the wind and waves. "Do you not care that we are perishing?"

When Jesus opened his eyes, he rebuked—overcame—the wind. The howling ceased. It was silent.

Then, he spoke to the sea. "Peace! Be still!" he commanded the water. The water calmed immediately.

To the startled but very relieved disciples, Jesus spoke next. "Why are you afraid? Do you still have no faith?" he asked them.

Awestruck, they spoke among themselves. "Who, then, is this, that even the wind and the sea obey him?" they questioned.

On the shore opposite the land of Galilee, Jesus and the disciples came to the land of Gerasa. The man who met them was possessed by demons. His condition was so extreme that he was naked. He had no house. Instead, he lived in the tombs of the city. No matter how many times the man had been kept under guard and bound with chains and shackles, the demons had forced him each time to break the chains and flee. When Jesus left the boat, the man fell to the ground before him and began to shout in the voices of the demons that controlled him.

"What have you to do with us, Son of the Most High God? Do not torment us," said the voices that even in their evil, recognized Jesus as the Son of God.

"What is your name?" Jesus asked the man.

"Legions," he answered, for an army of demons had entered him, pleading with him not to force them back into the abyss, the great empty void. A legion was a unit of 6,000 soldiers in the Roman army.

Seeing their defeat, the demons begged Jesus to allow them to enter the large herd of swine feeding on the hillside nearby, and Jesus rebuked them, "Go!" At that, the demons left the man. The entire herd then responded to their sudden possession. They fled down the steep hill and into the Sea of Galilee, and every one of the hogs drowned.

The astonished swineherds ran into the city where they told everyone they met what had happened to their herd. Word spread fast throughout the city and into the countryside. When the people of the area arrived to view the scene of the strange occurrence for themselves, they found the man that had been possessed by demons seated calmly at the feet of Jesus. He was clothed, and he was in his right mind.

For many, this was the first time ever that they had witnessed the man in his right mind. Fear seized them, and the people pleaded with Jesus to leave their land and to never return. The man whom Jesus had saved from the demons begged to accompany him, but Jesus refused his request.

"Return to your home and declare how much God has done for you," Jesus instructed him instead.

A third confrontation took place in Capernaum, a city across the sea in Galilee. Jesus visited the house of Simon Peter before Jesus named him a disciple. Simon's mother-in-law suffered from a very high fever at the time Jesus arrived. Showing the woman mercy, Jesus rebuked the fever. Immediately, the fever departed, leaving the woman in good health.

Word spread throughout the town of the woman's cure. By sunset, everyone within the surrounding region who was afflicted came in search of Jesus. He laid his hands on those sick with a multitude of diseases, and they were cured. Out of many of the formerly sick, there emerged nasty demons.

"You are the Son of God!" shouted the demons in horror.

But Jesus rebuked them, and he would not allow them to utter another word.

"Be gone!" he commanded. And they were gone in an instant.

A FEAST FOR FIVE THOUSAND PEOPLE

esus heard about the gruesome death of John the Baptist. He knew that John had been imprisoned by King Herod Antipas. The king wanted to marry Herodius, his half-niece. John told him this was unlawful. While Herod Antipas was ready to put John the Baptist to death for what he said, the king was afraid. The people regarded John as a prophet, and the king did not want to make the people angry.

What Jesus had not known was that, on the king's birthday, Salome, the daughter of Herodias danced for Herod Antipas. The king was most pleased with the dance, and he promised the young woman to give her anything she desired. Herodias told Salome to ask for the head of John the Baptist on a platter. The king granted the request, and John was killed. John's disciples buried John's body. Then they told Jesus what the king had done.

To mourn the death of the beloved John the Baptist, Jesus went away from the crowds that surrounded him. He traveled by boat. The crowds still followed from the towns along the shore. When Jesus saw how many people had come, he went ashore. He felt compassion for them, and he cured the sick in the crowd.

As evening approached, the disciples came to Jesus. They intended to ask him to send the people back to their villages. The location was very deserted, and there was no place to purchase food. Soon the crowd would be hungry. Then, it would be too dark for them to travel. Jesus read their thoughts. He decided to test the disciples.

"Where are we to buy bread for these people to eat?" Jesus asked Philip.

"Six months' wages would not buy enough bread for each of them to eat even a small portion," Philip answered.

"They need not go away. Give them something to eat here," Jesus instructed the disciples.

"A boy in the crowd has five loaves of barley bread and two fish. But what are they to so many people?" answered Andrew, Simon Peter's brother.

"Bring them to me," Jesus said about the five loaves of bread and two fish.

Jesus told the crowd to sit down on the grass. They sat in groups of hundreds and of fifties. Just the men in the crowd numbered five thousand people, not counting women and children. He lifted the loaves and fish up to heaven, and he blessed them. After he gave thanks to God, Jesus took the loaves of bread and told the disciples to distribute them to the seated crowd. He repeated the same steps with the two fish. He lifted them high to God, gave thanks for them, and his disciples distributed them to the people on the grass. When the crowd finished eating, Jesus spoke to the disciples.

"Gather up the fragments left over, so that nothing is lost," he instructed.

The fragments filled twelve baskets to the brim! The people sang the praises of the Son of God.

"This is indeed the prophet who was to come into the world," they sang.

The crowd was so excited that Jesus realized they intended to make him king. He did not want this, so he instructed the disciples to go ahead by boat to the northeast shore of the Sea of Galilee. Jesus escaped into the mountains to pray.

The disciples honored the wishes of Jesus. They boarded a boat and started rowing. The sky was dark. Later, the lake roughened as the wind blew stronger. Jesus saw that the disciples strained at the oars against the wind. He intended to quiet the sea. As the disciples struggled to get to land they saw something strange came toward them.

Walking on the water, Jesus approached the boat! The disciples were terrified, and they shrieked and screamed in their terror.

"Do not be afraid. It is I," said Jesus.

"If it is you, command me to come to you on the water," pleaded Peter.

"Come," said Jesus.

Peter exited the boat, and he started walking on the water in the direction of Jesus. The wind strengthened as he walked, and Peter became frightened. Peter began to sink. He cried out to Jesus to save him.

"You of little faith, why did you doubt?" Jesus asked Peter, as he extended his hand to him and pulled him from the water.

Jesus climbed into the boat with Peter. Immediately, the sea quieted. The boat was out of danger.

"Truly, you are the Son of God," said the disciples.

THE BREAD FROM HEAVEN

n the day after Jesus fed the crowd with five barley loaves and two fish, many of the people who had heard him speak and had eaten the bread and fish came to look for him. There was no sign of Jesus or his disciples. The people boarded their boats and crossed the Sea of Galilee from Tiberias on the southwestern shore to the city of Capernaum on the northern end of the sea. Capernaum, a prosperous city at the time, was where Jesus had established his ministry.

This is where the people found Jesus. They rushed to him, asking, "Rabbi, when did you come here?"

"I tell you why you are looking for me. It is because you ate your fill of the loaves yesterday. Do not work for food that perishes," he said. "Work for food that endures forever. That is the food that the Son of God will give you, because he has the mark of God's approval."

"What must we do to perform the work of God?" they asked Jesus.

"This is the work of God. Believe in him whom God has sent," Jesus answered.

"What sign will you give us, then, so that we may see it and believe in you?" responded the crowd. "Our ancestors ate the manna in the wilderness, according to what was written, 'He gave them bread from heaven to eat.'" They were referring to the book of Exodus.

"I tell you it was not Moses who gave the bread from heaven. It is my Father who gives you the true bread from heaven. The bread of God is he who comes down from heaven and gives life to the world," corrected Jesus.

"Sir, give us this bread always," they implored him.

Jesus responded, "I am the bread of life. Whoever comes to me will never be hungry, and whoever believes in me will never be thirsty. You have seen me and yet you do not believe. This is indeed the will of my Father, that all who see the Son and believe in him will have eternal life. I will raise them up on the last day."

The Jewish authorities in the crowd began to grumble aloud about Jesus. How could Jesus claim to be the bread that came down from heaven? Was he not the same Jesus whose father Joseph and mother Mary they knew personally? Then, how could he possibly have come down from God in heaven?

"Do not complain among yourselves. No one can come to me unless that person is driven to me by God. Everyone who has heard and learned from the Father comes to me," said Jesus to the Jewish authorities.

Still, they grumbled in displeasure at his words.

"Whoever believes has eternal life. I am the bread of life. Your ancestors ate the manna in the wilderness, and they died. Whoever eats of the bread of life will live forever. And the bread that I will give for the life of the world is my flesh," said Jesus to the crowd, which was silenced for the moment by the magnitude of what he had spoken.

But the grumbling grew in volume. How could this man say he would give them his flesh to eat? It was preposterous.

Jesus interrupted the complaining of the authorities once more. "I tell you that, unless you eat the flesh of the Son of God and drink his blood, you have no life in you. Those who eat my flesh and drink my blood have eternal life. I will raise them on the last day, because my flesh is the true food and my blood is the true drink."

Now, even among the followers, there was grumbling. What Jesus taught was difficult to understand. The idea of people eating his flesh and drinking his blood, referring to Jesus's body being crucified and his blood shed for forgiveness, was too much for them to handle.

"Does this offend you?" Jesus asked the grumblers. "Then what if you were to see the Son of God ascending to heaven where he was before? It is the spirit that gives life. The flesh is useless."

Many of the followers turned away. They no longer could believe the words that Jesus spoke. Jesus asked the twelve apostles if they, too, wished to leave.

Simon Peter was the first to answer. "To whom can we go? You have the words of eternal life. We have come to believe and know that you are the Holy One of God," he said to Jesus.

"Did I not choose you twelve?" responded Jesus. "Yet one of you is a devil."

The apostles were horrified that he would call one in their midst a devil. After all, they were true to him, and the thought of leaving never occurred to them. But Jesus spoke of Judas, son of Simon Iscariot, who was going to betray him.

THE GOOD SHEPHERD

 his story is a parable. It gives us a picture of sheepherding in ancient Palestine. At the same time, Jesus teaches his message. The parable takes place in a sheepfold. A sheepfold was an enclosure, often built of stone. At night, shepherds brought their flocks there to keep them safe.

Jesus spoke the parable to try to help the Jews who doubted him to understand his teachings. In particular, he spoke to the Pharisees, the Jewish authorities. Most of them were outraged and felt threatened by what he said about being the Son of God and about knowing the way to eternal life. Jesus began the parable about the good shepherd after he had healed the eyes of a blind man. He spoke the parable because the Pharisees doubted him after he cured the man of blindness.

Here is what Jesus spoke: "I tell you that anyone who does not enter the sheepfold by the gate is a thief and a bandit. The one who enters by the gate is the shepherd of the sheep." By bandit, Jesus spoke about the real bandits who stole sheep while the shepherds were away. They pretended the stolen sheep belonged to their own flocks. He also referred to the preachers who claimed to be the Messiah. In the time of Jesus, these fake preachers were called bandits.

"The gatekeeper opens the gate for the shepherd. The sheep hear his voice," said Jesus. "He calls his sheep by name, and he leads them out of the sheepfold. The sheep follow, because they know his voice. They will not follow a stranger, because they do not know the voices of strangers."

After he spoke the parable about the good shepherd, Jesus explained it to the crowd of listeners.

"I tell you, I am the gate for the sheep. Those who came before me are the thieves and bandits, but the sheep did not listen to them. Whoever enters the gate will be saved. They will come in and go out and find pastures to graze in," explained Jesus.

He continued. "I am the good shepherd who lays down his life for the sheep. The hired hand, who does not own the sheep, sees the wolf coming. He leaves the sheep and runs away. Then, the wolf snatches them and scatters them about. I know my own and my own know me. Just as the Father knows me and I know the father."

Jesus described himself as the good shepherd. The hired hand, or bad shepherds, were the leaders of Israel, such as the Pharisees, who disbelieved Jesus. When Jesus spoke of how he knew his own and his own knew him, he was talking about himself and the disciples.

Jesus finished the parable. "So there will be one flock and one shepherd. The Father loves me, because I lay down my life in order to take it up again. I have received this command from the Father."

Among the Jewish authorities in the crowd of listeners, there was considerable argument over whether or not Jesus spoke the truth.

"He has a demon and is out of his mind," proclaimed some who did not believe.

"Why listen to him?" agreed others.

But some answered, "These are not the words of one who has a demon."

"Yes, can a demon open the eyes of the blind?" shouted still others.

Jesus spoke the parable in the winter at the time of the festival of the Dedication in the city of Jerusalem. In Hebrew, Dedication meant Hanukkah, which takes place in modern times in December. The festival celebrated the rededication of the temple by Judas Maccabeus before Jesus was born. Jesus sat in the temple, in the portico of Solomon, a covered walkway on the temple's southeastern side. Some Jewish leaders surrounded him to state their demands.

"How long will you keep us in suspense?"

"If you are the Messiah, tell us plainly!"

Jesus answered them, "I have told you, and you do not believe. The works I do in my Father's name give testimony. But you do not believe, because you do not belong to my sheep."

The authorities were angry at the response of Jesus.

"My sheep hear my voice. I know them, and they follow me. I give them eternal life, and they will never perish. No one will snatch them out of my hand. What my Father gave me is greater than all else. Certainly, no one can snatch it out of the hand of my Father. The Father and I are one," said Jesus.

They took stones in their hands to throw at Jesus.

"I have shown you many good works from the Father. For which of these are you going to stone me?" Jesus demanded.

The angry Jews shouted, "It is not for a good work that we are going to stone you. It is because you, who are only a human being, are making yourself God."

Jesus responded once more. "If I am not doing the works of my Father, then do not believe me. But, if I do them, even though you do not believe me, believe the works. Thus, you may understand that the Father is in me, and I am in the Father."

They tried to arrest him, but Jesus escaped. He traveled across the Jordan River to the place where John had been baptizing. Many people came to see Jesus there, saying, 'John performed no signs. Yet everything that John said about this man was true.' Many of these people were willing to believe what Jesus taught.

MARY AND MARTHA
AND THE
MESSAGE OF JESUS

esus' visit to the home of Mary and Martha tells what Jesus expected from his followers. It is a short story in which Jesus taught the message that to believe in his teachings is the way to heaven. After this story, there are two others with similar messages. The first of the two is the story of Jesus and the seventy disciples. The second is the parable of the Good Samaritan.

Mary and Martha were sisters. When Jesus entered the village where they lived, Martha welcomed him into her home. Like all of the disciples, Mary sat at the feet of Jesus and listened to his teachings. Martha, while the teaching took place, was busy with the tasks of keeping house.

"Why do you not care that my sister lets me do all the work by myself?" Martha asked Jesus. "Please, tell her to help me," she added.

Jesus answered, "Martha, Martha, you are worried and distracted by many things. But there is need of only one thing. Mary has chosen better than you what to do. That will not be taken away from her."

In the next story, Jesus visited a town, and while he was there, he named seventy disciples. He sent them in pairs to every town and village where he planned to travel in the future to teach his message. He explained why he sent them.

He said, "The harvest is plentiful, but the laborers are few. Go on your way. I am sending you out like lambs into the midst of wolves."

Then, he gave the seventy disciples strict instructions for their journeys.

"Carry no purse, bag or sandals. Greet no one on the road. When you enter a house, say, 'Shalom! Peace to this house.' If anyone there shares peace with you, the peace of your greeting will remain with that person. If no one shares peace with you, the peace will stay with you," Jesus instructed the new disciples.

Then, he told them to remain in the house where peace was offered, not to move about from house to house. They were to accept food and drink and whatever the householder provided, because they were laborers who deserved to be paid. Their mission was to cure the sick in the village and say to them, "The kingdom of God is near for you."

If, by chance, the pair of disciples visited an unwelcoming town, they were to gather people around them in the town's streets. Then, they were to say, "Even the dust of your town that clings to our feet, we wipe off in protest against you. But know that the kingdom of God is near for you. On that day, God's punishment of the wicked city of Sodom would be more tolerable than what you will see."

The seventy disciples were joyous when they returned to Jesus after having followed his instructions on their journeys.

"In your name, even the demons give over power to us," they proclaimed.

Jesus welcomed them. He said, "See, I have given you authority to tread on snakes and scorpions. Nothing will hurt you. You reign over the power of the enemy. But, do not rejoice over this. Rejoice instead that your names are written in heaven."

The third story is the parable of the good Samaritan. The land of the Samaritans was far from the village where the Samaritan traveler in this story visited. The story begins with a question that a teacher of the law of Moses asked Jesus while he was preaching.

"Teacher," the Jewish scholar asked Jesus, "what must I do to inherit eternal life?"

"What is written in the law? What do you read there?" responded Jesus.

"You shall love God with all your heart, with all your soul, with all your strength and with all your mind. And, love your neighbor as yourself," answered the Jewish scholar.

Jesus said, "You have given the right answer. Do this and you will have eternal life."

But, the Jewish scholar wanted to make sure that Jesus saw him as a truly righteous man. "And, who is my neighbor?" the scholar asked to draw further attention to himself

Jesus replied with a parable to straighten out the scholar's thinking.

"A man was going down from Jerusalem to Jericho, and he fell into the hands of robbers. They stripped and beat him. Then, they went away, leaving him for dead. By chance, a priest happened down the road. When he saw the unfortunate man, he crossed to the other side. A Levite (from the priestly tribe of Levi, who worked in the temple), came down the road, observed the man and also crossed to the opposite side. A Samaritan traveler passed next. When he saw the man, he took pity on him, bandaged and cleaned his wounds, brought him to an inn and cared for him there.

The next day, the Samaritan had to continue his journey. So, he instruct-ed the innkeeper to care for the wounded man and to keep an account of what the care cost. The Samaritan promised to repay the man upon his return trip to the town."

Then, Jesus stopped and asked the Jewish scholar, "Which of these three was a neighbor to the man who fell into the hands of the robbers?"

"The one who showed him mercy," said the scholar.

"Go and do the same thing," said Jesus.

THE LOST SHEEP, THE LOST COIN AND THE PRODIGAL SON

 hile Jesus was preaching in the land of Galilee, some tax collectors and other sinners gathered close to listen to him. At that time, people who collected taxes were often dishonest and they were believed to have questionable dealings with foreign governments. The Pharisees in the temple grumbled among themselves about this.

"Look, this fellow welcomes sinners. He also eats with them," they said.

Their complaint about how Jesus ate with sinners related to the Pharisees' ideas that sharing food with a sinner made a person evil.

In response to the grumbling, Jesus told a parable to try to change the Pharisees' minds.

Jesus said, "Imagine having one hundred sheep and losing one of them. Which one of you does not leave the ninety-nine in the wilderness to search for the one that is lost until he finds it?"

The Pharisees looked back and forth between each other, but they did not respond.

Jesus continued, "When he has found it, he lifts the sheep onto his shoulders and rejoices. And when he comes home, he calls together his friends and neighbors. He says to them, 'Rejoice with me, because I have found my sheep that was lost.'"

The Pharisees said nothing, but the negative looks on their faces did not change.

"I tell you," said Jesus, "there will be more joy in heaven over one sinner who repents than over ninety-nine righteous persons who need no repentance."

Then, Jesus told another parable to clarify his lesson.

"What woman who has ten silver coins and who loses one of them does not light a lamp, sweep the house and carefully search until she finds the coin?" asked Jesus.

The Pharisees still said nothing.

"When she finds it," continued Jesus, "she calls together her friends and neighbors and says, 'Rejoice with me, because I have found the coin that I lost.'" Then, he explained, "I tell you there is joy in the presence of the angels of God over one sinner who repents."

Jesus spoke a third parable. "There was a man with two sons. The younger son said to his father, 'Father, give me now the share of the property that will belong to me when you die.' So, the man divided his property between his two sons. A few days later, the younger son gathered up all his possessions and he traveled to a distant land. In the new country, he lost all that he owned by the outrageous way he lived, spending everything on entertainment.

"A severe famine spread throughout the land where the younger son was living. In need of food and shelter, the young man found work with a pig farmer. Still, he was hungry. Then, he came to his senses. 'How many of my father's hired hands have bread to spare? Here I am dying of hunger! I will go to my father and tell him I have sinned against heaven and against him. I will ask him to treat me like one of his hired hands, because I am no longer worthy to be called his son.'

"While the younger son was still in the distance, the father saw him approach. Filled with compassion for this prodigal, or wasteful, son, the father ran to greet him. He put his arms around the young man, and he kissed him. 'Father, I have sinned against heaven and you. I am no longer worthy to be called your son,' said the young man.

"The father ordered his servants to bring out the best robe in the house for his son. He put a ring on the young man's finger and sandals on his feet. Then, he told the servants to find a fat calf and kill it so that they might eat and celebrate the son's return. 'This son of mine was dead and is alive again. He was lost and is found!' proclaimed the father in joy.

"The elder son had been in the field. When he approached the house, he heard music and dancing. One of the servants told him the cause of the celebration. Instead of happiness, the elder brother was filled with anger, and he refused to go inside. His father came out to him and pleaded with him to share the happiness over his brother's return. 'Listen, for all these years I have worked like a slave for you. I have never disobeyed what you asked. But you have never given me even a young goat to eat in celebration with my friends. When this son of yours returns after devouring all of the property you gave him, you kill a fat calf for him!' complained the elder son.

"'Son, you are always with me, and all that is mine is yours,' answered the father. 'But we must celebrate and rejoice, because your brother was dead and he has come to life. He was lost, and now he has been found.'"

This is how Jesus taught the lesson about welcoming back sinners.

THE DISHONEST MANAGER AND THE UNFORGIVING SERVANT

*J*esus told two parables about the dangers of money. The first is about the dishonest manager of a household, who had been given considerable responsibility by the rich owner of the house. The second parable describes how two different people act when someone owes them money. In it Jesus emphasizes the importance of forgiveness. As always, the Pharisees were in the crowd when Jesus spoke. These teachers of the Jewish faith ridiculed what Jesus taught.

Jesus told the first parable. "There was a rich man who had a manager. Other servants of the rich man reported tales to him of how his manager was squandering or wasting money that belonged to the man. So, the man called the manager to him.

"'What is this I have heard about you?' the rich man asked the manager. 'Give an accounting of your activities, because you are no longer my manager.'

"The manager was very anxious about his well-being now that he knew he would lose his position. He thought of his choices, 'I am not strong enough to dig. I am ashamed to beg. I will make sure that when the owner dismisses me, people will welcome me into their homes.'

"One by one, the dishonest manager called to him the people who owed debts to his master. He asked the first debtor, 'How much do you owe my master?' 'A hundred jugs of olive oil,' answered the first debtor. 'Take your bill and make it fifty,' ordered the manager.

"'How much do you owe my master?' he asked the second debtor. 'A hundred containers of wheat,' the second debtor responded. 'Take your bill and make it eighty,' said the dishonest manager.

"Soon the rich man heard what his former manager had done. The man complimented the manager not on his cheating, but on his shrewdness."

Then, Jesus explained the parable to his disciples. "I tell you, make friends for yourselves by means of worldly wealth. in that way you will gain heavenly treasure. Whoever is faithful with a very little is also faithful with much. No slave can serve two masters. A slave will either hate the one and love the other. Or he will be devoted to one and despise the other. You cannot serve God and wealth."

Peter asked Jesus a question. "If another believer sins against me, how often should I forgive him? As many as seven times?"

"Not seven times. I tell you, seventy times seven," corrected Jesus.

Then, Jesus told the disciples the parable of the unforgiving servant. "The kingdom of heaven may be compared to a king who wished to settle accounts with his servants. When he began the settling, the king saw that one servant owed him ten thousand talents (more than fifteen years of wages). He had the servant brought before him. When the servant explained that he was unable to pay, the king ordered that the servant, his wife, their children and all of their possessions be sold so that the debt would be repaid.

"The servant fell on his knees and begged the king, 'Have patience with me. I will repay everything.' Out of pity, the king released the servant and forgave the huge debt in its entirety.

"But, the very same servant then happened upon a fellow slave who owed him a mere one hundred denarii (one denarius was the usual day's wage at the time). 'Pay me what you owe,' demanded the first servant whose debt had been forgiven by the king. The second servant fell on his knees and begged, 'Have patience with me, and I will repay everything.' But, the first servant refused the plea. He had the second servant thrown into prison until he was able to repay the debt.

"The other servants were deeply distressed by the imprisonment of the second servant. They reported what had happened to the king. 'You wicked servant!' the king shouted at the first servant. 'I forgave you all that debt, because you pleaded with me. Should you not have had mercy on your fellow servant, just as I had mercy on you?' Then, in his anger, the king handed over the ungrateful servant to be tortured until he found the way to repay the entire debt."

Jesus explained the parable of the unforgiving servant to his disciples. "So, my heavenly Father will also do the same to every one of you if you do not forgive your brother or sister from your heart."

The Pharisees ridiculed the words of Jesus when they heard them.

"You appear righteous in the sight of others," Jesus accused the Pharisees. "But, God knows your hearts. Remember, what is prized by human beings is detestable in the sight of God."

THE VINEYARD LABORERS

esus and his disciples had recently left Galilee, and they had traveled through Judea across the Jordan river. Jesus was preaching when someone asked him about the most successful way to achieve eternal life.

"Teacher, what good deed must I do to have eternal life?" asked one of the listeners gathered around Jesus.

"Why do you ask me about what is good?" questioned Jesus. "There is only one who is good. If you wish to enter into the kingdom of heaven, keep the commandments," Jesus corrected.

"Which ones?" asked the same listener.

"You shall not murder. You shall not commit adultery. You shall not steal. You shall not bear false witness. Honor your father and mother. Also, you shall love your neighbor as yourself," answered Jesus.

The young man said, "I have kept all these. What am I still missing?"

Jesus looked at him closely and responded, "If you wish to be perfect, go and sell your possessions. Give the money to the poor, and you will have treasure in heaven. Then, come and follow me."

The young man departed in grief, because he owned many possessions and much property.

Jesus turned to speak to his disciples. "Truly, I tell you, it will be hard for a rich person to enter the kingdom of heaven. It is easier for a camel to move through the eye of a needle than for someone who is rich to enter the kingdom of God," he said.

"Then, who can be saved?" asked one of the disciples.

"All things are possible for God," Jesus replied.

But, Peter was not satisfied. "Look, we have left everything and followed you. What will we have then?"

Jesus consoled Peter. "When the Son of God is seated on the throne of his glory, you who have followed me will also sit on twelve thrones, judging the twelve tribes of Israel. And everyone who has left houses or brothers or sisters, father or mother, children or fields for the sake of my name will inherit eternal life. But many who are first will be last, and the last will be first."

Jesus spoke a parable to demonstrate the message. He said, "The kingdom of heaven is like a landowner who went out early in the morning (about 6 a.m.) to hire laborers for his vineyard. After agreeing with the laborers for the usual daily wage of one denarius, he sent the workers into the vineyard. At nine o'clock, the landowner noticed other laborers milling about idly in the marketplace. He said to them, 'Go also into the vineyard, and I will pay you the just wage.' And they did as he told them.

"He went out several more times, at noon, at three o'clock and again at five o'clock in the afternoon. Each time, he found laborers standing around, and he said to them, 'Why are you standing here idle all day?'

They answered him, 'Because no one has hired us.' 'Go into the vineyard,' was his response.

"Just before sunset, the vineyard owner said to his manager, 'Call the laborers and give them their pay. Begin with the last and then go down to the first.'

"When those hired at five o'clock came, they received the daily wage. When the first hired came, they thought they would receive more, but each got the same daily pay. They grumbled against the landowner, saying, 'These last hired worked only one hour. You have made them equal to us who have suffered the burden of the day and the scorching heat.'

"The landowner replied to one of those that grumbled, 'Friend, I am doing you no wrong. Did you not agree with me for the usual daily wage? Take what belongs to you and go. I choose to give to this last the same as I give to you. Am I not allowed to do what I choose with what belongs to me? Or are you envious because I am generous?'"

Then, Jesus repeated the message he gave the disciples before he spoke the parable, "So, the last will be first, and the first will be last."

The apostles asked Jesus on several occasions to increase their faith. On one occasion when they pleaded, "Increase our faith!" he replied, "If you had faith the size of a mustard seed, you could say to this mulberry tree, 'Be uprooted and be planted in the sea. The tree would obey you.'"

Then, Jesus gave another example. "Who among you would say to your servant who has just come in from plowing or from tending sheep in the field, 'Come here at once and take your place at the table?' Would you rather not say to him, 'Prepare supper for me, put on your apron and serve me while I eat and drink. Later, you may eat and drink.'

"Then, do you thank the servant for doing what you commanded? So, too, when you have done all that you were ordered to do, say to yourselves, 'We are worthless servants. We have done only what we ought to have done!'"

LAZARUS'S DEATH AND LIFE

This is the story of how Jesus brought his friend Lazarus back from death. Jesus risked his own life to help Lazarus. He had to travel from Galilee to Judea to a town named Bethany. The town was only two miles from Jerusalem, where many unbelieving Jewish leaders wanted Jesus dead.

Lazarus was Mary and Martha's brother. Mary was a woman who would anoint Jesus with perfume on the day before Palm Sunday. On that same occasion, she had wiped his feet with her hair. The sisters sent a message to Jesus, telling about their brother's illness. Though Jesus loved Mary, Martha and Lazarus, he waited two days before preparing to go to the bedside of Lazarus.

He explained, "This illness does not lead to death. Rather, it is for God's glory, so that the Son of God can be glorified through it."

On the third day, Jesus told the disciples, "Let us go to Judea once more."

What he suggested worried them. "Rabbi, the Jews there tried to stone you. Are you going to Judea again?"

Jesus answered the disciples. "Are there not twelve hours of daylight? They who walk during the day do not stumble, because they see the light of this world. They who walk at night stumble, because the light is not in them."

Although Jesus spoke to them of the daylight hours and the evening time, his words also meant that the hour of his death had not yet come. So, it was safe for them to set out for Judea that day. Then he explained to them what had happened to Lazarus.

"Our friend Lazarus has fallen asleep, but I am going there to awaken him," said Jesus.

"If he has fallen asleep, he will be all right," answered one of the disciples.

The others were relieved that, yes, Lazarus would be fine, because he was merely sleeping. But by sleep, Jesus meant Lazarus was dead. It was common at the time to refer to death as sleep. Jesus used a euphemism, an agreeable word for something that is unpleasant.

Then, to correct their misunderstanding, Jesus told the disciples, "Lazarus is dead. For your sake," he said, "I am glad I was not there, so that you may believe. But now let us go to him."

Thomas, who was called the Twin, was afraid of the danger they might find in the area around Jordan. Thomas said to the other disciples, "Let us also go, that we may die with him."

By the time they arrived at the village of Bethany, Lazarus had been in the tomb for four days. Jewish custom required that burial take place on the same day as death occurred. Many Jews believed the soul hovered near the deceased body for three days. Only on the fourth day was the death considered to be final. So, when Jesus and the disciples arrived, Lazarus was, in the opinion of all, truly dead.

Mary and Martha were mourning their brother, and many Jews were at the house with them to share their grief. When word reached the sisters that Jesus approached, Martha went to meet him on the road.

"If you had been here, my brother would not have died. But I know that God will give you whatever you ask of him."

Jesus said, "Your brother will rise again."

"I know that he will rise again in the resurrection on the last day," replied Martha, thinking that it was the resurrection that Jesus spoke of.

"I am the resurrection and the life. Those who believe in me, even though they die, will live. And everyone who lives and believes in me will never die. Do you believe this?" Jesus asked Martha.

"Yes, I believe that you are the Messiah, the Son of God, the one coming into the world," she answered.

Then, Martha returned home.

"The Teacher is calling for you," she told Mary.

The Jews who were mourning with them saw Mary get up quickly and go out. They followed her, thinking that she was going to mourn at her brother's tomb. But Mary met Jesus on the road as Martha had instructed her. When she saw Jesus, she knelt at his feet, unable to control her weeping.

"If you had been here, my brother would not have died," said Mary, in the same words that Martha had spoken earlier to Jesus.

He was deeply disturbed by Mary's tears.

"Where have you laid him?" Jesus asked her.

The Jews who had followed Mary answered, "Come and see where he is."

"See how he loved him!" said one of them, moved by the tears that Jesus shed for his friend. "Could he not have kept this man from dying? He opened the eyes of the blind man, didn't he?" said another.

"Take away the stone," instructed Jesus, because the tomb of Lazarus was a cave with a stone lying against its opening.

"But, Teacher, already there is a stench. He has been dead four days," said Martha.

"Did I not tell you that if you believed, you would see the glory of God?" Jesus consoled her.

When they removed the stone from the cave's opening, Jesus raised his eyes to heaven.

"Father, I thank you for having heard me. I know that you always hear me, but I have said this for the sake of the crowd standing here, that they may believe that you sent me," said Jesus. Then, in a loud voice, he cried, "Lazarus, come out!"

Lazarus appeared from inside the cave. Still wearing the trappings of burial, his hands and feet were bound with strips of cloth, and his face was wrapped in a cloth.

"Unbind him," said Jesus. "And let him walk."

THREE PARABLES ABOUT PRAYER

esus talked about prayer in three parables. The first parable taught the disciples how to pray. The second parable is the story of the widow and the unjust judge. The third parable is the story of the Pharisee and the tax collector.

Here is the first parable. After Jesus finished praying one day the disciples asked him for a lesson about how to pray.

"Lord, teach us to pray, as John taught his disciples," they asked.

Then, Jesus taught them "The Lord's Prayer." He said, "When you pray, say, 'Father, hallowed be your name. Your kingdom come. Your will be done, on earth as it is in heaven. Give us each day our daily bread. And forgive us our sins, for we ourselves forgive everyone indebted to us. And do not bring us to temptation.'"

Jesus explained the prayer by teaching a parable. "Suppose one of you has a friend, and you go to him at midnight. You say, 'Friend, lend me three loaves of bread, because another friend of mine has arrived and I have nothing to offer him.' He answers you, 'Do not bother me. The door is already locked, and my children are in bed. I cannot get up and give you anything.'

"Even though he will not get up and give you anything, he is your friend. If you persist in knocking, he will get up and give you whatever you need," said Jesus.

He explained that the parable was about prayer. "Ask, and it will be given to you. Search, and you will find. Knock, and the door will be opened for you. Because everyone who asks, receives. Everyone who searches, finds. And for everyone who knocks, the door will be opened. Is there anyone among you who, if your child asks for a fish, will give a snake instead? Or, is there anyone among you who, if the child asks for an egg, will give a scorpion? How much more will the heavenly Father give you in the name of the Holy Spirit if you ask him?"

In the second parable, Jesus gave the disciples instruction on how to prepare for the future days when he was no longer with them. Jesus told the story of the widow and the unjust judge to remind them that they needed to pray every day.

He taught, "In a certain city, there was a judge who neither feared God nor had respect for the people. In the same city, there was a widow who kept coming to the judge, saying, 'Grant me justice against my opponent.' The judge refused to hear the widow's case on many occasions when she came to him. But, finally, he said to himself, 'Though I have no fear of God and no respect for anyone, still this widow keeps bothering me. I will grant her justice, so that she will not wear me out by coming day after day.'"

Jesus explained the parable, "Listen to what the unjust judge said. Will not God grant justice to his chosen ones, who cry to him day and night? Will he delay long in helping them? I tell you, he will quickly grant them justice."

In the third parable, Jesus spoke to those people who might sing their own praises of how correct and righteous they were. At the same time, these people held others in contempt because of their own righteous behavior. Jesus said, "Two men went up to the temple to pray, one, a Pharisee and the other, a tax collector.

"The Pharisee, standing by himself, prayed, 'God, I thank you that I am not like other people, like thieves, rogues, adulterers or even like this tax collector. I fast twice a week. I give a tenth of my income in donations.'

"The tax collector, standing far off, would not even look to heaven. He beat his breast, saying, 'God, be merciful to me, a sinner!'"

Jesus explained the story of the Jewish teacher and the dishonest tax collector to his disciples, speaking first of the tax collector and next of the Pharisee in his explanation. He taught, "I tell you, this man went down to his home justified, not the other. All who exalt themselves will be humbled. But all who humble themselves will be exalted."

By "exalt," Jesus spoke of how the Pharisee tried to elevate himself in God's eyes because of what he saw as his own worth. By contrast, the tax collector humbled himself because of what he viewed as his own sins. The message was that God saw the opposite of what both men intended.

JESUS AND CHILDREN

esus loved children. He spoke often about children to his disciples. He described the goodness and honesty of children in his teachings. Sometimes, when he spoke about children, he really meant children, the youngest among the people. Other times he meant the true children of God, the believers in the word of God, no matter what their ages were.

One day, the disciples asked Jesus to help them understand about the kingdom of heaven.

"Who is the greatest in the kingdom of heaven?" they inquired of Jesus.

Jesus asked a child who was present to stand before him. When the child came close, Jesus welcomed him. Then, he answered the question.

"Truly, I tell you, unless you change and become like children, you will never enter the kingdom of heaven. Whoever becomes humble like this

child is the greatest in the kingdom of heaven. Whoever welcomes one such child in my name, welcomes me."

Jesus welcomed children to him on other occasions. One day, when he was teaching in the land of Judea, some Pharisees were asking him questions. As soon as he finished teaching his message, parents rushed forward and asked Jesus to bless their children. The disciples tried to push them away to give Jesus some breathing room.

Jesus corrected the disciples sternly. He said, "Let the little children come to me. Do not stop them, because it is to these that the kingdom of heaven belongs."

Then, he blessed the children. He took them into his arms, laid his hands on them, and he blessed them.

"Whoever does not receive the kingdom of God as a little child will never enter it," explained Jesus.

By his words, he was describing the characteristics of a little child. He spoke of the openness of children, how they met a new situation without any ideas that would stop them from seeing the truth. Jesus also described how a child entered the kingdom of God. The child would have no titles or achievements on earth that would make her or him more special than other people. Instead the child would enter with honesty and love.

Another day, the collectors of the temple tax came to Capernaum, where Jesus had his ministry. According to the law every Jewish male had to pay a tax each year to support the temple sacrifices. This was the law the Romans had decreed after the destruction of the Jewish temple and its rebuilding.

The collectors of the temple tax arrived at the house in Capernaum in the land of Galilee where Jesus most often taught. When they got there, Jesus was not at home. Peter came out to greet them. But the tax collectors tried to trick him. They expected him to answer that Jesus was unwilling to pay the tax they had come to collect.

"Does your teacher not pay the temple tax?" the tax collectors asked Peter.

"Yes, he does," responded Peter honestly.

When Jesus came back home, the tax collectors were no longer there. Yet, Jesus spoke to Simon, also called Peter, about the incident as the first thing he said to his disciple.

"What do you think, Simon? From whom do the kings of the earth take their toll or their tribute? From their children or from others?" asked Jesus.

Peter answered, "From others."

Jesus replied, "Then, the children are free. However, so we do not give offense to the tax collectors, go to the sea and cast a hook. Take the first fish that comes up, open its mouth and you will find a coin. Take that and give it to them for you and me."

When he spoke of children on this occasion, he spoke of the children of God. Jesus included not just the youngest, but all of the children of God who believed the word of God. The message of Jesus was that the children of God did not need to contribute to the upkeep of God's house. The kingdom of God did not belong to the earth. It belonged to heaven, and they did not need to pay to support it.

Jesus told his disciples on another day not to cause his "little ones" to stumble on the path to kingdom of God. Here, again, he meant the children of God as his little ones, not only the youngest alive on earth.

"If any of you put a stumbling block before one of these little ones who believe in me, it would be better for you if a great millstone were fastened around your neck and you were drowned in the depth of the sea," Jesus taught.

When he spoke of a great millstone, Jesus talked about a large round stone. The large stones were attached behind donkeys and were used to grind grain.

THE MAN BORN BLIND

One day, Jesus and the disciples met a blind beggar on the road.

"Rabbi, who sinned? Was it the sin of this man or his parents that he was born blind?" asked the disciples.

"Neither he nor his parents sinned," corrected Jesus. "He was born blind so that God's work of healing might be revealed in him."

Then, Jesus spoke to the disciples about the future. He used the symbol of night to refer to the end of his life on earth. This is what he said.

"We must do the work of him who sent me while it is day. Night is coming when no one can work. But as long as I am in the world, I am the light of the world," explained Jesus.

When Jesus finished speaking, he spat on the warm, dusty ground at his feet. He bent to mix the saliva with the dry dirt. With the mud on his fingers, Jesus reached out to the blind man. He spread the mud on the man's closed eyes.

"Go, wash in the pool of Siloam," he said. He instructed the blind man to cleanse the mud from his eyelids.

The pool of Siloam was fed by the Gihon spring which ran beneath the city of Jerusalem through the tunnel built during the reign of King Hezekiah. In Hebrew, Siloam meant "sent," so it was there that Jesus sent the blind man to wash.

When the man who had been blind returned from the pool, he could see. Some of the countrymen who had known him for years as a blind beggar in the vicinity of Jerusalem saw that he no longer was sightless. They spoke among themselves.

"Is this not the man who used to sit and beg?" one asked another.

"It is he," answered one of them.

"No, it is someone like him," said another neighbor.

The once-blind man overheard the conversation. "I am the man," he said to them.

"Then, how were your eyes opened?" asked someone.

"The man called Jesus made mud, spread it on my eyes and said, 'Go to Siloam and wash.' I went and washed and received my sight," he explained to the neighbors.

They demanded to know where Jesus was. "Where is he?" they shouted to the man no longer blind.

"I do not know," he responded.

The people in the crowd brought the former beggar to the Pharisees to tell his story. It was the sabbath, and the Pharisees strictly believed according to Jewish law that the day was reserved for worship only. When the man explained how he had regained his sight, the Pharisees were outraged by what Jesus had done on the sabbath.

"This man is not from God, because he does not observe the sabbath," proclaimed one of the Pharisees.

But another Pharisee protested what the first had said. "How can a man who is a sinner perform such signs?"

The Pharisees disagreed among themselves, so they turned to the former beggar to ask his opinion.

"He is a prophet," the man who was born blind said of Jesus.

Still disbelieving, the Pharisees called the man's parents to come before them. Surely, they would clear up the matter. Perhaps the beggar had only pretended to be blind all these years so that he could avoid work.

The man's parents explained, "We know that this is our son and we know that he was born blind. What we do not know is how it is that he now sees. Nor do we know who opened his eyes. Ask him. He is old enough to describe what happened. Let him speak for himself."

The Pharisees had proclaimed on an earlier occasion that anyone who testified that Jesus was the Messiah would be cast out of the synagogue. For this reason, the parents threw the matter back to their son. He was a grown man. They wanted him to answer for himself and take the consequences for what he said.

For the second time, the Jewish leaders asked the former beggar to explain. They asked him to judge whether Jesus was a sinner for what he had done on the sabbath.

"I do not know whether he is a sinner. One thing I do know is that though I was blind, I now see," said the man. Then, he added, "If this man were not from God, he could do nothing."

The Pharisees drove the man out of the synagogue, proclaiming him to have been born a sinner; therefore, he was unable to teach them anything. When Jesus heard what they had done to the man he cured, he looked for the man and found him.

"Do you believe in the Son of God?" Jesus asked the former beggar.

The man replied, "Who is he, sir? Tell me, so that I may believe in him."

Jesus said, "You have seen him, and the one speaking with you is he."

"I believe," responded the man.

"I came into the world for judgment, so that those who do not see may see. And those who do see may become blind," replied Jesus.

Among the Pharisees who overheard, one questioned Jesus. "Surely we are not blind, are we?" he asked.

"If you were blind, you would not have sin. But, now that you say, 'We see,' your sin remains," Jesus corrected the Pharisees.

ZACCHEUS AND THE TREE

esus and the disciples traveled to Jericho, the oasis of the Jordan Valley. It has been called the oldest inhabited city in the world. The city was called the Date City, famous for its fruits and its favorable but very warm climate. A crowd gathered on the road to see Jesus pass through the city. They hoped to hear him speak.

The chief tax collector named Zaccheus was in the crowd at Jericho. Zaccheus was a very rich man. He was also a very short man. Unfortunately, no matter how many times he tried to find a location from which to get a good view of Jesus, Zaccheus was unable to secure one. Everywhere he tried to enter the crowd, men, women and even some of the children towered over him.

A shady sycamore fig tree provided the solution. Zaccheus shimmied up its trunk and carefully climbed into the branches. He waited in the tree for

Jesus to pass, proud that he would now see the renowned teacher. When Jesus arrived, he looked up and saw the man in the branches of the tree.

"Zaccheus, hurry and come down," said Jesus to the chief tax collector. "Because I must stay at your house this night."

Delighted that Jesus noticed him, Zaccheus rushed down from his perch in the tree. Zaccheus was pleased to share his hospitality and his home with Jesus. But, many in the crowd grumbled loudly with what they saw.

"He is to be the guest of one who is a sinner," they complained, judging that Jesus should not reward the tax collector with his presence that evening, because people commonly believed that tax collectors were dishonest.

Zaccheus stood his ground before the crowd. "I will give half of my possessions to the poor," he said to Jesus. "If I have cheated anyone of anything, I will pay them back four times as much," he vowed.

"Today, salvation has come to your house, because you, too, are a son of Abraham. The Son of God has come to seek out and save the lost," said Jesus to Zaccheus.

Then, Jesus spoke this parable to the crowd. Because many Jewish leaders believed that the kingdom of God was about to appear immediately, Jesus wanted to correct their misunderstanding about salvation and eternal life.

He said, "A nobleman went to a distant country to achieve royal power for himself. Afterwards, he would return to his homeland." Those in the crowd who believed in the message of Jesus could see that he was talking about himself.

Jesus continued. "The nobleman summoned ten of his slaves. He gave them each ten mina (dollars), and he told them, 'Do business with these until I come back.' But the citizens of his country hated him. They sent a delegation after him, saying, 'We do not want this man to rule over us.'

"Nonetheless, the nobleman returned with the royal power he had gone to seek in the distant land. He again called forth the slaves to learn what they had gained through their trading with the money he had given them. The first slave said, 'Your pound has made ten more pounds.' The nobleman answered, 'Well done, good slave! Because you have been trustworthy in a very small thing, take charge of ten cities.'

"The second slave reported, 'Your pound has made five pounds.' The nobleman said, 'And, you, rule over five cities.' Then, the third slave came forward. 'Here is my pound,' he said to the nobleman. 'I wrapped it up in a piece of cloth, because I was afraid of you, as you are a harsh man. You take for yourself what you did not deposit, and you reap what you did not sow.' 'Wicked slave!' shouted the nobleman. 'You knew, did you, that I was a harsh man? Why then did you not put my money into the bank where I could have collected interest with it?'

"Then, the nobleman instructed the crowd of bystanders, 'Take the pound from him and give it to the one who has ten pounds.' 'But, he already has ten pounds,' they responded, confused by what he had ordered. 'I tell you, those who have will be given more. But, those who have nothing will have even more taken away from them,' corrected the nobleman."

In this parable, Jesus spoke of "having" as possessing the word of God. He hoped to explain that Zaccheus was saved, not because he was rich. Salvation came to Zaccheus, like everyone in the crowd who chose to believe, because he believed in the word of God.

THE RIDE INTO JERUSALEM

he feast of Passover was celebrated in the sacred city of Jerusalem by tens of thousands of people in the days of the adulthood of Jesus. The year that Jesus ate his last Passover supper with his apostles, he stopped, right before the meal, at the house of Lazarus, whom he had recently raised from the dead. At the house were the sisters of Lazarus, Mary and Martha.

After a dinner in Jesus's honor, where the apostles were also present, Mary got up from the table and prepared to anoint their esteemed guest. She took twelve ounces of a precious perfume called "nard," which came from the northern India. With it, she anointed the feet of Jesus, and wiped them dry with her hair. Judas Iscariot, who would betray Jesus very soon, spoke rudely to Mary. Judas was in fact already a thief. His responsibility as an apostle was to hold the purse of common monies. His habit was to steal from the purse for himself.

"Why have you not sold this perfume for three hundred denarii? You could have given the money to the poor," accused Judas, referring to a sum of money equal to the yearly wages of a laborer at the time.

"Leave her alone," commanded Jesus. "She bought it so that she might keep it for the day of my burial. You always have the poor with you, but you do not always have me."

By the next day, a great crowd had heard that Jesus was on his way to Jerusalem for Passover, and they came out to meet him. They carried branches of palm trees. When they saw him approach, they rushed forward, shouting, "Hosanna!" The word was Hebrew for "Please save us!"

They shouted, "Blessed is the one who comes in the name of the Lord, the King of Israel!" These words came from a psalm.

Jesus rode on young donkey. Then, the people shouted the words from Zechariah, "Do not be afraid, daughter of Zion. Look, your king is coming, sitting on a donkey's colt!"

Initially, the disciples did not understand the fervor of the crowd and the words that the people shouted at Jesus. But when Jesus was later glorified by his death, resurrection and ascension into heaven, disciples remembered what had been written about him in the scriptures. The Pharisees in the crowd were troubled, however, because they realized that there was nothing they could do to control such a huge crowd shouting praise at Jesus.

Some Greek people had come to worship at the temple for the festival of Passover, although they were not Jewish. They went to the apostle Philip and told him they wished to see Jesus. Philip told Andrew what the Greeks wanted. Together, Philip and Andrew went to Jesus and told him.

"The hour has come for the Son of God to be glorified," responded Jesus. "I tell you that unless a grain of wheat falls into the earth and dies, it is just a grain. But, if it dies, the grain bears much fruit. Those who love their life will lose it, and those who hate their life in this world will keep it for eternal life. Whoever serves me must follow me. Whoever serves me, the Father will honor."

Jesus continued speaking, and he turned his attention to the crowd at large. "Now, my soul is troubled. Should I say, 'Father, save me from this hour?' No, it is for this reason that I have come to this hour. Father, glory to your name."

A voice answered from heaven, "I have glorified it, and I will glorify it again."

The crowd heard the voice that sounded to them like thunder. Others said they had heard an angel speaking to Jesus.

Jesus said, "This voice has come for your sake, not mine. Now is the judgment of the world, because its ruler, the devil, is driven out. When I am lifted up from earth, I will draw all people to me."

"The law of the scriptures says that the Messiah remains forever," shouted the people in the crowd to Jesus.

Jesus answered them, "The light is with you for a little longer. Walk while you have the light, so that the darkness may not overtake you. If you walk in the darkness, you do not know where you are going. While you have the light, believe in the light, so that you may become children of the light." So Jesus told the people that he was the light.

THE
FIG TREE

eware of the scribes who like to walk around in long robes, love to be greeted with respect in the marketplaces and have the best seats in the synagogues and at banquets," said Jesus to the disciples within hearing of the same persons against whom he was warned.

Seated in the temple among the thousands who had gathered for Passover, Jesus watched as several rich worshippers deposit their gifts in the temple treasury. He saw a poor widow drop in two small copper coins. Then, he spoke to the crowd again.

He said, "Truly, I tell you this poor widow has put in more than all of them. They have contributed out of their abundance, but she has put in all she has to live on."

The words of some of the disciples reached the ears of Jesus. They marveled at the beautiful stones adorning the temple and the wonderful gifts which the rich worshippers gave to God. Jesus spoke directly to these admirers of wealth.

"As for the things that you see, the days will come when not one stone will be left upon another in this temple. They will all be thrown to the ground," said Jesus.

"Teacher, when will this be? And what will be the sign that this is about to happen?" they asked him.

Jesus warned, "Beware that you are not led astray by the many who will come in my name, saying, 'I am he!' and 'The time is near!' Beware that you do not go after them. When you hear word of wars and uprisings, do no be terrified." Jesus warned the people in the temple against false prophets. He also tried to tell them that the divine plan would take place in many phases.

He continued, "Nation will rise against nation, and kingdom against kingdom. There will be great earthquakes, and famines and plagues will take place in many places. There will be dreadful portents of suffering to come and great signs from heaven. But, before all this occurs, they will arrest you and persecute you. They will confine you in synagogues and prisons. You will be brought before kings and governors in my name. ... But not a hair of your head will perish. By your endurance, you will gain your souls."

Jesus told more about the destruction that would happen to the Jerusalem they knew.

"When you see Jerusalem surrounded by armies," he prophesied, "then know that its desolation has come near. Those in Judea must flee to the mountains, and those inside the city must leave it. And those out in the country must not enter. ... Jerusalem will be trampled on by the Gentiles until the times of the Gentiles are fulfilled," said Jesus, speaking of the dominance of the Roman Empire to come.

To emphasize that they should have faith, Jesus told them the parable of the fig tree. He said, "Look at the fig tree and all the trees. As soon as the trees sprout leaves, you see for yourselves that summer is near. So, also, when you see these things taking place, you will know that the kingdom of God is near. ... Be alert and pray for strength to stand for judgment before the Son of God."

The following day, Jesus and the disciples were hungry. Seeing a fig tree in the distance, Jesus went to search for some fruit to eat. The tree had nothing but leaves on its branches, because it was not the correct season for figs to have blossomed. Jesus cursed the tree within the hearing of his disciples, saying, "May no one ever eat fruit from you again."

The next day, Peter said, "Rabbi, look! The fig tree that you cursed has withered," pointing out the cursed fig tree to Jesus.

"Have faith in God," answered Jesus. "Truly, if you say to this mountain, 'Be uprooted and throw yourself into the sea,' and you do not doubt in your heart, but believe that what you say will come to pass, it will be done for you. So, I tell you, whatever you ask for in prayer, believe that you have received it, and it will be yours."

When they returned to the temple, they were met by the chief priests, scribes and elders of the Jewish faith, who were in an uproar over the words and practices of Jesus.

"By whose authority are you doing these things?" they asked.

"Who gave you the authority to do them?" demanded another.

Jesus responded, "I will ask you one question. Once you answer, I will tell you by whose authority I do these things." Then, he asked the question, "Did the baptism of John come from heaven?"

The priests, scribes and elders argued with one another. "If we say from heaven, he will say, 'Why then did you not believe John?'" said some. Others interrupted, "But, shall we say the authority was of human origin?"

They were afraid in the face of the large crowd in the temple, who regarded John as a prophet.

Unable to take a stand either way, they answered, "We do not know."

Because he knew they tried to trap him with the questions they asked, Jesus replied, "Neither will I tell you by whose authority I am doing these things."

THE LAST SUPPER OF JESUS

n the first day of Unleavened Bread, when the Passover lamb was sacrificed, the apostles approached Jesus with a question.

"Where do you want us to arrange for your Passover meal?" they asked.

"Go into the city," he said to two apostles, "and a man carrying a jar of water will meet you. Follow him, and whichever house he enters, say this to the owner. 'The Teacher asks which is the guest room where he may eat the Passover with his apostles.' He will take you upstairs and show you a large, furnished room. Make preparations for us there," said Jesus.

The two apostles went down to the city. There, they found a man carrying a jar of water. When they followed him to the house he entered, the owner showed them a room which was ready for them to use for the Passover meal. It happened just as Jesus had said.

During supper that evening, Jesus rose from the table. Even before the festival of the Passover, he knew that his hour had come to leave this world and return to the Father. When he looked at his reclining and seated apostles relaxed at their meal, Jesus was at peace, knowing that God had made everything possible for him and that he was returning to the Father. He removed his outer robe and tied a towel around his waist. Into a basin, he poured a good deal of water. Then, Jesus began to wash the apostles' feet, a job for the lowest servant in the household. He used the towel at his waist, to dry their feet. When he came to Peter, Jesus stopped.

"Lord, are you going to wash my feet?" asked the outraged Peter.

"You do not know what I am doing, but later you will understand," corrected Jesus.

"You will never wash my feet!" protested Peter.

"Unless I wash you, you have no share with me," Jesus answered him.

Peter thought he understood. "Lord, not my feet only, but also my hands and my head!"

Jesus again corrected the emotional Peter. "One who has bathed has only to wash the feet to be entirely clean. And you are clean, but not all of you are."

When Jesus finished washing their feet, he donned his robe and rejoined his apostles at the table.

"Do you know what I have done to you?" he asked them. "You call me Teacher and Lord, and you are right, because that is what I am. If I, your Lord and Teacher, have washed your feet, you, too, should wash each other's feet. By this example, I have shown you that you should do as I have done to you. Truly, I tell you that servants are not greater than their master, nor are messengers greater than the one who sent them. If you know these things, you are blessed if you do them."

Then, Jesus looked in the direction of Judas Iscariot. "I am not speaking of all of you. I know whom I have chosen. Yet, it fulfills the scripture, which says, 'The one who ate my bread has lifted his heel against me.' I tell you this now before it occurs, so that when it does occur, you will believe that I am he."

The spirit of Jesus was troubled, and he said sadly, "Very truly, I tell you, one of you will betray me."

"Who is it?" asked the apostle on Jesus's right side.

Jesus answered, "It is the one to whom I give this piece of bread after I dip it in the dish."

He handed the dipped piece of bread to Judas, son of Simon Iscariot. "Do quickly what you are going to do," Jesus instructed Judas.

The apostles had no idea what Jesus was talking about to Judas. What could be so important for him to do right then? Some thought that, because Judas kept the common purse for Jesus and the apostles, Jesus was sending him out to buy something he needed for the festival. Or, perhaps, Jesus wanted him to go then to give something to the poor. They watched Judas leave the room.

When Judas was gone, Jesus answered their unspoken questions. He said to them, "Now the Son of God has been glorified, and God has been glorified in him. Little children, I am with you only a little longer. Where I am going, you cannot come. I give you a new commandment. Love one another. Just as I have loved you, you also should love one another. By doing this, everyone will know that you are my disciples."

Then, Jesus took into his hands a loaf of bread, and he broke it into enough pieces to share. After blessing the bread, Jesus gave a piece to each apostle, saying, "Take, eat; this is my body."

After supper, Jesus took a cup of wine and held it gently in his raised palms. Giving thanks, he passed the cup to the apostles, saying, "Drink from it, all of you. This is my blood of the new covenant, which is poured out for many for the forgiveness of sins. I tell you, I will never again drink of this fruit of the vine until that day when I drink it new with you in my Father's kingdom."

Jesus and his eleven apostles finished the Passover meal with a hymn.

THE GARDEN
PRAYER

 t the close of the Passover meal that was now the Last Supper, Jesus was troubled. His betrayal by Judas Iscariot weighed heavily on Jesus. He had dismissed the traitor from the meal to do his work so that the scriptures would be fulfilled. It was time for Jesus to return to God and to leave his apostles behind to carry on his work.

"You will all become deserters because of me tonight," he said to the eleven apostles. "It is written, 'I will strike the shepherd, and the sheep of the flock will be scattered,'" he added, quoting the prophets Zechariah and Isaiah.

When the apostles protested that they would never desert Jesus that night, he comforted them, saying, "But, after I am raised up, I will go ahead of you to meet you in Galilee."

Peter still protested, "Though all of them become deserters, I will never desert you."

"Truly, I tell you, this very night before the cock crows twice, you will deny me three times," answered Jesus.

"Even if I have to die with you, I will not deny you," protested Peter. The other apostles echoed his protest.

With Jesus, they walked down to the west side of Mount Olive to a place called Gethsemane. Pointing to a spot on the hill, Jesus asked eight of the apostles to wait for him while he went on a little farther to pray. He invited Peter. James and John to accompany him. As they walked together, Jesus began to feel agitated, and he shared his thoughts.

"I am deeply grieved as I approach death. Remain here, but stay awake with me," said Jesus to the three apostles, and he proceeded a little farther to pray.

At that location, Jesus passionately threw himself to the ground. He prayed, "Father, if it is possible, let this cup pass from me. Yet, it is not what I want, but what you want."

Jesus raised himself up and went to the spot where he asked the three apostles to wait and stay awake. But, what did he find? Peter and the sons of Zebedee were fast asleep. Jesus woke Peter.

"So, could you not stay awake with me one hour? Stay awake and pray as you enter this time of temptation. Your spirit indeed is willing, but the flesh is weak," said Jesus to him.

A second time, Jesus went to pray. "Father, if this cannot pass unless I drink it, your will be done," he prayed. Then, he returned to find the apostles sound asleep.

The third time that Jesus prayed from the same spot, he repeated the words of the second prayer. He returned and again found the apostles fast asleep. He woke them.

"Are you still sleeping and taking your rest? See, the hour of the Son of God is at hand, and the Son of God is betrayed into the hands of sinners. Get up, let us be going. My betrayer is at hand," proclaimed Jesus.

While Jesus was talking Judas arrived, followed by a large crowd with swords and clubs. The group was formed mainly of the chief priests and the elders. Local inhabitants and the visitors from other lands who had come for the Passover festival came along to observe. Judas left his position as leader to place a kiss on the cheek of Jesus. This was a sign which he had arranged with the men who were going to arrest Jesus.

"Friend, do what you are here to do," said Jesus to Judas Iscariot.

The priests and their servants surrounded Jesus and restrained him with their hands. Peter drew his sword and struck the slave of the high priest, cutting off his ear. Jesus spoke to the apostle.

"Put your sword into its place. All who take up the sword will perish by the sword. Do you think that I cannot appeal to my Father? He will at once send me more than twelve legions of angels. But how, then, would the scriptures be fulfilled which say, 'At that hour, Jesus said to the crowds, "Have you come out with swords and clubs to arrest me as though I were a bandit? Day after day, I sat in the temple teaching, and you did not arrest me. Yet, all this has taken place so that the words of the prophets are fulfilled.'" The apostle replaced his sword in the sheath. Jesus healed the slave, but remained in the grip of the men who arrested him.

As Jesus had foretold, the apostles ran away. In the company of the scribes and the elders, Jesus was taken to the house of Caiaphas, the high priest. Peter followed at a distance and stopped in the courtyard of the house, staying close to the guards to try to learn what was going to happen. Inside, the chief priests and the council (which was the supreme Jewish court for the handling of religious affairs) questioned Jesus.

With difficulty, they found two people to testify against Jesus, as was required by law. The witnesses told the council that Jesus had said he could destroy the temple and build it in three days. Jesus's refusal to answer the accusation about the temple gave the high priest the chance to ask the main question on the priests' minds.

The chief priest spoke. "I put you under oath before the living God. Tell us if you are the Messiah, the Son of God," he demanded as the room full of priests, scribes and elders hushed.

Jesus spoke. "You have said so. From now on, you will see the Son of God seated at the right hand of Power and coming on the clouds of heaven."

"He has blasphemed!" shouted the high priest. "What is your verdict?" he asked the council.

"He deserves death," the council declared. Some of them even struck Jesus and spat in his face, ridiculing him.

Outside in the courtyard, Peter was approached by a servant. The girl said, "You, too, were with Jesus the Galilean."

"I do not know what you are talking about," denied Peter.

Looking for safety on the porch, Peter encountered another servant. The girl said to the others on the porch, "This man was with Jesus of Nazareth." This time, Peter denied the statement with an oath.

Then, some of the bystanders accused Peter of being with Jesus. "Surely, you are one of them. Your accent betrays you," they said. But Peter cursed their words, and he swore another oath, saying, "I do not know the man!"

Peter heard a rooster crow in the distance. It was the second time he had heard the crowing, and Peter wept bitterly because he had denied Jesus, as Jesus had said he would. The chief priests and the elders handed Jesus over to the Roman governor of the province of Judea early the next morning. His name was Pontius Pilate.

THE CROSS

hen the governor Pontius Pilate questioned Jesus whether he was the king of the Jews, Jesus said, "You say so." Still, Pontius Pilate tried to find another way to treat the case of Jesus without sentencing him to death. He realized that the priests were jealous of Jesus, and for that reason, they had handed the fate of Jesus over to him.

During the Passover festival, one of the customs was for the Roman governor to release someone in prison to the crowd. Barabbas was a notorious prisoner of the time, having committed many awful crimes. Pilate offered the priests the choice of freeing Barabbas or Jesus. The priests and the scribes discussed the matter among themselves.

At that moment, the wife of Pontius Pilate sent word to him through a messenger. The message was, "Have nothing to do with that innocent man. Today I have suffered a great deal because of a dream I had about him."

She was referring to Jesus, because she had no way of knowing the details of Pilate's offer to free Jesus or Barabbas.

But the chief priests and the elders persuaded the crowd to demand Barabbas instead of Jesus. Pilate asked them what he should do about Jesus.

"Let him be crucified!" shouted the crowd that had been primed by the priests.

Taking water into his hands to wash them, Pilate said to the crowd, "I am innocent of this man's blood. See to it yourselves."

The governors' soldiers brought Jesus to their headquarters where they stripped him and made him wear a scarlet robe. Twisting thorns, they forced him to wear what looked like a crown on his head. They made him hold a reed in his right hand. Then, they kneeled before Jesus and mockingly hailed him as the king of the Jews. The soldiers spat at Jesus, and they struck him with the very reed they had forced him to hold. Finally, they stripped off the robe and dressed him again in his own clothes. Then, they led Jesus away to be crucified.

Outside, the soldiers found a man from the land of Cyrene, named Simon. Simon was ordered to help Jesus carry the cross upon which he would be hanged by the soldiers. At a place called Golgotha, which means "Place of a Skull" in Hebrew, the soldiers offered Jesus some wine which they had mixed with gall, a mixture which killed pain. Jesus refused the drink, despite his thirst.

The soldiers prepared to crucify Jesus. The act of crucifixion was slow and painful. They nailed Jesus to the cross he had carried, attaching him at both hands with spikes and through both feet bound together. This punishment was used most of the time for only the most dangerous criminals like murderers or those in rebellion against the state. The accusers of Jesus were so jealous that they had asked for this kind of death!

Jesus hung on the cross while the soldiers cast lots for his clothes, as the psalm had said. Many people passed below the cross, shaking their heads and speaking derisively, saying such things as "You would destroy the temple and build it in three days, save yourself now! If you are the Son of God, come down from the cross." Or, "He saved others; he cannot save himself." Or, "He is the king of Israel. Let him come down from the cross now, and we will believe in him." Or, "He trusts in God. Let God deliver him now if he wants to, because he said, 'I am God's Son.'" Even the bandits that hung on crosses on either side of Jesus mocked him.

At noon, darkness funneled through the land until it was as black as pitch. The darkness lasted three hours. Jesus cried out, "Eli, Eli, lema sabachthani?" which meant, "My God, my God, why have you forsaken me?"

One of the bystanders proclaimed, "This man is calling for Elijah."

"Let us see whether Elijah will save him," said another.

When someone extended a stick toward him, offering sour wine on a sponge, Jesus cried out his last cry and exhaled his last breath. At that very moment, the curtain of the temple tore down the middle from top to bottom. The earth shook so hard that the rocks split on the cliffs. Tombs opened as the boulders securing them were hurled away from the entrances.

"Truly, this man was God's Son!" said one of the centurions on watch.

When it was evening, a rich Jewish man named Joseph from the town of Arimathea visited Pontius Pilate. Joseph asked Pilate for the deceased body of Jesus. And Pilate ordered that the body be given to Joseph. Wrapping it in a clean linen cloth, Joseph laid the body of Jesus in a new tomb, one which he had recently hewn in the rock. Joseph rolled a great stone to cover the door of the tomb, and then he went away.

THE
RESURRECTION

At early dawn on Sunday, Mary Magdalene and Mary the mother of James and Joanna went to the tomb of Jesus to anoint his body according to the customs of those days. They carried oils and spices for the anointing. As they had walked together in the first light of the day, they wondered how they would move the large circular stone away from the tomb so they could enter.

"Who will roll away the stone from the entrance?" they wondered as they approached the burial site.

To their amazement to find the large wheel-shaped stone lay apart from the tomb's entrance. They hurried inside the cave-like tomb, afraid that the body of Jesus had been stolen by his enemies. Suddenly, two men in dazzling robes appeared alongside them. The terrified women folded to the ground and hid their eyes from God's angels.

"Why do you look for the living among the dead? He is not here; he has risen. Remember what he told you in Galilee? The Son of God must be handed over to sinners, be crucified and rise again on the third day," the angels told the women.

The women nodded in agreement. They now remembered the words that Jesus had spoken. Then, the angels spoke again.

"Go, tell his disciples and Peter that he is going ahead of you to Galilee. There you will see him, just as he told you," said the angels.

The women obeyed the angels' words. A combination of terror and amazement propelled them forward. When they arrived at the quarters of the apostles in Jerusalem, they told them had happened and repeated the words of the angel. The apostles found the story hard to believe, and did not pay much attention to what the women told them. Still, Peter ran to the tomb to investigate for himself. He was greeted by the opened tomb and the linen cloths that had wrapped the dead body of Jesus.

About seven miles from Jerusalem in the direction of Galilee was the village of Emmaus. That day, two disciples of Jesus were en route to Emmaus when they encountered a fellow traveler whom they had not seen approach. This traveler was Jesus, risen from the tomb.

"What are you discussing with each other while you walk?" the traveler asked the disciples.

The disciple named Cleopas answered the traveler sadly, "Are you the only stranger in Jerusalem who does not know the things that have taken place there recently?"

"What things?" inquired the traveler.

The disciples were impatient. "The things about Jesus of Nazareth, who was a prophet mighty in deed and word before God and all the people. Our chief priests and leaders handed him over to be condemned to death, and they crucified him. We had hoped he was the one to redeem Israel. Besides all this, it is now the third day since these things took place."

They continued speaking to the traveler, "Earlier, some women of our group astounded us. They were at the tomb this morning. When they did not find his body there, they came back and told us that they saw a vision of angels who said he was alive. Some of our group went to the tomb and found it just as the women had said. But they did not see him."

Then, the traveler said, "How foolish you are and how slow of heart to believe what the prophets have declared! Was it not necessary that the Messiah should suffer these things and enter into his glory?" In answer to his own question, Jesus recounted for them what had been written about himself in the scriptures, beginning with Moses and through the books of the prophets.

The two disciples invited the stranger to stay with them, because it was nearly evening. When they were seated at dinner, Jesus made his identity clear to the disciples. He took bread, blessed and broke it and gave it to them. Then, he vanished from their sight.

Later, Jesus appeared to his apostles and said, "Peace be with you."

The startled apostles thought they were looking at his ghost. But, Jesus invited them to inspect his hands and his feet, to touch his wounds and to see for themselves that he was no ghost. In their joy, they remained in a state between disbelief and wonder.

"Have you anything to eat?" Jesus asked, ending their stupor.

The apostles brought him a piece of broiled fish, which he ate. Then, Jesus helped them understand the scriptures more fully. Jesus told them to remain in Jerusalem until he could send them what his Father promised. He would send them the Holy Spirit on Pentecost, when he took his seat at the right side of the throne of God.

BELIEVING JESUS

his is a story about believing Jesus. The first part of the story talks about the reaction of Thomas, whom many have since named "Doubting Thomas." The second part is a conversation between Peter and Jesus when Jesus appears for the last time to the disciples as they are fishing.

When Jesus showed himself the first time to his apostles after he rose from the tomb, Thomas, who was called the Twin, was not with them. The excited apostles were eager to tell Thomas the news after he returned to the house where they were living.

"We have seen Jesus," they exclaimed.

Yet, Thomas questioned what they told him. "Unless I see the mark of the nails in his hands, and I put my finger in the mark of the nails and my hand in his side, I will not believe," he protested.

Thomas was very doubtful. The following week, however, Thomas was at home with the other apostles. The doors remained shut, and, there in the presence of the apostles, Jesus stood in full view.

"Peace be with you," said Jesus to the twelve apostles.

Then, Jesus spoke directly to Thomas. "Put your finger here and see my hands," he said, showing Thomas the mark of the nails in his hands, and Thomas did as Jesus asked.

"Reach out your hand and put it in my side," Jesus instructed Thomas. "Do not doubt, but believe," Jesus said, and Thomas once more did as Jesus asked.

"My Lord and my God," exclaimed Thomas.

Jesus spoke to him again. "Have you believed because you have seen me? Blessed are those who have not seen and yet believe."

After this meeting with Thomas and the eleven apostles, Jesus appeared for the last time to his disciples. He showed himself at the Sea of Tiberias, another name for the Sea of Galilee. Thomas was present. The other disciples were Peter, Nathaniel of Cana, located in the land of Galilee, the sons of Zebedee and two others.

"I am going fishing," said Peter to the disciples.

"We will go with you," they answered.

All night long, they caught nothing. At daybreak, Jesus stood on the beach nearby. But the disciples did not recognize him.

"Children, you have no fish, have you?" asked Jesus.

"No," they answered.

"Cast the net to the right side of the boat, and you will find some," instructed Jesus.

When they did as Jesus told them, they caught so many fish they were unable to haul in the catch. One of the disciples then recognized who it was that had spoken to them. Peter, who was naked, put on clothes and jumped into the sea. The other disciples, who were only about one hundred yards out to sea in their boat, dragged the net full of fish to shore. Awaiting them was a fire where fish were cooking and some bread.

"Bring some of the fish that you have just caught," Jesus told them. So, Peter went aboard and hauled the net closer. The fish were large and the count was one-hundred-fifty-three in all. Even though the catch was so tremendous, the net was untorn.

"Come and have breakfast," Jesus instructed his disciples.

None of them dared ask his identity, because they knew who he was. Jesus took bread and gave it to them. He did the same with the fish. Now, he had appeared to his disciples three times since he rose from the dead. When they finished eating, Jesus spoke directly to Simon Peter.

"Simon, son of John, do you love me more than these others?" asked Jesus.

"Yes, Lord. You know that I love you," Peter responded.

Jesus answered, "Feed my lambs."

A second time, Jesus said to Peter, "Simon, son of John, do you love me?"

"Yes, Lord. You know that I love you," Peter responded like before.

"Jesus answered, "Tend my sheep."

A third time, Jesus said, "Simon, son of John, do you love me?" His feelings were hurt by the questioning from Jesus, and Peter said, "Lord, you know everything. You know that I love you."

Jesus answered, "Feed my sheep."

The three times that Peter told Jesus he loved him were the opposite of the three times that Peter had denied knowing Jesus. Peter's denials had been in the courtyard and on the porch of the house of the high priest Caiaphas. When Jesus told Peter to care for his lambs and his sheep, Jesus was referring to Peter's leadership in the early days of the

church. Then, Jesus spoke of Peter's future death, which would also be by crucifixion.

Jesus said to Peter, "When you were younger, you used to fasten your own belt and go wherever you wished. But, when you grow old, you will stretch out your hands. Someone else will fasten a belt around you and take you where you do not wish to go." Then, Jesus told Peter, "Follow me."

THE ASCENSION OF JESUS TO HEAVEN

 orty days after he rose from the tomb, Jesus went back to heaven. Just before this time Jesus and the apostles were speaking about the kingdom of God. The apostles were asking questions.

"These are my words that I spoke to you while I was still with you," said Jesus, speaking about the time before he was put to death. "Everything written about me in the law of Moses, spoken by the prophets and sung by the psalms must be fulfilled," Jesus declared to the apostles.

The apostles were thoughtful. Jesus helped them understand even more of the scriptures, especially what he had taught them about the kingdom of heaven and salvation. When Jesus spoke again, the apostles listened with new wisdom.

"It is written that the Messiah must suffer and rise from the dead on the third day. Repentance for the sins of humankind and God's forgiveness will be proclaimed in his name to all nations, starting with Jerusalem. You are witnesses to the fulfillment of what is written. Now I will make way for what my Father promised. You must stay in the city until you have been clothed with power from on high," instructed Jesus.

The apostles now understood the scriptures in a new, enlightened way. They traveled to the Mount of Olives. Zechariah had spoken that God would appear at this spot on the day of the Lord and become king over all the earth. Jesus was going to say goodbye to his apostles.

"Lord, is this the time when you will restore the kingdom to Israel?" asked one of the apostles. The others kept quiet, because the thought was in their heads, too.

"It is not for you to know the times or periods set by the Father's authority. But you will receive such power when the Holy Spirit comes upon you," replied Jesus. He reminded them that they must remain in the city of Jerusalem to await the promise of God.

The apostles were still. When Jesus finished speaking, he lifted gradually from the ground just as he was standing, and he disappeared into a cloud. The cloud rose until the apostles could see it no longer. Two men in white robes materialized on the ground directly before the astonished apostles.

The angels said, "Men of Galilee, why do you stand looking up toward heaven? This Jesus who has been taken away from you into heaven will come in the same way as you saw him go into heaven."

Shaken, the apostles walked back to Jerusalem, slowly climbing the rise of the Judean Mountains to the city on the cliffs. All eleven of them, Peter, John, James, Andrew, Philip, Thomas, Bartholomew, Matthew, James son of Alphaeus, Simon the Zealot and Judas brother of James ascended the stairs to the quarters where they were staying. Missing was Judas Iscariot, who had betrayed Jesus. They were met by many believers, including certain women, among whom was Mary, the mother of Jesus. Quiet prayer and discussion were the reasons they were all gathered there.

Peter stood among the sizable crowd. "Friends," he said, "the scripture had to be fulfilled. What the Holy Spirit told to David in particular about Judas has come to pass."

They discussed among themselves what had happened to Judas Iscariot after the betrayal. With his bounty of silver, Judas had purchased a field. And there he had died. Everyone in Jerusalem knew the story by now, and the field had been renamed by the people in Hebrew, "Akeldama," which means "field of blood."

"It is written in the book of Psalms, 'Let his homestead become desolate, and let there be no one to live in it. ... Let another take his position as overseer,'" said Peter.

The apostles decided they must choose a twelfth apostle, to take the place of Judas Iscariot, whom God had punished for betraying Jesus to his accusers. The appointment must go to someone who had been with Jesus from the baptism of John to that very day, the day of the ascension of Jesus. The new apostle would have to be a witness to the fulfillment of the scriptures like the other eleven were. The names of two men were proposed. Joseph called Barsabbas, also known as Justus, was one name. Matthias was the other.

"Lord, you know everyone's heart. Show us which one of these two you have chosen to take the place in this ministry which Judas turned aside to go to his own place," they prayed.

Then, they cast lots. When the lots fell, Matthias was identified as the choice of Jesus. So, Matthias became the new twelfth apostle to witness the unfolding of the scriptures.

THE COMING
OF THE HOLY SPIRIT

entecost means "fiftieth" in Hebrew, and it was the Jewish festival that took place fifty days after Passover. On the first Christian Pentecost, the Holy Spirit entered the temple of Jerusalem in a spectacular display. Jewish people of all nations were gatherd in the city. Some lived in distant lands and had remained in Jerusalem after Passover. Others were in the city doing business that required their presence.

But the main reason for the crowd was the feast of Pentecost, and the temple was filled with worshippers. Suddenly, a sound like the rush of a violent wind from heaven filled the house. Tongues like fire hung above each apostle. The apostles began to speak in other languages than their own, and worshippers were puzzled.

People asked themselves, "Are not all these men Galileans who are speaking thus?"

"How is it that we each hear our own language?" asked others.

"We are Parthians, Medes, Elamites, residents of Mesopotamia, Judea and Cappadocia, Pontus and Asia, Phrygia and Pamphylia, Egypt and the parts of Libya that belong to Cyrene and visitors from Rome. How can we hear them speak about God's deeds of power in our own languages?" demanded another large group.

"They are filled with new wine!" ridiculed others, who knew of the practice of drinking wine before making a proclamation about the future.

Then, Peter stood apart from the other eleven apostles and spoke to the assembly. "Men of Judea and all who live in Jerusalem, listen to what I have to say. We are not drunk, for it is only nine o'clock in the morning. No, what has happened was spoken by the prophet Joel, who said these words, 'God declared I will pour out my Spirit, and they shall prophesy. And I will show signs in the heaven above and signs on the earth below, signs of blood, fire and smoky mist.'"

Peter continued to address the astonished crowd, "You who are Israelites, this is what I have to say. Jesus of Nazareth was a man through whom God showed his power, wonders and signs among you, as you yourselves know. This man was handed over to you according to God's plan. He was crucified and killed by those outside the law. But, God raised him up and freed him from death, because it was impossible for him to be held by death's inferior power. David spoke of the resurrection of the Messiah when he said, 'He was not abandoned to Hades, nor did his flesh experience the corruption of death.'

"All of us are witnesses to the raising up of Jesus by God," said Peter. "Honored at the right hand of God and having received from God the Holy Spirit, Jesus has shown you today that God has kept his promise to David. David both died and was buried, and his tomb is with us to this day. He was a prophet, and he knew that God had sworn an oath to him to put one of his descendants on God's throne. That is why David said that Jesus was not abandoned to death by God. While David did not ascend into heaven, he saw into the future that Jesus would rise to God."

Peter finished speaking with a dramatic tone as he spoke of Jesus as the descendant of David on the throne of Israel. With a loud voice, he spoke to everyone in the assembly, "Therefore, let the entire house of Israel know with certainty that God has made Jesus the Messiah. This is the Jesus that you crucified."

"Brothers, what should we do?" the people cried out one after another to Peter and the other apostles.

Peter answered, "Repent and be baptized every one of you in the name of Jesus Christ so that your sins may be forgiven. You will then receive the gift of the Holy Spirit. God's promise is for you, your children and also for those who live far away. It is for everyone that God calls to him."

The people who welcomed the message of Peter rushed to be baptized. On that very day of Pentecost, the apostles baptized three thousand people. Three thousand people received the Holy Spirit according to God's promise.

The new converts sold their possessions and distributed the money they earned among anyone with a need. Day after day, they spent time together in the temple. Going from house to house, they broke bread in the name of Jesus. They ate their food with glad and generous hearts. During this time, the apostles performed many wondrous signs in the name of God.

PHILIP AND THE
ETHIOPIAN

hilip was one of the seven men of good standing which the apostles selected to help them in the early days of the church of Jerusalem. Like the other six men, he was wise and full of the Holy Spirit. One day, an angel appeared to Philip in Jerusalem.

"Get up and travel south on the road that leads from Jerusalem to Gaza," said the angel to Philip.

Philip started on the journey into the wilderness region. He knew the angel had been sent from God, so he did not question the angel's words. Philip's trust in God told him that he would learn for himself what it was he must do in this region. Before long, Philip saw a fellow traveler in the distance. When he was close behind the traveler, he felt the presence of the Holy Spirit.

"Go over to the chariot and join it," said the Holy Spirit to him.

Once again, Philip did as he was told. He learned that the man was from Ethiopia. A court official of the Candace, the queen of the Ethiopians, the man had just come from Jerusalem where he was allowed to worship in the outer court of the temple as a Gentile. The man was reading from the prophet Isaiah as he sat in his chariot.

"Do you understand what you are reading?" Philip asked him.

"How can I, unless someone guides me?" the traveler answered.

The traveler invited Philip to sit beside him in the chariot. Philip, who traveled on foot, accepted the Ethiopian's hospitality. He glanced at the passage the Ethiopian read. It was Isaiah 53.7-8,

"Like a sheep he was led to the slaughter,

and like a lamb silent before its shearer,

so he does not open his mouth.

In his humiliation, justice was denied to him.

Who can describe his generation?

For his life is taken away from the earth."

The Ethiopian asked Philip, "About whom, may I ask you, does the prophet say this? About himself? Or about someone else?"

Perhaps Philip remembered Peter's sermon to the first converts to Christianity after Jesus died. Peter told them, "Repent, and be baptized every one of you in the name of Jesus Christ so that your sins may be forgiven. And you will receive the Holy Spirit. For the promise is for you, for your children and for all who are far away, for everyone whom our God calls to him." The promise Peter spoke of was the gift of the Holy Spirit, and the salvation which God promised to Israel and which was offered by Jesus. The Ethiopian was a traveler from "far away," just as Peter had said. Philip understood that God wanted him to tell the Ethiopian the good news about Jesus.

In the words that Jesus spoke after he rose from the dead, Philip started the story with Moses and the prophets. He explained the things about Jesus in the scriptures. The message of asking forgiveness for one's sins, baptism, and receiving forgiveness and the Holy Spirit was a message that the Ethiopian was glad to hear.

Along the road, the chariot passed a stream. The Ethiopian pointed to it.

"Look, here is water! What is to prevent me from being baptized?" he asked Philip excitedly.

Philip directed the chariot to stop. He and the Ethiopian walked down to the stream. There, Philip baptized the traveler from "far away." The Holy Spirit appeared and blessed the Ethiopian.

At the same time, the Holy Spirit removed Philip from the road. The Ethiopian official never saw him again, and he returned to his home, rejoicing that he had been baptized. In the city of Azotus, about twenty-two miles north of Gaza, near the Mediterranean coast, Philip found himself on a new mission to proclaim the good news about Jesus.

A certain man named Simon amazed the people of the city with his magic. They were so impressed by his magic they believed Simon to have the power of God.

But when Philip arrived in Samaria to proclaim the good news about the kingdom of God and the name of Jesus Christ, the inhabitants believed the words he spoke to them. Philip accompanied his teaching with signs. He healed people of their unclean spirits, and he cured the paralyzed and the lame. The Samaritans, including Simon, asked Philip to baptize them. When the apostles in Jerusalem heard that the people of Samaria had accepted the word of God, they sent Peter and John to that land to pray that the people might receive the Holy Spirit.

Peter and John laid their hands on the newly baptized Samaritans, and the Holy Spirit filled them. When Simon saw that the people received the

Spirit through the laying on of the apostles' hands, he wanted the power that belonged to Peter and John in the name of God.

"Give me also this power so that anyone on whom I lay my hands may receive the Holy Spirit," asked Simon, and he tried to pay the apostles.

"May your silver perish with you, because you thought you could obtain God's gift with money! Repent of this wickedness of yours, and pray to God to forgive the wicked intent of your heart," said Peter.

What the magician asked was unacceptable to the ministers of God. What the Ethiopian asked was given by God, because the Ethiopian asked with a pure heart.

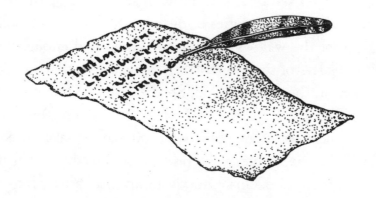

STEPHEN, FULL OF GRACE

tephen was one of seven men appointed by the apostles to help with the duties of the church, which included making sure the widows and their children had enough food. The leaders of the church in Jerusalem saw that he was full of grace and power. In the name of God, Stephen worked many wonders and signs among the people.

Some of the members of one of the synagogues in Jerusalem liked to argue with Stephen. But, when Stephen spoke, his words showed the wisdom that could only have been given by God. Unable to win an argument against him, the group plotted against him. Some of them told lies about Stephen to the temple leaders.

"We have heard him say blasphemous words against Moses and God," they lied.

Their false words stirred up even more people against Stephen. Before long, the temple elders and scribes, along with some ordinary Jewish people, believed the evil lies. They confronted Stephen in a mob, surrounded him and forced him to appear before the temple council. False witnesses against him came forward.

"This man never stops saying things against this holy place and the law," said one witness.

"We have heard him say that Jesus of Nazareth will destroy this place," said another witness.

"He wants to change the customs that Moses handed down to us," said a third false witness.

In spite of this, everyone in the temple who looked at Stephen saw that his face was the face of an angel.

"Are these things true?" demanded the high priest.

Stephen's answer to the high priest's question quieted the crowd. He told them the lengthy story of God's people, from Abraham, Isaac and Jacob to Joseph in Egypt. They all knew the story but he wanted to remind them of their history.

"So Abraham became the father of Isaac, and Isaac became the father of Jacob, and Jacob, the father of the twelve patriarchs. The patriarchs, jealous of Joseph, sold him into Egypt. But, God was with Joseph, and he allowed him to show wisdom when he stood before Pharaoh, king of Egypt. ... Then Joseph invited his father Jacob and all of his relatives to come to him, seventy-five in total. Jacob did well in Egypt," said Stephen during the long speech to the high priest and the people in the council.

He spoke to them about the birth of Moses and his adoption by Pharaoh's daughter.

"Then, another king who had not known Joseph ruled over Egypt. He dealt craftily with our race and forced our ancestors to abandon their infants so that they would die. At this time, Moses was born, and he was beautiful before God. Pharaoh's daughter adopted him and brought him up as her own son."

Stephen told of the angel who appeared to Moses in the wilderness of Mount Sinai in the flame of the burning bush. "And, as he approached to look, there came the voice of God, 'I am the God of your ancestors, the God of Abraham, Isaac and Jacob.'"

Afterward, Stephen recounted the Israelites' journey across the desert to the promised land and their disobedience toward Moses. "Our ancestors were unwilling to obey him. Instead, they pushed him aside, and in their hearts, they turned back to Egypt. ... They made a calf. ... But God turned away from them and handed them over to worship the host of heaven."

Then, Stephen accused the high priest, the council and the other leaders of the temple. "The Most High does not dwell in houses made with human hands as the prophet Isaiah says. You stiff-necked people, you are forever opposing the Holy Spirit, just as your ancestors used to do. Which of the prophets did your ancestors not persecute? They killed those who told of the coming of Jesus, the Righteous One, and now you have become his betrayers and murderers. You are the ones that received the law, which was made holy by the angels. Yet, you have not kept it."

When Stephen finished, he radiated before the crowd in the light of the Holy Spirit. He looked to heaven, and he saw the glory of God and Jesus at the right hand of God. He was overcome with the beauty that he witnessed.

"Look!" he said. "I see the heavens opened and the Son of God standing at the right hand of God!"

But, the people covered their ears. With a loud shout, many of them rushed against Stephen. They dragged him with the fury of a mob outside the city. Then, they stoned him.

Stephen prayed, "Jesus, receive my spirit." He cried in a loud voice, "Lord, do not hold this sin against them." When he said these words, he died.

Still, many in the crowd were not convinced of his innocence. But, some must have seen that he was full of grace, even as he died.

PETER AND CORNELIUS

man named Cornelius lived in the city of Caesarea. Cornelius was a centurion, a Roman army officer in charge of one hundred men. Like other people living in the seaside city on the Mediterranean coast, Cornelius was a Gentile. This is the story of how God taught Peter to accept the Gentiles as believers, too. Before the lesson, Peter, like most Jewish people of his time, thought that the Jews were the only chosen ones of God.

Cornelius was a devout man who feared God. He gave money and food to the poor, and he prayed constantly. The rest of his household followed his example.

One afternoon at three o'clock, Cornelius had a vision. An angel of God appeared to him and clearly spoke his name.

"What is it?" asked Cornelius.

"Your prayers and your alms for the poor have risen to the notice of God.

Now, send men to Joppa for a certain Simon who is called Peter. He is lodging with Simon the tanner, whose house is by the seaside," replied the angel.

Following the angel's instructions, Cornelius called before him two slaves and a soldier from his ranks of one hundred. He told them to go to Joppa and to bring back Peter from the house of Simon the tanner by the sea.

Around noon on the following day, as the servants of Cornelius were on their journey to find him, Peter went up to Simon's roof to pray. Once there, he became very hungry, Peter asked Simon's servant to bring him some food. While the servant prepared his food, Peter fell into a trance.

He saw the heavens open. Something like a large sheet floated to the ground, outstretched at its four corners. All kinds of four-footed animals, reptiles and birds were supported by the sheet. Then, Peter heard a voice speaking to him.

"Get up, Peter. Kill and eat," said the voice of God.

"By no means. I have never eaten anything profane or unclean," he answered God, because some of the species on the sheet were prohibited as food by Jewish law.

The voice spoke to him again. "What God has made clean, you must not call profane."

Three times, the voice told Peter to kill and eat the animals. Three times, Peter refused. And three times, God told his apostle not to call his creations unclean. Peter was very puzzled. Then, the sheet and all the animals disappeared into the heavens.

Meanwhile, the three men sent by Cornelius appeared at the tanner's gate. They asked whether someone called Peter was staying at the house. The Holy Spirit instructed Peter to go down from the roof without hesitation, because the visitors were sent by God.

"I am the one you are looking for. What is your reason for coming?" Peter asked the men at the front gate.

They answered, "Cornelius, a centurion, an upright and God-fearing man, who is spoken of highly by the Jewish people, was directed by a holy angel to have you come to his house so that he may hear what you speak."

Peter invited the men to spend the night. The following day, he and some of his companions accompanied them to Caesarea. When they arrived at the home of Cornelius, the centurion bowed to Peter and fell at his feet as a sign of worship.

"Stand," Peter told the centurion. "I am only a mortal."

When Peter entered the house, he saw many Gentiles assembled there.

"You know that it is unlawful for a Jew to associate with a Gentile. Yet, God has shown me that I should not call anyone profane or unclean. Now, may I ask why you sent for me?" Peter asked. As he spoke his first words to Cornelius, he understood the meaning of God's vision on the roof.

"Four days ago, at this very hour of three o'clock," answered Cornelius, "I was praying in my house when suddenly a man in dazzling clothes stood before me, saying, 'Cornelius, your prayer has been heard and your alms have been remembered by God. Send therefore to Joppa and ask for Simon called Peter, who is staying at the home of Simon the tanner.' Now, all of us are here together in the presence of God to listen to what God has commanded you to say."

Then, Peter spoke to the crowd in the house of Cornelius. "I truly understand now that God shows no favoritism. In every nation, anyone who fears him and does what is right is acceptable to him."

When the Holy Spirit came to every person in the house, Peter said, "Can anyone withhold the water for baptizing these people? We see they have received the Holy Spirit just as we have."

And, Peter ordered the Gentiles to be baptized in the name of Jesus Christ. At their invitation, he stayed with them for several days, something he would not have considered before God showed him how.

PAUL AND SILAS IN PRISON

P aul and Silas, followers of Christ in the early days of the church, were preaching in the southern cities of the land of Macedonia in part of present-day Greece. One day, when they were on their way to the church to pray, they met a slave girl. The girl was possessed by what was called the Spirit of the Python, the spirit that inspired the oracle at nearby Delphi. Because of the presence of this spirit, the slave girl was able to make a lot of money as a fortune teller. And, because she was a slave, the money that she earned belonged to her owner. The girl was impressed with her power, and she trailed behind Paul and Silas, making fun of them.

"These men are slaves of the Most High God," she shouted to the townspeople on the street where Paul and Silas walked. "How can they show to us the way of salvation," she said.

Paul was very annoyed by the slave girl's words. He was particularly annoyed, because he knew the words were the words of the spirit that possessed her. "I order you in the name of Jesus Christ to come out of her," demanded Paul of the spirit.

Instantly, the spirit was gone from the slave girl. While she was relieved to be free of this spirit, her owners were furious to see their source of income depart. They seized Paul and Silas and dragged them in the marketplace in front of the authorities assembled.

The owners spoke to the chief officials of the Roman colony of Philippi, called magistrates, "These men are disturbing our city. They are Jews, and they want us to follow customs which are unlawful for us Romans to observe."

The crowd joined in the attack on Paul and Silas. The magistrates ordered that the two followers of Christ be stripped of their clothing. Then, they were beaten with rods. After a severe flogging, they were thrown into prison. The jailer was instructed to keep them under close scrutiny, so he put them in the innermost cell of the prison and fastened their feet to guard against an escape.

About midnight, Paul and Silas were praying and singing hymns to God, and the other prisoners listened to them. Just then, an earthquake violently shook the prison's very foundation. All the prison doors flew open, free of their locks. The stocks that bound the feet of Paul and Silas flew open, too. When the jailer awoke and saw the cells wide open, he drew his sword and was about to kill himself. His death would be an act of honor, because it was his responsibility to safeguard the prisoners. If he did not kill himself, the magistrates would order that he be killed for failing in his responsibility to Rome.

But, Paul interrupted the jailer, shouting, "Do not harm yourself. We are all here."

When the jailer demanded that the lights be lit, he saw that Paul told the truth. None of the prisoners had escaped into the horrendous earthquake outside.

"Sirs, what must I do to be saved?" he asked Paul and Silas.

They answered, "Believe in Jesus, and you will be saved, you and your whole household."

The jailer took Paul and Silas to his house under his custody, and he washed their wounds. Paul and Silas baptized him and his family. Then, the jailer set out food for them, and they ate with the family. After dinner, everyone in the household rejoiced that they had become believers in God. In the morning, the magistrates ordered the jailer to free Paul and Silas. But, instead of welcoming the news, Paul refused to leave the prison.

"They have beaten us in public, yet we are not condemned. We are Roman citizens, whom they have thrown into prison. Now they are going to discharge us in secret? Certainly not. Let them come and take us out themselves," Paul proclaimed to the police officers sent by the magistrates.

When the police officers reported to the magistrates that Paul and Silas were citizens of Rome, they became afraid. The magistrates had broken Roman law by torturing and imprisoning them without a fair trial. As Paul had suggested, they went directly to the prison themselves. They apologized to the two followers of Christ, and they released them.

After leaving the jail, Paul and Silas went to the house of Lydia, a follower of Jesus. They encouraged the brothers and sisters in the house who believed in the teachings of Jesus. When they had stayed enough time with Lydia, they departed under the guidance of the Holy Spirit, who instructed them where they should go to spread the word.

PAUL IN
A SHIPWRECK

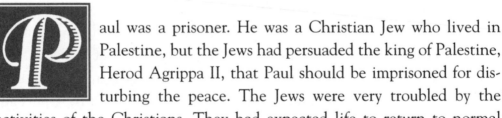

aul was a prisoner. He was a Christian Jew who lived in Palestine, but the Jews had persuaded the king of Palestine, Herod Agrippa II, that Paul should be imprisoned for disturbing the peace. The Jews were very troubled by the activities of the Christians. They had expected life to return to normal after Jesus was killed. But, they were wrong.

Paul (also called Saul) was a Roman citizen. He had been born into a family of citizens in Tarsus, so he had the right to be tried for his crimes in Rome as a Roman. The Roman governor decided that Paul should travel from Palestine to Rome and state his case to the emperor.

Paul had once been a Pharisee, and he had done many things against the name of Jesus of Nazareth under the authority of the chief priests of the temple of Jerusalem. Paul jailed many of the followers of Jesus. In synagogues, he tried to get them to speak against God. He followed the disciples of Jesus even to foreign cities to persecute them.

One day, things changed for Paul. He was on the road to Damascus on a commission from the high priests against the followers of Jesus. It was midday, and, in the heavens, he saw a light brighter than even the noontime sun. Paul and his companions fell to the ground, because of the glow around them.

"Saul, Saul, why are you persecuting me?" said a voice from above in the Hebrew language.

"Who are you?" asked Paul.

"I am Jesus, whom you are persecuting. Get up and stand on your feet. I have appeared to you to appoint you to testify to the things you have seen. I will rescue you from your people and from the Gentiles to whom I am sending you. You will open their eyes so they may turn from Satan to God."

After the vision and the appointment by Jesus, Paul began to declare, first in the city of Damascus, then in Jerusalem, then throughout the land of Judea, that the people should repent and turn to God. Because of his message, Paul infuriated the Jews. They seized him in the temple and tried to kill him. For this reason, Paul had to go to Rome to be tried by the emperor.

Paul boarded the ship bound for Rome with some other prisoners. A centurion, an officer commanded by the emperor, was to guard him. The ship was to follow the coast of Asia. Sailing to the north and east of the island of Cyprus, the ship was shielded from the winds of the west. The ship docked on the southern coast of Crete. Beyond this point lay the open sea with no further protection from any islands.

Paul advised the centurion, "I can see that the voyage will be in danger of heavy loss, not only of the cargo we carry and the ship itself, but also of our lives."

But the centurion ignored Paul's warnings. The ship set sail from Crete, with a moderate south wind blowing. Soon, however, a violent wind called a northeaster blew from the direction of Crete. The wind drove the ship away from the safety of the island she had just left. The sailors were scarcely able to control her. Fearing total loss of control, they dropped anchor. Still, the wind moved the ship. The next day, the storm pounded them, so the sailors threw the cargo overboard. On the third day, they dropped the ship's tackle overboard. Neither sun nor stars appeared in the sky for many days, and all hope of survival was abandoned by the passengers, who had not eaten since the cargo was let loose.

Paul stood and spoke again. "Men, you should have listened when I advised you not to leave Crete. I urge you now to keep up your courage. There will be no loss of life among you. Only the ship will be lost. Last night, an angel of God told me I would stand before the emperor. The angel said that all those sailing with me would be safe."

After fourteen days at sea, the ship headed for an island the sailors did not recognize. They cast off the anchors and left them at sea. Loosening the ropes that tied the steering oars, they hoisted the sail to the wind. They aimed the ship at the beach. But, striking a reef, the ship ran aground. The bow stuck and remained immovable. The force of the waves broke up the stern. Against the judgment of the soldiers on board who wished to kill the prisoners, the centurion prevailed. He instructed the prisoners to jump overboard and swim toward land. Once ashore, they learned that they had found safety on the island of Malta.

After three months on Malta, Paul and the others set sail for Rome on a ship that had wintered on the island. Paul became a prisoner of the emperor in Rome, living in a house for two years at his own expense, under house arrest. He continued to preach the word of God, teaching openly about Jesus Christ.

TIMOTHY, THE BELIEVER

his story is about letters. It takes place in the early days of
the church after the ascension of Christ. The subject of the
letters was how to be a good Christian.

The first letter was written on parchment by the elders
of the church in Jerusalem. The letter was addressed to the Gentiles who
had decided to turn to God. Gentiles were people from other nations
besides Israel who did not practice the Jewish faith. Gentile people, like
the Jewish people, were also included in God's plan for salvation. The letter from the church in Jerusalem welcomed the Gentiles as followers of the
law of Moses and the teachings of Jesus Christ.

Of course, there was no postal service in those days. So, the letter was
carried in person to the Gentiles by members of the church. The group
chosen to accompany the letter included Paul, Barnabas and several others.

The first stop for the letter was the ancient city of Antioch on the continent of Asia. After Antioch, Paul decided to visit the believers of Christ in every city in Asia. He stopped in Lystra, where he became acquainted with a believer named Timothy. Timothy was the son of a Jewish mother named Eunice. With help from Eunice's mother Lois, who was Timothy's grandmother, Eunice taught her son the message of Jesus. Paul invited Timothy to accompany him on his travels to the cities of Asia. In each city, they read the letter from the elders of the church in Jerusalem. They followed the visions they received from God which told them what routes to take. The Gentiles in the cities they visited welcomed the message of the letter, and the churches increased their membership because of them.

Finally, it was important for Paul to return to the elders in Jerusalem. He appointed Timothy to remain in Asia and to continue preaching to the believers of Christ in the cities of that continent. But, a conspiracy of Jewish non-believers plotted against Paul in Jerusalem. He was arrested. Then, because he was a Roman citizen, he had to travel to Rome to plead his innocence before the emperor.

The second letter in this story was written by Paul to Timothy. It was passed along to him from believer to believer until Timothy received it. Here is part of Paul's letter. It is written in the words he might use today to speak to Timothy if he were alive.

Dear Timothy,

I rejoice in the name of God that you are his loyal child. Please remain in the city of Ephesus. Teach the people to be on guard against any beliefs that are different from ours and which others may try to teach them. Teach them the love that comes from a pure heart, a good conscience and sincere faith.

Pray and give thanks to God for everyone, even for kings and all who are in high positions. Teach the people to lead a quiet and peaceful life in dignity, according to God's wishes. Remind them that there is only one God. Tell them there is one messenger between God and mankind. This is Christ Jesus, who gave himself to save us.

When you speak to an older man, speak to him as a father. Speak to younger men as brothers, speak to older women as mothers and to younger women as sisters. If someone accuses an elder of the church, do not believe it without the word of two or three witnesses.

Tell those who are rich not to be proud or to set their hopes on the uncertainty of riches. Tell them instead to trust God who richly provides us with everything for our enjoyment. They are to do good, to be rich in good works, generous and ready to share their wealth.

No longer drink only water, as the false teachers claim. Take a little wine for the sake of your stomach and your frequent ailments. Fight the good fight of the faith. Keep in mind the eternal life to which you were called and follow the commandments.

As for me, I am already marked for death. I am a libation, a liquid to be poured in sacrifice to God. I have fought the good fight, I have finished the race, I have kept the faith.

Do your best to come to me here in Rome before winter. When you come, please bring the cloak that I left with Carpus at Troas. Bring also the books, and, above all, the parchments.

Grace be with you,

Paul

John's Vision of Heaven

 his story is an apocalypse. "Apocalypse" means "unveiling" or "disclosure." This story is a vision of heaven from God. The vision was seen by a man named John whom many people believe is the John who wrote the Gospel. He lived in Palestine, and he was a Christian prophet who was well-known in his time.

The vision in this story is a heavenly Jerusalem. It is more than a match for the earthly Jerusalem where God asked Solomon to build his house. These are John's words about his vision.

"Then I saw a new heaven and a new earth. The first heaven and the first earth had passed away. And the sea was no more. I saw the holy city, the new Jerusalem, coming down out of heaven from God. And I heard a loud voice from the throne. It was God's voice that said, 'Death will be no more. Mourning and crying and pain will be no more, because the first things have passed away.'"

"The one who was seated on the throne said, 'See, I am making all things new. To the thirsty I will give water as a gift from the spring of the water of life. Those who are faithful until their death will inherit these things. I will be their God, and they will be my children. But, as for the rebels and all those who do not believe, their place will be in the lake that burns with fire and sulfur, which is their second death.'"

"One of seven angels with seven bowls full of the seven last plagues said to me, 'Come, I will show you the bride, the wife of the Lamb.' (Here, John is talking about the church as the bride, and Christ as the Lamb, or the bridegroom.) The angel carried me away to a great, high mountain to the holy city of Jerusalem which came down out of heaven from God.

"It has the glory of God and a radiance like a very rare jewel, like jasper, as clear as a crystal. It has a great high wall with twelve gates, three gates to the east, three gates to the north, three gates to the south and three gates to the west. At the gates are twelve angels. On the gates are inscribed the names of the twelve tribes of the Israelites. The wall of the city has twelve foundations. On them are the twelve names of the apostles of the Lamb.

"The angel had a measuring rod of gold to measure the city with its gates and walls. The city is a gigantic cube. The length is the same as the width. The wall is built of jasper, and the city is pure gold, clear as glass. The foundations of the wall are adorned with every jewel. The first foundation is jasper, the second sapphire, the third agate, the fourth emerald, the fifth onyx, the sixth carnelian, the seventh crysolite, the eighth beryl, the ninth topaz, the tenth chrysoprase, the eleventh jacinth, and the twelfth amethyst. The twelve gates are twelve pearls. The street of the city is pure gold, as transparent as glass.

"There is no temple in the city. Its temple is God the Almighty and the Lamb. The city has no need of sun or moon to shine on it. The glory of God is its light, and its lamp was the Lamb. The gates will never be shut by day, and there will be no night there. People will bring into the city the glory and honor of the nations. But, nothing unclean will enter it; only those whose names are written in the Lamb's book of life.

"The angel showed me the river of the water of life, as bright as crystal, flowing from the throne of God and the Lamb through the middle of the city's street. On either side of the river is the tree of life with its twelve kinds of fruit that produce fruit each month. The leaves of the tree of life are for the healing of the nations.

"Nothing cursed will be found there any more. The throne of God and the Lamb will be in it. His servants, the faithful, would worship him. They will see his face. And his name will be on their foreheads. God will be their light forever and ever.

"And God said to me, 'Do not seal up the words of this book, the Lamb's book of life, for the time is near. Let the evildoer still do evil, the filthy still be filthy, the righteous still do right, and the holy still be holy.'

"Blessed are those who make their robes white in the blood of the Lamb. They will have the right to the tree of life, and they may enter the city by the gate. Outside is everyone who loves and practices falsehood.

"Then, I heard, 'It is I, Jesus, who sent my angel to you with this testimony. I am the root and the descendant of David, the bright morning star.'"

INDEX OF CITATIONS

Believing Jesus   John 20.24-29; 21.1-19
The Ascension of Jesus to Heaven   Mark 16.19-20;Luke 24.50-53;
                                         Acts 1

The Coming of the Holy Spirit   Acts 2
Philip and the Ethiopian   Acts 8.4-40
Stephen, Full of Grace   Acts 6.8-15;7
Peter and Cornelius   Acts 10
Paul and Silas in Prison   Acts 16.16-40
Paul in a Shipwreck   Acts 27.9-44
Timothy, the Believer   Acts 16.1-5;1 Timothy;2 Timothy
John's Vision of Heaven   Revelations 21-22.1-7